THE
ONLY FOOLS and HORSES
STORY

Only Fools and Horses
☆☆☆☆☆☆

Stick a pony in me pocket
I'll fetch the suitcase from the van
Coz if you want the best 'uns
And you don't ask questions
Then, brother, I'm your man
•
Where it all comes from
Is a mystery
It's like the changing of the seasons
And the tides of the sea
But here's the one what's driving me berserk
Why do only fools and horses work
La la lala – la la la la la la (etc)

Hooky Street
☆☆☆☆☆☆

We've got some half-priced cracked-ice
And miles and miles of carpet tiles
TVs, deep-freeze and David Bowie LPs
Pool games, gold chains, wossnames
And at a push
Some Trevor Francis track-suits
From a mush in Shepherd's Bush, Bush, Bush, Bush
•
No income-tax, no VAT
No money back, no guarantee
Black or white, rich or broke
We'll cut prices at a stroke
•
God bless Hooky Street
Long live Hooky Street
C'est magnifique Hooky Street
Magnifique Hooky Street, Hooky Street (etc)

Words and music
by John Sullivan

THE

ONLY FOOLS
and
HORSES

STORY

STEVE CLARK

Series created and written by
JOHN SULLIVAN

BBC

Acknowledgements

I am deeply grateful to everyone who helped with the preparation and research for this book. In particular I would like to thank the following for giving up their time so generously to be interviewed: Jonathan Betts of the National Maritime Museum, Greenwich, Jim Broadbent, Ray Butt, who has always been so supportive, John Challis, Phoebe De Gaye, who also allowed us to reproduce her costume designs, Lynn Faulds Wood, Gareth Gwenlan, Roy Heather, Sue Holderness, Carole James, David Jason, Sydney Lotterby, Roger Lloyd Pack, Nick Lyndhurst, Ken MacDonald, Buster Merryfield, Patrick Murray, Daniel Peacock, Tessa Peake-Jones, Tony Snoaden, Gwyneth Strong and Donal Woods, who allowed us to print one of his set designs.

I would also like to express my sincere thanks for their help to: Perry Aghajanoff, who does a fine job running *The Only Fools and Horses* Appreciation Society, Ronnie Barker, for giving his thoughts on the show, Debbie Carey, for her encouragement, Tony Dow, Sir Anthony Hopkins for taking time out of his busy schedule to write the foreword, and Adrian Pegg, whose help over the years has been greatly appreciated.

My thanks also go to Jenny Clark for her help compiling the episode guide, Anna Stock for her constant support and help, Kathryn Perkins for secretarial back-up, Sheila Ableman at BBC Books for her faith in the project, Linda Blakemore for her enthusiasm and brilliant designs, my editor Anna Ottewill for her practical help and support, diligent picture researcher Miriam Hyman, editorial assistant Debbi Francis, Jane Redmond and Richard Hamilton-Jones at BBC TV Locations and the staff of the BBC Archives at Caversham.

Most of all though I'd like to thank John Sullivan for his support and for being so generous with his time and for writing a show which has given me – and so many millions of others so much pleasure, not to mention aching ribs, over the years. *Steve Clark*

Series producers: Ray Butt and Gareth Gwenlan

Published by BBC Worldwide Limited,
Woodlands, 80 Wood Lane, London W12 0TT

First published 1998
Only Fools and Horses format and television scripts © John Sullivan 1998
This book © Steve Clark 1998
The moral right of the author has been asserted.
Reprinted 1998

ISBN 0 563 38445 X

Commissioning Editor: Sheila Ableman
Project Editor: Anna Ottewill
Copy Editor: Kelly Davies
Designer: Linda Blakemore
Picture Researcher: Miriam Hyman

Set in Janson and Gill Sans by BBC Books
Printed and bound in Belgium by Proost NV

CONTENTS

*For John, Maria and Jenny
and for Anna
and in memory of Lennard Pearce*

Only Fools and Horses deserves every bit of its colossal success. Since its
very first episode it has grown and grown in popularity and I am only one
among millions who love and admire its quality as entertainment.

At worst it is excellent, at best brilliant. In my view, its unrivalled and
universal appeal is due to three things; one, the continual skill and perception
of its writer John Sullivan, who, ever since he knocked on my dressing-room
door at Television Centre and offered me a sketch for *The Two Ronnies*,
has not looked back. He goes from strength to strength.

The second ingredient of this happy concoction is the supporting cast,
each one talented, solid and reliable to a man, including the women.
One must single out Nicholas Lyndhurst's Rodney, a droll foil to Del Boy,
and an accomplished comedian in his own right.

The third and by far the greatest contribution comes, of course, from my
old dear friend and colleague in so many treasured comedy moments, the
inimitable David Jason. He is without doubt one of Britain's finest actors and
comedians. He inhabits the character of the little scheming loser that is
Del Boy as no other actor could. I would say that no less than seventy-five
per cent of the success of the show is due to him and his energy,
his timing and his brilliance.

RONNIE BARKER

ANTHONY HOPKINS

I *am very surprised and honoured to have been asked to write the foreword for this book because I think* Only Fools and Horses *is such a great programme and ranks alongside classic series like* Steptoe and Son *and* Morecambe and Wise. *I've watched the show from way back when Lennard Pearce was in it and what appeals to me about it, and I know I am stating the obvious when I say this, is that it is simply very, very funny.*

John Sullivan's writing is just terrific and his scripts are way up there with the very best of them, like the work Galton and Simpson did for Tony Hancock. Like theirs, his characters are drawn from real life and very well observed.

I always love those exchanges between Trigger and the guys. One of my favourite moments was in the final episode when they are in the Nag's Head talking about everyone having fifteen minutes of fame during a lifetime and Trig says, 'Like Gandhi'. And Rodney says, 'Gandhi?' and Trig says, 'He made one great film and then you never saw him again.' Also the time Del and Rodney burst into the funeral dressed as Batman and Robin was just brilliant.

Another reason I'm such a great fan is because the acting is absolutely first rate. The skill of the actors in the situations that are presented to them is spot on – it's as simple as that. David Jason and Nicholas Lyndhurst are superb actors. It is obvious that they work really well together. They play their scenes straight and they make us laugh because they are just so convincing. Their timing is superb and having lived in London for many years now I love cockney humour. As a young actor I certainly knew a couple of Del Boys in the Waterloo Road area! I used to hang around in The Windmill pub where you'd come across traders of all sorts – fishmongers, florists, barrow boys and spivs – all great characters to chat to.

The show is such a great ensemble piece. It works like a well-oiled machine with all the other characters that appear played by an excellent array of supporting actors.

I would have been delighted to have had a part in the programme but I know my limitations and I'm not a Londoner so I don't think I'd have fitted in unless I'd played a Welshman.

Only Fools and Horses *is a classic, and will remain so. I can't offer any mystical insights into it; it's simply wonderful comedy.*

Page 10
How It All Began

How It All Began

John Sullivan will always remember 1980 as the year his second television series was cancelled by a senior executive at BBC Television. For the young writer, with a family to support, it was nothing short of a disaster. Three years previously he'd had a meteoric rise from his job as a scene shifter at BBC Television Centre in Wood Lane, London, working on programmes like *The Morecambe and Wise Show, Porridge, I Claudius,* and *To The Manor Born,* to become a writer on a BBC contract with a hit series, *Citizen Smith,* to his name.

The show, which starred Robert Lindsay as Tooting revolutionary Wolfie Smith, had been a hit with viewers and Sullivan went on to write a further three series. However, during the filming of the fourth series, it became apparent that it would be the last. John had decided that he'd gone as far as he could with the character of Wolfie and Robert Lindsay had indicated that he would like to move on and try his hand at something new.

Robert Lindsay as Wolfie in John Sullivan's first hit television series Citizen Smith. *The show established John as a comedy writer and four series were produced by the BBC.*

John wasn't too worried, as he had another idea up his sleeve, a sitcom called *Over the Moon* about a football manager running a down-at-heel club but with great aspirations that were never likely to be fulfilled. A pilot episode was recorded on 30 November at Television Centre, starring Brian Wilde (best known as Foggy in *Last of the Summer Wine*) as Ron Wilson, the manager.

The show also starred George Baker (now Inspector Wexford in the ITV drama) as the club's chairman Major Gormley, and Paula Tilbrook (who now stars as Betty Eagleton in *Emmerdale*) as Wilson's landlady Mrs Allardyce. 'The BBC liked the pilot and commissioned a series and I went off and wrote a second and third episode,' John recalls. 'I had high hopes for the show and was confident it would work.'

The man in charge of the series was to be a senior BBC producer and director called Ray Butt, who had already made the successful pilot episode. He and Sullivan had met before, when Ray had been called in to direct several episodes of the second series of *Citizen Smith* and sort out some problems over cast punctuality – 'to kick some backsides,' as John puts it.

The two men had gained a healthy respect for one another. They both had working-class backgrounds which produced a natural rapport and they shared a mutual passion for television comedy. They became friends and began a fruitful working partnership that would last for many years.

'The first good thing was that we had similar accents,' says Ray Butt, a genial and likeable man who joined the BBC in 1955, after doing National Service in the RAF, when a lot of vacancies were created at the Corporation, following an exodus of employees to the newly formed ITV. 'John is a South London boy and I'm an East London boy so we seemed to talk the same language.'

Everything was looking good for *Over the Moon* and John Sullivan was busy writing the fourth episode when suddenly disaster struck. Ray Butt was called into a meeting at Television Centre and told that the show was to be cancelled. He rang John Sullivan and broke the bad news. Sullivan remembers the moment well. 'I was working on the fourth episode when Bill Cotton, who was the Controller of BBC1, came back from a trip to America and killed it. As you can imagine, I wasn't very happy. Ironically, one of the reasons that they decided to shelve the idea was because they'd decided to make a new series about a boxer called *Seconds Out,* starring Robert Lindsay, and they didn't want two comedies with sporting themes, so I lost out.'

For John it was terrible news. He was overdrawn and had been banking on *Over the Moon* to keep him and his family afloat. 'I had no work in the pipeline,' he says. 'We'd just bought our first house down in Sutton in Surrey, and frankly I was worried about being able to pay the mortgage because prior to that we'd only been renting somewhere.

The idea that wouldn't go away – a series about London market traders. Nicholas Lyndhurst and David Jason get into their roles on the first day of filming of **Only Fools and Horses.**

I was under contract for a year but after that the future looked very uncertain. Not only that but no show on the box meant no repeat fees.'

He and Ray arranged to meet for a lunchtime drink the following week at Ray's local, The Three Kings, in North End Road. Over several pints the two friends talked of their disappointment and Sullivan looked for inspiration. Their conversation covered a plethora of subjects, including their childhoods and their families, and now and again John would bounce ideas off Ray and make suggestions about new characters.

John had one hazy idea at the back of his mind that wouldn't go away – about a wheeler-dealer street market trader who dealt only in cash and would sell anything to anyone. But he knew the BBC didn't like it because he'd already talked to the Corporation's Head of Light Entertainment, Jimmy Gilbert, a few years before and it had been given a very firm thumbs down.

'I'd written a one-page treatment thing explaining the idea,' says John. 'It was all about modern working-class London. I was sick to death of the kind of comedies I saw on telly which were almost always based in the forties or earlier, with toffs and that sort of tugging-the-forelock, Gor-Bless-You-Guv type of stuff which didn't exist. Now

we had a modern, vibrant, multi-racial, new slang London where a lot of working-class guys had suits and a bit of dosh in their pockets and that was a very different thing.

'That's what I wanted to write about. It would be a bit more aggressive and it would feature the pubs, clubs and tower blocks and even touch on the drug problem. Jimmy just looked at me for a while and then he went away and I got a message back some time later, through someone else, that the BBC didn't want to go along that road and that was that.'

Ray Butt, though, thought it was a great idea. He recalls: 'At the time the papers were full of all this stuff about the black economy and this fella John talked about was that sort of bloke. He'd only deal in cash. He was a guy who would do anything for readies and he didn't pay any tax. He didn't take anything from the state but wouldn't give anything to the state either. He was a readies man, simple as that.'

Both men liked the idea and both knew a fair bit about the world that the character lived in. Ray Butt's father Bill had come out of the RAF after the Second World War and, finding his pre-war job as a printer rather dull, pooled his money with a friend, bought an old NAAFI wagon and set

WHY ONLY FOOLS AND HORSES?

John Sullivan had to fight his corner over the title of the show. As far as he was concerned, *Readies* had simply been a working title.

'I always thought longer titles grabbed people's eyes and obviously I wanted to make viewers aware of us,' he says. 'I liked the idea of calling the show *Only Fools and Horses*, from the old expression "Only fools and horses work", because Del's main aim in life is not to work and yet he scurries around till 11 at night working his socks off not to work.

'The man himself is a contradiction. So I wanted to call it that and Jimmy Gilbert said: "What does it mean? Oh, it's a London saying." In the end we found out it was an American saying from Vaudeville theatre days that came over here through music halls. One day we did a straw poll in the BBC bar and we asked people what the expression meant to them and the answers ranged from "A quote from Shakespeare" to "The life and times of Lester Piggott – his autobiography".'

Other names were considered – including *Big Brother*, but it was thought that viewers might confuse it with George Orwell's book *1984* (with the real year 1984 being just over two years away). John was due to have a final meeting with Jimmy Gilbert and Head of Comedy, John Howard Davis, over the show's name and spent a weekend trying to come up with an acceptable alternative. He couldn't.

Gareth Gwenlan, who was at that time an executive producer in the BBC comedy department, and later became the show's producer, had heard the saying, supported John Sullivan's argument and helped him win the day. 'Gareth is a great politician,' says John Sullivan. 'He said: "Go into the meeting and say you haven't got a clue what else to call it. Tell them it's up to them to come up with another title and they won't be able to and you'll get your title."

'That was just what happened. They looked at each other and said: "OK, you can have it." After weeks of haggling, finally they decided to go with the name *Only Fools and Horses*.'

Opposite: The brothers, Rodney and Del (Derek), played by Nicholas Lyndhurst and David Jason. The big age gap between them was inspired by John Sullivan's own experiences of having a sister who was thirteen years his senior and those of two friends who had siblings of very different ages.

up a business selling ice-creams round markets. That was fine as a summer trade, but to earn a living in winter Bill Butt had to diversify. He set up a stall on the Roman Road market near his home, selling everything from ladies' stockings to toffee apples, and as a youngster Ray used to work the stall at weekends and during his school holidays.

The family would also travel to other markets in Ashford and Maidstone in Kent and Epsom in Surrey, and Ray spent time working for another street market trader who later became a legend of the entertainment world – Tommy Cooper. 'Tommy was a market grafter long before he was a comic,' says Ray. 'And I worked for him as a kid in the markets. He used to sell saccharine and elastic and stuff like that but he was wonderful. His selling routine was great, as you might imagine.'

'In the eighties people were talking about the black economy like it was something new but after the war it was all the rage,' says Ray. 'Market traders were all working for readies. They had this cash and there was no way they were going to declare all of it to the Inland Revenue. You had to declare something but basically the vast majority went straight into your bin and the tax man never saw it.'

'Ray and I decided that the most interesting market characters were the fly pitchers,' says John. 'They were funny guys who'd turn up with their gear in a box or a suitcase. They'd never have a licence and they'd just flog their stuff to passers-by. You never knew their names and we wondered where they came from and where they went back to, after a day selling their wares.' A few pints on, the pair decided that there might be some merit in John's trader idea.

'This idea didn't come as some great blinding flash,' says Ray Butt. 'It was just one of a number of ideas John was bouncing off me. I just told him to go away and see what he came up with and that was pretty much that.' John Sullivan went back home that afternoon full of renewed enthusiasm. 'I took the archetypal fly pitcher with the gold watch and the battered suitcase and decided to give him a family and a home life,' he says. 'I made him a guy with a burning ambition to make it big – but who never quite managed it.

'Part of my inspiration for Del was a guy I knew called Chicky Stocker. He was a working-class Londoner and a tough man but always dressed very neatly. He wasn't the sort of bloke that you'd go out of your way to annoy but nevertheless he was a very nice man. He was very genuine and I liked his attitude to life. He was very loyal to his family

and I tried to instil that into Del. Other aspects of his character, like buying drinks for people down the pub even when he couldn't really afford to, came from people I knew in the car trade. Even if they were doing badly, they'd borrow money to flash about, to let everyone think they were doing well, and wearing lots of gold rings was part of that.

'I was also fascinated by the idea of having a big age gap between him and his younger brother. That idea came from three different sources. Firstly my sister Maureen is thirteen years older than me and because of that she was never really like a sister until I was twenty or so. It was weird. She wasn't like a mother but it was odd because of the age gap, and it took a few years when I was older to catch up with that.

'Secondly the brother of my oldest friend Colin was eleven or so years older than him, and thirdly another mate of mine also had a much younger brother. In both cases the older guy had some little business going and took the younger brother in, so there was this continual big brother thing throughout their lives and that fascinated me.

'The character of Grandad gave the situation the voice of an old man who'd seen all of life. He'd witnessed the end of the First World War and lived through the Second and now couldn't really give a monkey's about the world. Del Boy was the man in the middle, with enough experience of life to know the pitfalls, but still young enough to have a dream and be ambitious. Rodney was the naïve young lad at the beginning of the road who was very, very green. With the three ages you had a balance.

'Rodney reminds me of myself when I was young. I was a dreamer and an idealist, just like Rodders is. There was a kid in school with us who had two GCEs – and he went round acting like he was Einstein. Whenever there was an argument he'd behave like his two GCEs made him automatically right. I used that idea for Rodney who is so proud

Above: Lennard Pearce as Grandad Trotter, the voice of experience and a man who'd seen all of life.

of his two 'O' Levels. On one side Del would use them to praise him and on the other he'd send him up because of them.'

To bond the brothers even more closely, John brought in the idea that their father had deserted them and that their mother Joan had died when Rodney was just three, leaving Del to bring up his little brother. 'In those cockney and Irish working-class worlds the mother figure, particularly the late mother figure, was so incredibly important,' says John. 'Over the years people would still be crying about her, even if she'd actually been horrible. That means there's warmth and love there but you can also paint the picture that she was nothing like how Del describes her. Rodney doesn't really remember her and Del just can't see what she was really like.'

A few weeks after John's initial conversation with Ray in the pub, he arrived at Ray's office at BBC Television Centre with a draft script for *Readies*, as he called the show at that time. Butt was impressed. 'I read it, liked it and sent it to Head of Comedy, John Howard Davis,' he recalls. 'He read it and then sent me a memo back saying he quite liked the script but that he didn't think it was an opener, a first episode.

'I kept that memo on my wall until the day I left the BBC and I treasured it. He was totally and utterly wrong because we made that episode and it stayed as the first episode, "Big Brother". Despite his reluctance over the first episode, however, John Howard Davis did see the potential in the series and, with pressure from Ray Butt, commissioned Sullivan to write a full series, although there was no guarantee that it would ever actually go into production. 'It was a tremendous moment for me,' John recalls. 'I think they were a little bit shocked about how colourful it was but they went with it.'

Several factors counted in John's favour this time, in contrast to the first time he'd talked to the BBC about

Readies. Firstly the Corporation had to pay him anyway, under the terms of his contract, so they felt they might as well get him to write something. Secondly, they had a gap in their transmission schedules left by *Over the Moon.* Thirdly, *Minder* had begun on ITV and was proving to be a big ratings success. So there was a growing realisation that there was an audience for shows about modern-day, rough, tough, London wheeler-dealers and the BBC wasn't yet tapping it.

'When *Minder* first came out I was choked because I thought that they'd done that modern London,' says John Sullivan. 'They weren't doing markets or tower blocks but it was modern London and it was very good and I just thought: "Shit. That's that idea gone". But after *Over the Moon* was axed and I wrote *Readies* the BBC changed their minds. And I've always given credit to *Minder* for opening that door for me, because without it I don't think that idea would have ever got used.'

Within two weeks John Sullivan had written a second episode and the rest followed quickly. Senior executives liked them and the show was given the green light to actually go into production. Ray Butt set about finding a cast for the series and this proved terribly simple on one side – and fiendishly tough on the other. Nicholas Lyndhurst, who'd begun his career as a child star and gone on to find fame as Wendy Craig's screen son Adam in Carla Lane's BBC comedy series *Butterflies,* was first to be cast – in the role of Rodney Trotter.

John Sullivan recalls: 'John Howard Davis came down to the production office and told us, sort of point blank, that Nick Lyndhurst was going to play Rodney. He thought Nick was right for the part and neither Ray nor I disagreed. The only thing I doubted, and it was only for a moment, was whether Nick could play working-class convincingly.

'That was because I'd only seen him as middle-class in *Butterflies* and, as I really hate false accents, I didn't want some middle-class boy coming in, trying to do his version of cockney. John told me about Nick having played Ronnie Barker's cockney son Raymond in *Going Straight,* the follow-up to *Porridge,* and convinced me about him – and of course, once I'd seen him in action, I was happy. There was no argument.'

Lennard Pearce only landed the role of the Trotter boys' elderly grandad by chance. Ray Butt rang an agent he knew well, and trusted, called Carole James and told her what he was looking for. 'What I was really after was almost

an old man Steptoe character but I didn't want to use Wilfrid Brambell because he was so well known from *Steptoe and Son,* but it was that sort of part,' says Ray Butt.

'Carole said she didn't have anyone who fitted the bill on her book but she knew of this actor called Lennard Pearce who was with another agent. So I rang the other agent and we got Lennard in to see us and I thought he was perfect.'

John Sullivan recalls: 'We saw two or three actors for the part and then Lennard came in and he read a bit for us and we just heard that lovely old growly voice of his and when he'd gone I said to Ray: "That's him."'

'Ray said: "Let's see the others" and I said: "Well, we can see the others but that's him". There was no doubt in my mind whatsoever that he was right as our grandad. To me his voice was just like everyone's grandad.' He was perfect for the part – except in one way, as John Sullivan explains. 'Being an old man, I assumed he had some false teeth in there so I wrote one episode, "It Never Rains", where he didn't have his teeth in and Lennard read it and piped up: "But I've got all my own teeth!"'

Casting Del proved to be the biggest headache. First choice was actor Enn Reitel. 'I thought Enn was right for the original character of Del as written,' says Ray Butt. 'With hindsight, he is physically very different to David Jason, and much taller, but I thought casting him would appease Jimmy Gilbert because he looked more like Nick Lyndhurst and Jimmy felt the pair should look like traditional brothers.'

Ray Butt approached Enn Reitel's agent only to find that he was busy filming a series for Yorkshire Television called *Misfits* and would not be available. Enn went on to find fame in the BBC series *The Adventures of Lucky Jim* and the ITV series *Mog* but it is his versatility with voices which has been the key to his success. He provided many of the voices for *Spitting Image,* including Lester Piggott, Dustin Hoffman and Donald Sinden, and is now one of Britain's top voice-over artists.

John Howard Davis then suggested to Ray Butt that he should go to see another actor, Jim Broadbent, who was appearing in Mike Leigh's play *Goosepimples* at the Hampstead Theatre in North London. 'I went to see him and he was very good and afterwards we had a drink and I offered him the part,' recalls Ray Butt. 'He turned it down because the play was transferring to the West End. He didn't think he could split his energies between opening in the West End and doing a new sitcom series. I understood

his problem and thought it was very nice of him to be so upfront about it.'

However Jim did appear in three episodes of the show as dodgy detective Roy Slater, who viewers later found out had once been married to Del's long-time girl-friend Raquel. Two other actors in the frame at one stage were Robin Nedwell and Billy Murray, who was starring in the West End play *Moving* with Roger Lloyd Pack and Penelope Keith. Ray didn't think Billy, who now stars in ITV's *The Bill* as Detective Sergeant Don Beech, would be right for Del Boy but the trip to the theatre wasn't a complete waste of time, as Ray spotted Roger Lloyd Pack who he thought would be perfect for the role of dozy roadsweeper Trigger who first appeared in episode one.

Ray Butt was getting nowhere fast. Sitting in his flat off North End Road, West Kensington, one Sunday evening, he was getting increasingly worried. 'I remember thinking: "Christ, we start filming in a couple of weeks and we're still missing a main character." Time was getting tighter and tighter and we were getting close to being up the creek without a paddle.'

What might have been. This could have been how you saw the Trotter brothers and their friend Trigger. Actor Jim Broadbent was offered the role of Del. He did appear in the series though, playing the role of dodgy detective Roy Slater.

There was a real possibility of losing Nick Lyndhurst and Lennard Pearce, because he didn't have the budget to contract them to the show until it was due to go into production and so there was a chance that they'd be signed up for other work in the meantime. Ray then switched on his television and happened to catch a repeat of *Open All Hours*, written by Roy Clarke, a hugely successful comedy series about stuttering Northern corner-shopkeeper Arkwright, played by Ronnie Barker, and his delivery boy nephew Granville, played by David Jason.

One particular part of the episode caught Ray's attention. Granville was in the shop's storeroom and had a long solo scene. 'The penny dropped,' Ray recalls. 'I thought: "David could be just right for Del."' The following morning Ray arrived at his office at BBC Television Centre and immediately telephoned John Sullivan to put forward his suggestion about David Jason playing the lead role.

'John was a bit tepid, to put it mildly,' he recalls. 'He wasn't that keen at all because his first impression was that David wasn't right for the role. He wasn't dead against him and was willing to listen but he wanted time to think about the idea.'

'It wasn't that I was against the idea of David for the role as such,' says John. 'It was more that I couldn't actually see him in the part. I was terrified that he couldn't play that sharp edge that you needed for Del.'

'John had it very fixed in his mind what sort of character Del Boy was,' says David Jason. 'And he didn't think I could play that.'

Ray Butt had another ally in senior producer Syd Lotterby. He'd worked with David Jason on shows like *Porridge* and *Open All Hours*, and had produced and directed a pilot show, starring David and written by Roy Clarke, called *It's Only Me Whoever I Am*, which was never transmitted.

'It just didn't work,' says David. 'It was loosely based on the character of Granville and they thought there might be something in it for me. It was about a guy who lived with his mother in the North and wasn't allowed to grow up, basically.'

Ray Butt had worked on that show as Production Manager alongside Syd Lotterby, and after filming he, Syd and David would play pool at the hotel where they were staying. David was fascinated by Ray's strong East London accent and often used to mimic him. It was all good-humoured and no offence was ever meant or taken. When Ray said he was going to get David Jason in to read the part of Del Boy, Syd reminded Ray of those times. This only added to Ray's certainty that he'd found the right man for the part.

The only resistance to David being cast came from the BBC's Head of Light Entertainment, Jimmy Gilbert, and other senior executives. One reason was that they feared casting him in his own series could jeopardise their relationship with Ronnie Barker. At that stage Ronnie was Britain's number one TV star and a major asset to BBC Television. Both *Open All Hours* and *The Two Ronnies* were huge successes for the Corporation and the risk of offending Ronnie was deemed too great.

David Jason, cast in the part of Del just weeks before the series began filming. It now seems inconceivable that anyone else could have played the part.

Yet Ronnie saw David Jason almost as his prodigy and it seems unlikely that he would have been anything other than delighted that his friend and colleague should gain the recognition he was due by way of his own starring vehicle. Nevertheless, it seems there was major reluctance high up at the BBC to promote David Jason in case for some reason it caused difficulties with Barker. The other reason for their reluctance to consider Jason was that he didn't look at all like Nicholas Lyndhurst, a fact which was actually a key part of John Sullivan's Trotter mythology.

For, as John Sullivan says: 'The whole point is that Del and Rodney are actually the only ones who think they are brothers. Everyone else thinks they might well have different fathers. They had to be counterpoints to each other – one tall, one short, one blond and the other dark-haired. They had to look different to each other and at one point when we were casting there was even a suggestion that we had one of them mixed-race.

'The age difference between them was important too because Del is almost a father figure to Rodney and he is supposed to be about fifteen years older than him.'

The more Ray Butt thought about David Jason as Del – not to mention the closer his filming deadline grew – the more he convinced himself that David was right for the job. 'I always knew that he was a fine actor,' says Ray. 'And a particularly fine comedy actor. He's also capable of playing very heavy drama and has shown that time and time again.'

As soon as he saw a script for *Only Fools and Horses*, David Jason was determined to get the part of Del Boy. 'I thought it was one of the funniest things I'd ever read,' he recalls. 'I couldn't wait to turn over the page.'

However, at that point David wasn't sure which part he was being considered for. 'The reason I wasn't certain was that at that stage in my career I'd been playing a lot of old men. I was a character actor and they were the sort of parts I was getting.

TROTTERS
INDEPENDENT
NEW YORK · PARIS

'I'd played the 100-year-old gardener Dithers in *His Lordship Entertains* and old Blanco in *Porridge* and I thought they might have thought that I'd wanted to play Grandad or even Rodney because it could have been cast any way.'

Eventually Ray Butt asked David to come in and read for the part of Del Boy with Nicholas Lyndhurst. 'I was sort of past auditioning for jobs at that stage in my career,' David says. 'But this script was so good and Del was the sort of character I'd never played. In addition to playing old men, I'd also been playing a lot of hapless characters like Granville in *Open All Hours,* which I was still doing, and the parts I'd played in *Lucky Fella* and *A Sharp Intake of Breath*.

'I was known for playing losers and then here was the part of Del – this sharp, bright, upfront guy with all this bounce and quick chat. It was the sort of part that normally nobody would ever have considered me for. I went to that meeting desperately wanting the job. I thought it was one of the best things I'd ever read. It was just very funny, although there was no guarantee it would be successful. I suppose I just had a gut feeling that it would work out.'

David, knowing it would be him who missed out if the

Above: Just weeks before filming began, David Jason joined Nicholas Lyndhurst and Lennard Pearce to complete the casting of the Trotter family.
Opposite: Proof positive that they got it right – Nicholas Lyndhurst and David Jason at a BAFTA awards ceremony.

BBC bosses couldn't be convinced to let him and Nicholas Lyndhurst play brothers because they didn't look alike, had his own explanation prepared for their differences. 'Just because they were brothers didn't mean they had to look alike and they might not genetically have the same father,' he says. 'One of them could actually be the milkman's! Of course we didn't know that at the time but later John quite rightly exploited the fact that they don't necessarily look like brothers. After all, there's one who's three foot five and the other's eight foot six!'

The following day David was asked to come back and read with Nicholas Lyndhurst and Lennard Pearce. This time John Sullivan was at the meeting and he was impressed. 'He read with Nick and Lennard for about a quarter of an hour and that was it,' says John. 'Ray and I looked at each other and nodded. We had our Del and Rodney.

'Ray suddenly said: "OK, thanks. We're going to go with you three," recalls David Jason. 'As you can imagine I was delighted. Then we all shook hands and went off for a drink.'

That was it. After all the discussions and disagreements it was finally decided in fifteen minutes. Within weeks the show went into production.

PART

2

John Sullivan THE WRITER

Above: John Sullivan in the late 70s when he had made the amazing move from being a scene shifter at the BBC to writer of the hit comedy series Citizen Smith.
Opposite: A recent picture of John.

Ohn Sullivan did what was expected of him in 1957 and failed his eleven-plus. Four years later he left school without any qualifications and took the first of a long line of fill-in jobs to make ends meet. He's come a very long way since, although his journey to fame and fortune has been neither easy nor quick.

Born in 1946, he grew up in Balham, South London. His father, also John, was a plumber and his mother Hilda was a housewife who occasionally worked as a charlady. 'My childhood was almost clichéd working class,' he says. 'Our house had three floors and another family lived at the top. There was a tin bath hanging out in the yard that would come into the scullery on a Friday and we'd heat water up on the stove for it. We didn't have an inside toilet until I was about five.'

John had little ambition and school was something to be tolerated until he could get out and begin earning a living. However, from the age of twelve, one lesson began to hold his attention – English. And the British viewing public owe a great debt of gratitude to a certain Mr Trowers, a young English master with an eye patch, who taught at Telferscot School. Jim Trowers, more than anyone else, inspired John to take an interest in the subject, an interest that would eventually lead him to try his hand at writing scripts.

'Up until Jim Trowers started teaching us, all we had done during English classes was to be given a book and told to read it in silence,' says John. 'Afterwards we'd be asked questions about it and we never really took it in. You'd rather go to sleep. Suddenly Mr Trowers came along and, instead of just letting us read the books, he'd read them to us, acting it out and doing all the voices. He made it come alive.

'I remember being almost hypnotised by Charles Dickens' *David Copperfield*. I was enthralled by it and for the first time in all my school days I was actually look-ing forward to something other than football. From that moment on I was very keen on English and I started to enjoy writing. I liked Dickens because he was the first author whose work had come alive for me and had colour in it. He was writing about areas that I knew about and the class system that was familiar to me. From then on he became my favourite author.'

Even so, John ended up leaving school at fifteen without any qualifications. 'The middle-class kids in their school uniforms would do "O" Levels but us working-class mob from the poor areas didn't,' he says. 'Their parents worked in offices and they knew they might be going somewhere. That didn't apply to the rest of us. We wanted to get out and earn some money to help the family out.'

John Sullivan

…it never seemed to matter if we passed or not because we were all going to work in factories anyway.

It had been the same with the eleven-plus. 'I remember taking the exam but it never seemed to matter if we passed or not because we were all going to work in factories anyway. That's how it was and so we approached it with that attitude. Teachers would say how important the exam was and our attitude was: "Yeah, right." We knew we were going to be factory fodder so there seemed to be no point trying.'

His first job was as a messenger with Reuters. Then, at sixteen he joined advertising agency, Collett, Dickinson and Pearce, again as a messenger, where he worked for, among others, David Puttnam and Alan Parker, who would later become famous film-makers. A year later, fed up with earning just £3.50 a week, he joined his best friend Colin Humphries, cleaning cars for a second-hand motor trader, and his wages shot up to a respectable £20 a week. 'Suddenly I was earning more money than my father and I could afford to do up the family home a bit and have a phone line put in,' he says.

Later John and Colin began selling cars. 'But I wasn't a very successful salesman,' he laughs. 'I used to do stupid things, like one time when I was asked to go out and test a car my boss was thinking of buying in, and all I did was go out and test how good the radio was. I thought it was great driving this fast MG and didn't bother listening to the engine. I came back and said it was brilliant and he bought

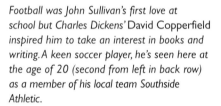

Football was John Sullivan's first love at school but Charles Dickens' David Copperfield *inspired him to take an interest in books and writing. A keen soccer player, he's seen here at the age of 20 (second from left in back row) as a member of his local team Southside Athletic.*

it on my word. He came in the following day furious. It turned out the engine was knackered but I hadn't heard it over the noise of the radio. In the end I decided that it wasn't the job for me.'

His next job was at Watney's Brewery and it was there that he first decided to try his hand at scriptwriting. 'I had a job stacking crates of beer and going out delivering to pubs,' he says. 'I worked with a guy called Paul Saunders, who I knew from school. He was a very funny bloke with a very dry wit and we got on well. The job was so dull that we used humour to keep us from going mad. One day he read an article about Johnny Speight which said he earned £1000 a script for *Till Death Us Do Part* and Paul said: "We're pretty funny guys. We could do this."

'I said: "Yeah, anything for a laugh" and I went out and bought an old typewriter for about £2 and for the next two months we wrote this idea we had for a sitcom which we then sent off to the BBC. It was called *Gentleman* and it was about an old ex-soldier who ran an old-fashioned gents' toilet with brass pipes and china trough. It was his pride and joy and he had his regular people who used to come in every morning. Then suddenly he started to lose his customers because the council opened a brand-new loo down the road, with piped muzak and aftershave on tap and hot air hand-dryers. After three months we got a letter back saying, "We are not looking for this kind of material" which was quite right because it was awful.'

The rejection put Paul off the idea of writing but John was undaunted. 'I'd enjoyed the process of writing and developing characters so much that I carried on on my own and wrote various scripts. One was about a family called the Leeches who lived off the state and knew every fiddle there was, and another was about a football team. I'd send them off to the BBC and get nowhere, so I'd rewrite them, change the names and send them in again, giving myself a different name. Everything I wrote about was based on people that I knew, places I was familiar with, and that hasn't really changed much over the years.'

It isn't just the British who love *Only Fools and Horses*. It has been sold all round the world and dubbed into a host of foreign languages. Among the countries who've bought the show are: Ireland, Hong Kong, Spain, Yugoslavia, Belgium, New Zealand, Croatia, Australia, South Africa, Israel, Poland, Cyprus, Greece, Pakistan, Serbia, Barbados and Malta. The Netherlands went one better and as well as buying the BBC version also made their own called *Wat schuift't? (What's it Worth?)*. Pictured (l–r) are Johnny Kraaykamp jr as Stef (Del), Sacco van der Made as Granpa (Grandad) and Kasper van Kooten as Robbie (Rodney).

My dad was my greatest influence… he was a prisoner of war, a bookies' runner and an illegal boxer… he had some great stories.

John's working-class roots have given him most of his writing ideas. 'My dad was my greatest influence,' he says. 'He was a prisoner of war, a bookies' runner and an illegal boxer, and he had some great stories. He swore blind that he saw Hitler after the war. It was after the Americans had released him from his POW camp. He went scavenging for food and went into a barn and there was a tall German in a full-length leather coat who pulled a gun out. With him was Hitler wearing a suit and Eva Braun and they asked if my dad could get clothes from anywhere. He said yes and he went off and never said a word to anyone at the time about seeing them – nor did he get them any clothes. I once asked him why and I think it was because he hated the British army so much because of the class system in the POW camp that by the end of the war I don't think he was too sure which side he was fighting on!'

John Sullivan

After his brewery job John went to work with his father as a plumber. 'But I was an even worse plumber than I was a car salesman,' he admits. 'I was terrible. The last guy I worked for said that I flooded more houses than Hurricane Hilda. I just didn't check things properly and then I'd switch the water on and would have forgotten to tighten something up somewhere and water would start pouring from some joint or start coming through a ceiling!'

...we only had two books in the house. One was the Bible and the other was a Littlewoods' football pools perm book.

At the same time as working, John tried to learn more about some of the subjects he'd missed out on at school. 'Most weeks, after I got paid, I'd go and buy one of those "teach yourself" books, like on maths or English,' he recalls. 'I was always keen on buying books and reading as much as I could. My parents hadn't been big book lovers. In fact we only had two books in the house. One was the Bible and the other was a Littlewoods' football pools perm book.'

In 1972 John met a pretty secretary called Sharon in The Drugstore pub in London's King's Road. 'I was working as a plumber at the time and I went out with her a few times before I told her about my ideas of becoming a writer,' he says. 'At the time she said, "Oh really" but later she admitted she thought, "Oh God, I've got a weirdo!" She thought I must be a bit of a dreamer.' She was earning more than him at the time, but decided she could put up with his writing ambitions. Two years later they married and she then had to put up with him bashing away at his typewriter on the kitchen table for the next few years.

As an aspiring writer, John would make up stories and situations at random by picking bits out of newspapers. 'As a brain exercise, I'd decided to open a paper on, say, page two and write something about whatever I read on the top of column two,' he says. 'It could be anything, from a company crashing to a court report, and I'd try to think of what I'd write about it if I was given it as subject matter. When would-be writers come to me for advice I now recommend the idea to them as a way of challenging themselves and of giving themselves flexibility and encouraging them to be ready to change and adapt their scripts.'

Every time he had a rejection letter from the BBC he redoubled his efforts. But he also had a theory about the staff of the Corporation's script-reading department who had to sift through the mountains of ideas from would-be writers, filtering out the ones they thought had potential for producers and sending rejection slips to the writers of the rest. 'I used to think that if these people were that good then why were they just reading scripts all day?' he says. 'Surely if they were any good they'd be producing shows and doing things. I didn't have much faith in them.'

One day he came up with the idea for *Citizen Smith* – about a Tooting man who planned to start a revolution – based upon a man he knew from a South London pub who was always talking about doing the same thing. 'I knew it was my best idea yet,' he says. 'I thought it had lots of potential as talk of revolution was topical in the seventies. I was almost frightened to send it in and have it rejected. It was

Only Fools and Horses has won a stack of awards over the years including: Television Situation Comedy of the Year 1984, 1997 (Television and Radio Industries Club – TRIC), Best Comedy Series 1986, 1988 and 1997 (BAFTA), Funniest Television Programme, 1989 (SOS Award), Best Situation Comedy Award and Best Comedy Drama Award 1997 (Royal Television Society Programmes Awards)... and that's not counting individual awards to writer John Sullivan and actor David Jason.

like having an ace in a poker game. I didn't know when to throw it! I figured that if *Smith* didn't go I'd have to give up the idea of writing because I had nothing else.'

He decided his best bet was to get a job at the BBC, any job, learn more about the business and then meet someone who might actually take some notice of his script. 'I wrote a letter to them, telling them what I wanted to do, and the moment I posted it, I regretted it,' he says. 'I thought they'd think I was a maniac and I wouldn't get considered.' Fortunately they didn't and John was interviewed and given a job at BBC Television in the props department, on the understanding that he wouldn't annoy the stars. He soon switched jobs and became a scene shifter because it was a studio job and brought him closer to actual filming.

John had been biding his time, waiting to meet a producer to talk to about his idea for *Citizen Smith*. One Sunday a colleague pointed out a dapper man. He said he was a producer called Dennis Main Wilson who John knew was a bit of a legend at the BBC and the producer of hit shows like *Till Death Us Do Part*. At last John had someone he could talk to who had some creative influence. 'But I was a bit intimidated by the fact he had a double-barrelled name and that he had a sort of ex-RAF officer air about him,' John says.

'A few evenings later I found him in the small BBC bar which I thought was reserved for producers and directors but I was too nervous to approach him. Twice I started walking across to him and both times I bottled it. The third time he spotted me. Our eyes met and I had no choice but to actually go over and introduce myself. Everyone else in there was smartly dressed and I felt very conspicuous in my scruffy jeans and big boots. I thought: "I'm going to get sacked for this."

'I said, "Dennis. I'm John Sullivan. I thought I'd introduce myself because we're going to be working together soon." And he said, "Oh, what on?" thinking I was going to be working on one of his shows and I said, "On this new thing I've just written" and he just roared with laughter. He said, "Buy me a drink", and I did and we sat at the bar chatting and he gave me lots of advice and encouragement. I think he liked my cheek and I later found out that he liked people who were upfront so I obviously picked the right guy to approach.'

One of his main pieces of advice was that John should go off and write sketches for shows like *The Two Ronnies* and *The Dave Allen Show*. Breaking his promise not to bother the stars, while working on *Porridge* John asked Ronnie Barker for advice. He told Ronnie that he had some ideas for sketches and the star told him to bring them in. A week later he did and Barker took them home to read. The following Sunday Ronnie called John over and asked him if he could write any more. 'He was terrific to me,' says John. 'He said he liked them and he put me on a contract. I was ecstatic.'

Five weeks later John met Dennis again, still keen to write *Citizen Smith*. This time, impressed by the fact that he'd been hired to write material for *The Two Ronnies*, Main Wilson told John to go off and write it. John didn't wait around. He took two weeks' leave and went to Sharon's parents' home in Crystal Palace where he bashed out a pilot script for *Citizen Smith* which he delivered to Dennis as soon as it was finished. He then promptly took another week off, which he again spent at his in-laws'.

★★★*Did you know?*

'Only Fools and Horses' was the title of a 1979 episode of John Sullivan's first series *Citizen Smith*, which featured a guest appearance by *Steptoe and Son* star Wilfrid Brambell.

AN EYE FOR THE CAST TOO
John Sullivan isn't just a dab hand at writing scripts. He also has a good eye for spotting the right people to star in his shows. He cast Robert Lindsay in *Citizen Smith*, Paul Nicholas in *Just Good Friends*, Ralph Bates in *Dear John*, Diane Bull in *Sitting Pretty* and Robert Daws in *Roger, Roger*. John Sullivan's wife Sharon also takes an active role in his writing and makes suggestions on casting and scripts. So much so, that when *Only Fools and Horses* producer Ray Butt moved to a new job with Central Television, he wanted Sharon to join him as a casting director.

John Sullivan

DEFENDING DEL BOY

In the aftermath of the success of the final three stories, Chris Woodhead, the Government's Chief Inspector of Schools, launched an attack on the morals of the show and concluded that: 'If Del Boy and Rodney are the only role models available to the young then we have a problem.'

John Sullivan was persuaded to hit back and in a short article for *The Sunday Times* he defended his creations. He pointed out that Del had brought up his younger brother after they lost both parents, cared for and fed his ageing Grandfather and later his old Uncle Albert and strove to make sure he could always provide for them.

He admitted that some of Del's 'business arrangements' may not have fared well in a court of law but said that compared with the activities of some politicians and captains of industry, Del was squeaky clean. Rodney, he said, was a decent, law-abiding young man and the first to warn against anything unsavoury. Albert had spent his life fighting Nazism and his only fault was in constantly reminding everyone of the fact.

He asked if Mr Woodhead believed that youngsters were so stupid that they would copy everything they saw on screen or stage. Did Shakespeare's Romeo and Juliet induce young people to commit suicide, he wondered, or did Charles Dickens endorse pickpocketing as a fun career in *Oliver Twist*.

'Throughout the series,' he conclude, 'I have tried to emphasise the basic decency of the Trotters. They are not violent, they don't take drugs and they don't drink and drive. They respect the old and the very young. More importantly, they have strong family values, loyalty and love and the ability to laugh at themselves. If more people followed their example, Britain might be a happier place.'

Main Wilson loved the script and so did his boss, Jimmy Gilbert. They wanted to make it for a Comedy Playhouse series which tried out new ideas with a view to them becoming series. When he returned home a week later the writer phoned Main Wilson for his verdict. John remembers the response. '"Where the hell have you been?" came the reply. "We've been looking for you everywhere. We're doing it!" I couldn't believe it. After ten years of trying, something was finally happening. It was a great moment. It went into production and eight weeks later it was on the telly.'

The show did well and a full series was commissioned. Sullivan was on his way. After two years shifting scenery he quit his job and decided to throw himself into writing full time. The rest, to quote a well-known cliché, is history. Although there are plenty of comedy writers working in television who create popular shows that have good ratings, none seem to have quite matched John Sullivan's ability to capture such a wide-ranging audience and no comedy is likely to better the huge ratings he's achieved with *Only Fools and Horses*. He is generally considered to be in a class of his own.

As David Jason puts it, 'There are some great writers but John is the best. I saw the strengths in his work and what he was capable of very early on, and would encourage him to be bolder and braver about the emotional side of his characters. A lot of people would dismiss things in a comedy and say: "Hang on, this is a comedy and you are getting too serious here." But I realised that that was his strength and the way he wrote he made them more human and not just sitcom characters.'

'John writes about real people,' says Nick Lyndhurst. 'He's so clever because he can lead you up one garden path with his writing and you can be convinced that you think you know where it is going and then suddenly something completely different happens.'

Only Fools and Horses may be the show that everyone talks about but John has also had great success with the other shows he's created. *Just Good Friends* was a smash hit and *Dear John*, about a hapless divorcee, was very popular and a Hollywood version became a huge hit in the United States. The 1992 sitcom *Sitting Pretty*, about the life of sixties good-time girl Annie Briggs, wasn't a big hit but he bounced back with a two-part comedy drama set during the war, *Over Here*, which starred Martin Clunes. *Roger, Roger*, based around a mini-cab firm and starring Robert Daws, is his newest hit, and his latest project, *Heartburn Hotel*, which he has co-written with Steve Glover, stars Tim Healy as a Falklands vet running a downmarket hotel. He's also been commissioned by the BBC to adapt his favourite novel *David Copperfield* for television.

His success has earned him a decent lifestyle and a large house in a leafy part of Surrey, where he lives with his wife Sharon, their sons Daniel and Jim and daughter Amy, but he remains a quiet, unassuming and down-to-earth man. He's passionate and enthusiastic about his work but still worries about whether the next script will be as funny as his last one. 'And I'm sure that will always be the case,' he says. 'But that's probably no bad thing.'

Writer John Sullivan, director Tony Dow and the cast gather together on the set of the Nag's Head after filming the final episode.

David Jason
DEL

Whenever he thinks about the circumstances that led to him landing the part of Del Trotter, David Jason chuckles to himself. It was, after all, pretty well all down to fate, mixed with a fair measure of good luck.

Above and opposite: David Jason in his role of Del Trotter, the main character in the BBC's most successful comedy series of all time, Only Fools and Horses. A time span of ten years separates the two photographs which were taken in 1981 and 1991.

It all began over a decade before, when David missed out on a role which would have given him his biggest television break and probably would have made him a major star. Back in the autumn of 1967, television producer David Croft and his writing partner Jimmy Perry were casting for a new BBC comedy series. The show, called *Dad's Army*, was all about the exploits of a group of old men who were members of a South Coast town's wartime Home Guard platoon.

They had already cast most of the major parts but there was one more role that needed filling – that of bumbling, elderly butcher Lance Corporal Jack Jones – and it was offered to character actor Clive Dunn. However he was busy at the time, in *The Spike Milligan Show,* and had to turn it down. Croft then thought of David Jason, a young character actor, who, although still only in his late twenties, was skilled at playing old men. Croft thought highly of Jason and had used him a couple of times before in a BBC sitcom he produced called *Hugh and I*, starring Hugh Lloyd and Terry Scott as two friends who lived together in South London.

David Jason was called in to read for the part and two hours later his agent rang to tell him he'd got the job. Three hours after that she rang back to say she had very bad news and that he hadn't got it at all. In the meantime Clive Dunn had discovered that no more Spike Milligan shows were being made at that time and so he had decided to accept the part in *Dad's Army* after all. Understandably, David was hugely disappointed to lose a part that would have been his first big break in mainstream television, especially when *Dad's Army* became a major success and ran for nine years. But these days he's rather glad it happened that way.

For life would have been very different if he *had* starred in *Dad's Army*. He would have been busy filming that series when the part of dopey corner-shop assistant Granville, in Roy Clarke's *Open All Hours,* came up. That would have

David Jason DEL

meant that he would never have worked with Ray Butt on that show – or been cast in *It's Only Me Whoever I Am,* where he showed off his ability with accents by mimicking Ray's strong London accent.

Then he would never even have been considered for the part of Del Trotter – the role that has made him famous and allowed him to demonstrate the brilliant acting skills that have since led to straight roles in *Porterhouse Blue* and *A Touch of Frost.*

'After I lost the part in *Dad's Army* and it started to become really successful there were times when I'd watch it and see Corporal Jones and I'd say, "I was offered that bloody part!"' he recalls.

'You can't help thinking like that. At the time I thought it would have changed my life because I would have been recognised as a television actor, which I wasn't at that stage. That's all history now but not getting that part had a major effect on my career. When I think about it, the whole thing that led to me getting the part of Del is littered with ifs and buts. Obviously if John Sullivan's other show hadn't been cancelled then he would never have written *Only Fools.* If Jim Broadbent or Enn Reitel had been free to play the part of Del then I would have never done it, and if Ray Butt hadn't been determined to cast me then I would have never got the job at all.'

David Jason was born David John White on 2 February 1940. His father, Arthur, was a fish porter at Billingsgate Fish Market, his mother Olwen was a charlady, and the family – David, his elder brother Arthur and younger sister June – lived in a modest terraced home in Finchley, North London.

I didn't want to be in the school play. Only girls were in plays.

He did his first acting in a school play, *Wayside War,* at the age of fourteen. He only got the part when a classmate dropped out with measles, and he was a reluctant performer. 'I didn't want to be in the school play,' he says. 'Only girls were in plays.' He played a cavalier in the Civil War drama and, to his surprise, he loved every minute of it and joined an amateur dramatic society straight afterwards.

He left school at fifteen and, as his parents had always wanted him to get a trade, he worked in a garage as a trainee mechanic but left after a year and became an apprentice electrician. By night he was treading the boards in a string of amateur productions and he soon set his heart on acting professionally, just like his elder brother Arthur.

By the time he reached his mid-twenties David was working as an electrician with his friend Bob Bevil, with whom he'd set up a company called B. and W. Installations. The urge to act professionally was too strong though, and he began thinking about turning professional. His chance came in March 1965 when his brother Arthur was offered a part in the BBC police drama *Z Cars* which would earn him £25. In order to take the television job, Arthur gave up a forthcoming £9-a-week part in the Noël Coward play *South Sea Bubble* at Bromley Rep in Kent.

But before leaving Arthur recommended his brother to the director who, after watching David in action in an amateur play, offered him the job. It was the

DEL *David Jason*

spur he needed. He gave his share in B. and W. Installations to his partner, took the plunge and made his professional debut on 5 April 1965. Other minor work followed, interspersed with long spells out of work, before he went back to Bromley Rep on a year-long contract, playing all sorts of parts, with directors usually recognising his skills as a comic actor and casting him in humorous roles. 'I was a resident so I had to do any part that came up in any play every two weeks,' he recalls. 'I was always playing something from a vicar to a Derek Royle lookalike, falling over or jumping through hoops.'

Derek Royle was an acrobat employed by the Brian Rix Company to appear in his West End farces who was forever tumbling over or being knocked down. When Bromley Rep staged the farces, the part Royle had played would inevitably fall to David Jason. 'I enjoyed doing them and I could do all that stuff but in those days I couldn't get on the West End stage,' he says.

It was while he was appearing at Bromley Rep that David first met Lennard Pearce, the actor who was later to become his co-star in *Only Fools and Horses*. 'We were doing the eighteenth-century comedy *The Rivals*,' he recalls. 'I was playing Bob Acres, the country bumpkin, and Lennard came in to play Sir Lucius O'Trigger, the Irish wheeler-dealer. He was a lovely character actor and one of many who would come in and play a part for a few weeks. We got on very well but after that I didn't see him for about fifteen years until we met again at the BBC.'

Afterwards David continued to work on the stage in a variety of roles and took a number of parts in summer seasons, appearing with stars like Bob Monkhouse and Dick Emery. In the autumn of 1967 he got his first television job in the children's comedy series *Do Not Adjust Your Set*, alongside Eric Idle, Michael Palin and Terry Jones. It was around the same time that David lost out on the *Dad's Army* part. 'At that stage in my career I was winning and losing parts like any other average actor,' he says.

'You'd audition for parts and meet people who you didn't know and they didn't know you or your work. It was a struggle, the way it is for anybody trying to forge a career, prove their worth and make a living as an actor. That's why I was happy to go away and do summer seasons, and I was really happy on stage and enjoyed it. When I missed out on a television part… like anybody, I got disappointed because that was a rung on a different ladder.'

When *Do Not Adjust Your Set* ended in 1969 David landed a small role in the ITV soap *Crossroads* playing a gardener, but it was his next job that gave him his major break. London Weekend Television's *Hark at Barker*, starring Ronnie Barker,

FACT FILE

NAME *David Jason*
DATE OF BIRTH *2.2.1940*
BORN *London*
OTHER TV WORK INCLUDES
Crossroads, Do Not Adjust Your Set, Hark at Barker, The Top Secret Life of Edgar Briggs, Lucky Feller, Open All Hours, A Sharp Intake of Breath, Porterhouse Blue, A Bit of a Do, Amongst Barbarians, The Chemist, The Darling Buds of May, The Bullion Boys, A Touch of Frost, and *March In Windy City*

A young David Jason (left) in one of his first television appearances – the children's comedy series Do Not Adjust Your Set. *With David are Michael Palin, Terry Jones and Eric Idle.*

David Jason DEL

Above: David as Granville and Ronnie Barker as Arkwright in the hugely successful series Open All Hours.
Opposite: An early photograph of David Jason as Del Trotter. Both David and writer John Sullivan had very definite ideas of how the character would dress and behave, drawing heavily on their own backgrounds and experiences.

was produced by Humphrey Barclay, the man behind *Do Not Adjust Your Set,* and he thought David would be great as Dithers, the 100-year-old gardener.

'They were looking for a bloke to play Dithers who was capable of being knocked over and could fall down,' says David. 'You can't get old men to fall down for real because if you do they'll probably break something.' The show was a success, but more important for David was the impression he made on Ronnie Barker. The two got on famously and when Barker came to make a series of seven one-off comedies for the BBC in 1973 he recommended David for a part in one of them, called *Open All Hours,* which later became a hugely popular series.

Similarly, when another of the plays, *Prisoner and Escort* by Dick Clement and Ian le Frenais, was commissioned as a full series in 1974 and renamed *Porridge,* Ronnie suggested David for the part of aged prison lag Blanco Webb, a role he played in three episodes. In 1974 David gained his first starring role in the ITV comedy series *The Top Secret Life of Edgar Briggs,* followed in 1976 by the series *Lucky Feller.* The same year, the first full series of *Open All Hours* was made. Some episodes were directed by Ray Butt and it was he who, five years later, realised that David would make the perfect Del Trotter.

Immediately after being confirmed in the part of Del, David went off with his new co-stars Lennard Pearce and Nicholas Lyndhurst for a celebration drink at the BBC bar at Television Centre in Wood Lane, White City. David had already spotted what Ray Butt and John Howard Davis had realised (as had Dennis Main Wilson back in 1977, when he backed *Citizen Smith),* that they were dealing with scripts by a rare talent.

David recalls, 'I remember saying to Lennard and Nick in the bar, "I think we've got something really unusual here and we're going to have to play this very differently".

'It wasn't like your typical sitcom with very obvious, in your face, jokes. This was much more based around characters. It meant we'd have to approach it differently. I didn't realise at the time, though, that it had the potential that John Sullivan had seen in it and that it would later grow and grow. John had this marvellous ability to make it move with the times and develop in a natural way.'

... *He's got more front than Blackpool and I'm not like that.*

David and Nicholas Lyndhurst had met before they started on **Only Fools and Horses**. Nick had interviewed him about his series *Lucky Feller* when he presented an LWT children's programme called *Our Show.* 'I'd forgotten that,' says David. 'Much later Nick reminded me of it.'

David's enthusiasm for the part and the world in which Del lived also came from the fact that he understood that world. 'I came from the same sort of roots as Del,' he says. 'We both came from poor working-class families and went to the same sort of school. But, from there on, we go our separate ways. For example, he's far more confident than I ever was. He's got more front than Blackpool and I'm not like that.'

David, John Sullivan and Ray Butt were all working-class London boys and all spoke the same language. 'There was a tremendous amount of empathy between us so we could communicate quite quickly,' David recalls. 'Time and time again, John would bring dialogue into the script that we'd used when we were lads, that wasn't heard any more. I'd read a line in a script and that would spark off another one in me, either that my father had said or we had said as kids.'

David Jason DEL

*…I'm the business,
look at me, I'm the
cat's whiskers,
I've got style,
I've got class…*

With John Sullivan's script for the first episode, 'Big Brother', David had a decent idea of the character he was to play but he needed to flesh it out more and bring him to life. It was then that he remembered someone he knew from his days as an electrician. When they ran B. and W. Installations David and his partner Bob Bevil went to great lengths to try to get work. 'One time we were so desperate for work that we did a mail shot,' he recalls. 'We sent hundreds of letters out to every builder, plumber and contractor in London and we got a letter back from this bloke called Derek Hockley. He ran a building firm and he had contracts to do up pubs all over East London and he called us down to his office at his builder's yard in the East End.

'He had a little goatee beard and was terribly well turned out. He always had a clean shirt on that was immaculately pressed, a sharp suit, all the jewellery, highly polished shoes and a camel-hair coat and he just looked the business. He thought he was very smart and what I couldn't get out of my mind was a guy looking as elegantly dressed as he did and yet he spoke like a gorblimey cockney. That really left a great impression on me.

'He looked like he could have been an accountant or an army officer or even a member of the royal family but he spoke like a barrow boy, with an East End accent you could cut with a knife, very similar to Del Boy's. He was a great character and, as I got to know him more, it became clear that he was a real ducker and diver and his watchwords were very much "What costs you nothing can't be dear" and "Don't ask where it came from".

'I think the reason why Derek Hockley stuck in my memory so much was that back then I'd never met anybody who spoke with a strong working-class accent who looked like a posh person. He was a wheeler-dealer and a marvellous character. As far as I was concerned, there was no way he did anything dishonest or illegal but you just knew – he was so sharp.

'We'd give him a price and we'd be making a little bit of a profit, which he'd accept, and then, instead of putting on 10 per cent, he'd double or treble our price and put it in to his customer and get it accepted. His father had started the business and he'd expanded it and he was always after bigger contracts, and we got involved with him after he'd become one of the major contractors for Ind Coope Brewery who had hundreds of pubs in the East End.

'He realised that, in order to win contracts, you didn't just turn up to meetings with brewery managers and architects looking like a wally, so he'd go very, very well dressed. They say "Clothes maketh the man" and I think he was very wise to that, and other rival builders hadn't quite got that panache. They'd go to meetings looking reasonably tidy but when Derek went people would remember him. He looked like money, he looked well dressed and he'd make an impression on people and I think that's why he did it. He was very clever like that.

'So when I came to do *Only Fools and Horses,* I decided to have this character always trying to look the bees' knees and trying to be elegant and smart, even if

DEL *David Jason*

his taste wasn't quite as conservative as people might have liked. I decided to use some of Derek Hockley's attitudes and his dress-sense and apply it to Del Boy. And all that smart, sharp dressing stuff in Del came from Derek. So, even though Del, Rodney and Grandad were living in a Peckham Council flat, it seemed quite funny to find the head of the family spending a lot of money on his image.

'They could starve for want of a slice of bread but Del would still have to have a new tie. Rodney, by contrast, always had the same clothes on, and Grandad, well he wasn't really too worried. Even Del's jeans would have a crease put in the side of them because he thought that looked neat. He wasn't aware that he might look naff. He thought all these things looked smart. Some of them did but some of them just looked terrible.'

David discussed his ideas with writer John Sullivan and costume designer Phoebe De Gaye and, between the three of them, Del Boy, as seen in 'Big Brother', emerged. 'John described him as a medallion man with a sovereign ring on each finger but I felt the medallion was too big and the rings were too many,' remembers David. 'I said I didn't think he'd have a ring on each finger, as that would look common rather than elegant. So we cut the number back to just a couple on each hand, the medallion became a chain with his initial on that he'd often wear over his shirt or jumper, and we added a chunky bracelet.'

Derek Hockley, who sadly died some years ago, recognised the fact that David had taken some inspiration from him when he played Del Boy in *Only Fools and Horses,* and wrote to him. 'He was delighted and very proud of the fact that he had been inspirational to me and that he was the original for Derek Trotter, if you like,' David recalls. 'He was flattered and pleased that I'd likened Del to him but, funnily enough, he was never known as Del.'

…a chain with his initial on that he'd often wear over his shirt or jumper…

Del's confident swagger was David Jason's addition. 'I'd seen it so many times with guys who fancy themselves,' he says. 'They develop a body language that is supposed to impress the birds I suppose. It's like a signal that says "I'm the business, look at me, I'm the cat's whiskers, I've got style, I've got class" which is really sort of wrong but it seemed to fit his personality because Del was full of it, especially when it came to chatting up girls. Like writers, actors are like magpies. They observe people and then sometimes pick things up from them and store them away and that's where that came from. It's just something I'd seen over the years. So you've got your character as created by the writer. Then you pinch an idea from here, an observation from there, and you hope that, once you put it all together, it makes a nice picture.'

David has always had a soft spot for Derek Trotter. 'He's a great character and I enjoy playing him so much because you can play all sides of him,' he says. 'Whatever happens to him, he always bounces back, like a beach ball. However hard you push him down, Del will always bounce back.

'Del's heart has always been in the right place. In terms of human relationships he is a diamond because he'd give you any-

David Jason DEL

thing ultimately and he cares for his family and his friends. I've always seen him as a sort of modern-day Robin Hood although he didn't really ever rob anyone. He's just into deals. It didn't matter if his gear was a bit hooky and he never asked where it came from. To him what was really important was how much he could knock it out for. One of the reasons why he was a failure was if he'd put as much energy into applying his brain to bigger things as he did to making a couple of quid on some bit of junk then they would have been millionaires twenty years ago.

'In his manor he's the sort of bloke who knows everyone. There is no side to him and he doesn't care who he sells to — black, white, Chinese, Jewish or whatever. Del treats them all the same. He'll rip off anyone he can — to him they are all equal. Having said that, he treats people fairly. He'd never take money off the old, the infirm, the crippled. He'd never take advantage of people like that. And at the same time he would look after people. He cares about people and I think that's part of his charm. In a way he's a very moral character and very honest — well, honestly dishonest!'

David has always rejected the suggestion that the show glamorises petty crime. 'The whole point about Del Trotter is that he isn't that successful in what he does,' he says. 'It's easy come and easy go with him and some of what he sells is a bit iffy but most of it is just rubbish. How many times has he ever made any money out of the stuff he's sold? Hardly ever. He's forever getting burnt. Occasionally he makes a bit on a deal but then he loses it all on the next daft idea. So I can't actually see him glorifying living outside the law. It's a difficult one to quantify and I can't really defend him 100 per cent.'

David's own theory is that most of the stuff Del sells is junk or fake rather than stolen. 'If you go up to Oxford Street even now you'll see fly pitchers flogging their gear,' he says. 'You wouldn't believe that it still goes on. Just like Del Boy, there they are with their suitcases and a couple of lookouts selling something like dodgy scent. It's a tenner for three bottles. Everybody who goes up and buys it thinks it's knocked off but they don't say anything.

'The fact of the matter is, it isn't stolen, it's fake. They buy it from a wholesaler, then sell it to people who think they are getting a bargain and that's the way I assume that Del Boy gets most of his gear. It's made somewhere like Taiwan or Singapore and they get it very cheap and so he doesn't mind selling it for a tenner because he's paid next to nothing for it and the punters are going potty for it. Sometimes when I'm in Oxford Street I stand there and watch and it just makes me laugh. I think, "Who are the fools?" The guy has probably bought the fakes legitimately but he's giving people the impression it's knocked off to explain why he can afford to sell it so cheap!'

David has fallen prey to such a con himself. 'I was on a tour in the Far East with Derek Nimmo's theatre company and I went to this place in Dubai where they sell cheap perfume and aftershave. It was like a warehouse and it had every single scent

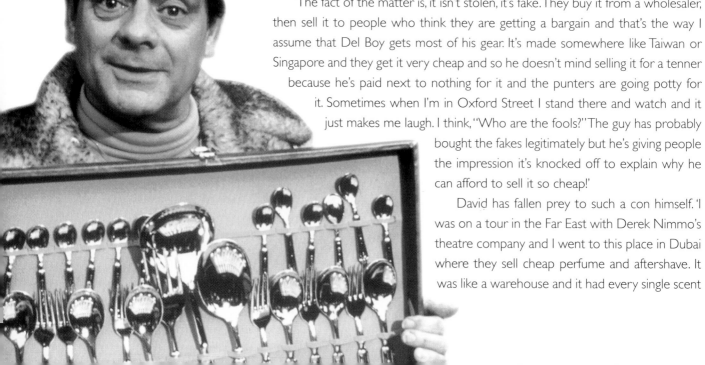

> *…I've always seen him as a sort of modern-day Robin Hood although he didn't really ever rob anyone. He's just into deals.*

in the world in exactly the right bottle with the right label and box. It was really cheap – it only cost me a fiver for half a dozen bottles.

'Later I found out why. What is in it is nothing more than water with a drop of the real stuff in. So that when you take the top off it smells OK but, a few days after you've opened it, it smells like cabbage water and it just stinks. It had gone off and I had to throw it away. So much for my bargain aftershave!'

Del's family is central to his life. He's sacrificed a great deal, not least his chance of getting married as a young man, to bring up his younger brother Rodney when their father Reg walked out and Joan, their mum, died. 'The family tie has always been very strong for Del,' says David. 'He wasn't prepared to leave his family. So if the girl didn't love him enough to take on the rest of the family then, as far as Del was concerned, she wasn't good enough for Del Boy, and he'd elbow her. That would happen time and time again.

'At first Rodney was the younger brother who relied on Del. So Del was the breadwinner who had to go out and earn the money to put food on the table for him and Grandad. As they got older and we first saw them on screen, we'd see them bickering like all families do. It was usually something about Rodney not wanting to carry boxes round or be a lookout. It then became a battle of wits, with Del trying to turn it all round, to manoeuvre the situation to make Rodney feel important. Rodney would try to get out of the work and Del would have to use his brain and outwit him.

'Rodney would refuse to do something and then Del would say something like: "But I can't do this without you Rodney, you are the brains of the outfit. You've got GCEs in maths and art. You are part of my design team and I need your artistic input into this." He'd con him and then, after a while, Rodney would realise that he was being conned and used. He'd started to see through Del but, rather than saying, "Up yours" and walking out, he would basically just do what Del asked. It was his loyalty back to Del, I suppose. The bond between them was stronger than any argument and ultimately they both recognised that.'

Of course Grandad, and later Uncle Albert, would frequently get caught in the crossfire. 'Grandad was family and, yes, Del loved him, but it didn't stop Derek Trotter being Derek Trotter,' says David. 'If Grandad decided to take Rodney's side in an argument Del

Above: Nicholas Lyndhurst (Rodney) and David Jason (Del) as the Trotter brothers. Far left: David Jason as Del with his latest line – a bargain-priced canteen of cutlery.

DEL'S LINGO

John Sullivan's inspiration for Del's daft foreign phrases come from sauce bottles to clothes' labels, says John. 'Del would read things, think that they were impressive and then he'd start to use them, very inappropriately.' Other words, like cushty – which means great or smashing – is an old London saying which comes from Britain's colonial days when a posting to Custibar in India was considered to be easy. Lovely jubbly comes from an ice-lolly called Jubbly, popular in the 50s, which was advertised with the slogan 'Lovely Jubbly'.

Here are some of the best of the rest, and what Del means when he uses them:

Fabrique Belgique: I agree
Plume de ma tante: Used when he's exasperated instead of something like Gordon Bennett
Bonjour: Used to mean goodbye
Au revoir: Used to mean hello
Twonk, Dipstick, Plonker, Pranny, Div and *Wally*: All mean idiot
Allemagne dix points: Such is life
Noofter or Woofter: A gay man
Pucker (Pukka): Perfect

And when he's talking money:
Grand: £1000, *Monkey*: £500, *Century*: £100, *Pony*: £25, *Score*: £20
Douce in bunce: £200 in cash

David Jason DEL

Opposite: David Jason as Detective Inspector Jack Frost in Yorkshire Television's popular drama series A Touch of Frost.

would say, "Shut up, you old git, what do you know? You're going senile. You don't know what you're talking about" but if he took Del Boy's side then he'd praise him. It would be, "There you are see, Grandad agrees. There you are Rodney, did you hear what Grandad said?" Grandad was used as a pawn. Del didn't mean any harm – it was simply that he wanted to get his own way and if it meant using Grandad then he'd use him.'

The public have certainly taken David to their hearts. He's indisputably Britain's best-loved actor and there was delight throughout the country in 1993 when he was awarded an OBE. Yet, despite his success, David Jason is a man who shuns fame. He has never courted publicity and avoids showbusiness parties. He's happier staying at home in Buckinghamshire, tinkering with his old motorbikes, than appearing on chat shows. He loves his work, be it *Only Fools, The Darling Buds of May* or dramas like *A Touch of Frost* or *Porterhouse Blue*, but if he had a choice he would rather be without the attention he receives for it.

…it does become wearing when someone asks him for the fortieth time that day: 'Where's Rodney?'

Not an hour goes by when David is out that someone doesn't shout something along the lines of 'Oi, Del Boy' or 'You plonker'. It's something he's had to get used to. Nevertheless it means it's hard for him to lead a normal life. Having a quiet drink in pubs with friends has become impossible, due to constant interruptions from fans of the show. And, while David understands their interest and is delighted that so many people love *Only Fools*, it does become wearing when someone asks him for the fortieth time that day: 'Where's Rodney?'

'I tend not to go anywhere that I don't have to,' he says. 'I don't go shopping or into pubs or the cinema much, mainly because I know what's going to happen. It's part of the job and it is the downside but it is a small price to pay for the fun that we've had making the show and the enjoyment that it's brought people.'

Indeed David is genuinely thrilled by the laughs that he knows he and his colleagues on *Only Fools and Horses* have given the public. 'When you realise that you bring so much joy to people's lives, through television for Christ's sake, then it isn't all bad, is it?' he says. 'It's very satisfying and it makes me feel extremely privileged. Much of the mail I get is from people saying, "Please don't stop making the series because we love it so much!"'

Only Fools and Horses has also given David the chance to make a difference in a way that few people ever can – and it's not something he has ever made public before. On several occasions he's helped bring people out of comas by recording tapes for them as Del Boy.

'Their families wrote to me, asking me to do Del Boy on tape and asking me to talk to them in the character because it was their favourite show and they thought it might help,' he says. 'And it did, because they've written back to thank me. To me, that has been the very best side of playing Del Boy. I felt very fortunate that I was able to help. It's an unbelievable power and shows just what a powerful medicine comedy is.'

David is no great collector of souvenirs but he has kept a few things to remind him of *Only Fools and Horses*. He says: 'I've got one of Del's caps and I've got a couple of bottles of Peckham Spring water. I'll keep that forever. I won't drink it. After all it's BBC water and not only that, would *you* drink something Del Trotter had made?'

Nicholas Lyndhurst
RODNEY

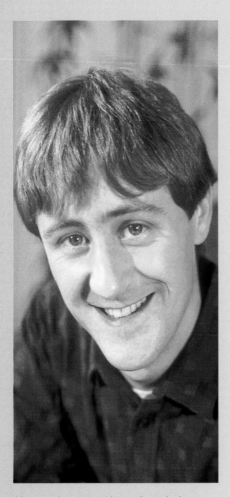

Above and opposite: Not really a plonker. Despite playing the fool on screen, there's nothing daft in real-life about Nicholas Lyndhurst.

Nicholas Lyndhurst was sitting at home in his London flat at around 5p.m. on a Thursday in the spring of 1981 when he heard the double thwack of two packages landing on his doormat. The thick envelopes bearing BBC Television stickers contained six scripts, and a covering letter from Ray Butt explaining that they were for a new series called *Only Fools and Horses* and asking him to read them with a view to being considered for the part of Rodney.

Nick put the scripts aside. He was pushed for time, as he was meeting friends for a drink at 6 o'clock. 'I thought, "I'll read them tomorrow" and I went out,' he recalls. 'I came home about 11p.m. that night, slightly the worse for wear and read the covering note again and noticed a line I hadn't seen before which read, "Could you come and see us tomorrow afternoon." I thought, "Christ – an audition. I'd better start reading these things."

'I had two options: to start reading them there and then or get up early in the morning. I decided to start reading one before I went to bed. That was it. I started reading the first one and I ended up reading the whole lot and didn't finish until about 2a.m. I just couldn't wait to turn over the page. I was laughing out loud and it's been like that ever since – except these days I tear the envelope open if I know there's a *Fools* script inside!'

Nick went off to the BBC the following afternoon thinking he was going to audition. He didn't know at the time that he was the first and only choice to play Rodney. Some weeks later he was called back to read with David Jason and the day after that was asked to read with both David and Lennard Pearce. 'I was oblivious to the fact that I was cast until the moment that they said, "We'd like to go with you three," at the third meeting,' he says.

…He's always trying to be cool and failing miserably…

Nick liked the idea of playing Rodney. 'He's very much an innocent and quite sheltered from the real world and has always had his brother to look after the real nasties,' he says. 'I was – and probably still am – quite awkward and gawky and I accentuated that for the character. I also based him on the younger brother of a friend of mine who was always trying to be one of the lads. Rodney is like that. He's always trying to be cool and failing miserably and you see that a lot with young blokes.

Nicholas Lyndhurst **RODNEY**

FACT FILE

NAME *Nicholas Lyndhurst*
DATE OF BIRTH *21.4.61*
BORN *Emsworth, West Sussex*
OTHER TV WORK INCLUDES
Our Show, Anne of Avonlea, Heidi, The Prince and the Pauper, Going Straight, Butterflies, To Serve Them All Our Days, The Two of Us, The Piglet Files, Stalag Luft, Goodnight Sweetheart and *Gulliver's Travels*

'Rodney relies on Del a great deal and, although in the early days he wanted to break free from him, he never knew how to. They were always rowing with each other but David and I decided that they would be scoring points off each other rather than shouting at each other all the time because that would just get boring for the audience. It's no real wonder, though, that Rodney never got his own enterprise off the ground. After all, who was his role model? Del Trotter and he's not really a great success. Poor Rodney was bound to fail.

'Rodney would moan about having to be Del's lookout or carrying boxes around but ultimately he owes Del a lot and he knows that. Del was sixteen years old when their mum died and Rodney was just two. Del could have cleared off and he knows he could have gone into care and probably should have gone into care. These days he would be taken into care just like that. They wouldn't let a sixteen-year-old bring up a two-year-old.

...if the chips were down Rodney would die for him.

'They fight like cat and dog but actually they care about each other deeply. Del also needs Rodney and as the series progressed we realised that more and more. In "The Jolly Boys' Outing" there's a scene at the end of the breakwater where Del is saying he's never achieved anything and Rodney is saying: "Yeah but you will." There is a very strong bond with them and if the chips were down Rodney would die for him.'

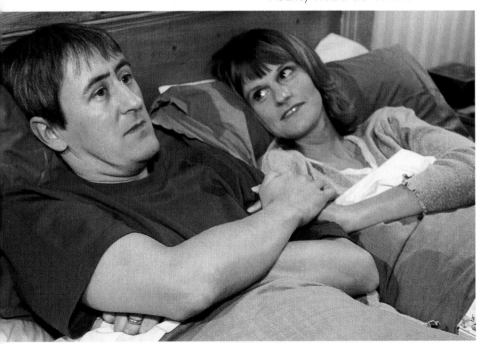

Rodney eventually moved on and fell in love with Cassandra. 'Up until he met Cassie he'd not had a lot of luck with girlfriends,' says Nick. 'He failed repeatedly and never had a steady girl-friend. Rodney was getting a bit old to stay that way so I was glad when he met someone and it worked out. Also, as far as viewers were concerned, Rodney had always been in lust rather than in love and now he was really smitten.

'Their relationship has never been easy though. Rodney got riled by her job at the bank in a childish way and Cassandra gave as good as she got and that's what started the fighting. She

Above: Poor Rodney had many unsuccessful attempts at forming relationships before meeting and marrying Cassandra (Gwyneth Strong).
Opposite (top): Nicholas Lyndhurst, aged 10, in Anne of Avonlea and (bottom) as Adam in Butterflies. With Nicholas in the photograph are, from left to right, Geoffrey Palmer, Andrew Hall and Wendy Craig.

also teased him a lot, hoping he'd see the funny side of it, but often he'd just sulk. He didn't like the way her job at the bank took up so much of her time but he was never jealous of her success.'

Nick began acting at the age of six, albeit only in a school nativity play. 'I was a donkey and my only line was hee-haw,' he laughs. 'I don't think that was what got me interested in acting and I honestly couldn't tell you what did. I remember thinking I wanted to be in an advert, maybe because I thought it was a way of

RODNEY *Nicholas Lyndhurst*

getting lots of chocolate, but I don't recall ever wanting to be in films or on telly. Eventually I did three adverts but only my hands were featured!'

At the age of eight he began asking his mum if he could go to drama school and after two years she gave in and he went off to the Corona Drama Academy in West London. 'I think my mum thought it would get it out of my system,' he says. It didn't and he stayed there until he was eighteen using money he earned from adverts to pay his tuition fees.

His first television work came in two BBC Schools productions, followed by lots of non-speaking work as an extra. His first big part was in a BBC production of *Anne of Avonlea*, a period drama. That was followed soon after by a leading role as Peter in an adaptation of the classic children's book *Heidi*, again for the BBC. Fame came at fourteen when he landed the starring role in *The Prince and the Pauper* which saw him performing the dual role of both peasant and royal.

Nick then had a lean time for a few years, around the time he took his 'O' Levels. He was also growing at a rate of knots. 'Producers were seeing me in *The Prince and the Pauper*, which was transmitted a year after we'd filmed it, and deciding to get that little lad Nick Lyndhurst in to audition for something. The trouble was, by the time they did, that little lad was getting on for 6 foot and was a bit of a spotty herbert by then!'

Nicholas Lyndhurst **RODNEY**

Opposite: Dave (Rodney) and Trigger alias Nicholas Lyndhurst and Roger Lloyd Pack.

'Work went a bit quiet at that age and I remember thinking that it was because a lot of kids don't make the transition to becoming an adult actor,' he says. Fortunately Nick's quiet spell was only temporary and in 1978 he landed the role of Ronnie Barker's cockney son Raymond in *Going Straight*, the follow-up to *Porridge*, followed soon after by the part of Adam in the comedy series *Butterflies*. It was that role as Wendy Craig's awkward, teenage son that led directly to him being cast as Rodney in *Only Fools and Horses*.

Nick has never forgotten his first day filming *Only Fools and Horses*. 'We were at Chapel Street Market and we had all these market stalls set up,' he says. 'We took a break from filming because it was pouring with rain and I was standing there with an umbrella, waiting for the rain to stop so we could continue. All the production team were standing around, a lot of them without umbrellas, getting soaked.

'I saw a little girl hurrying to school, using our stalls to keep out of the rain, and then she suddenly ran and stood next to me, using my umbrella to keep dry. She could see there was a camera and people standing about and she said to me, "What are you doing, mister?" and I said, "We're making a television programme" and she said, "What's it called then?" I said, "It's called *Only Fools and Horses*." And she considered that and she looked at us standing in the bucketing rain and she said, "Where are the horses then?"

'I thought that was classic. She didn't know how funny what she said was but it was obvious that she really meant, "Everyone else in London is under cover and you bloody idiots are standing in the rain getting soaked." It was pure John Sullivan!'

…The window came down and this voice boomed out, 'Rodney, you plonker.'

Over the years Nick has met more than his fair share of real-life Rodneys, but none of them sticks in his memory as much as the driver of a Capri who spotted him in Sloane Avenue in London. 'I was walking home with a couple of bags of shopping one day and it was pouring with rain,' he recalls. 'I was soaked and there was a line of traffic waiting at a red light. Suddenly I was aware of the thump-thump of a loud stereo system.

'I walked past this Capri – a real Rodney-mobile – and then the lights changed and this car came parallel with me. I was aware of being clocked by this real geezer with a little earring and his two mates and I could hear them going, "Yeah, it's definitely him." The window came down and this voice boomed out, "Rodney, you plonker." He then laughed loudly. I heard a wheel spin and he drove straight bang into the van in front. This guy had seen the lights change and the traffic move up a bit but the van in front hadn't got through and he was too busy clocking me and he wrote off his Capri.

'I then had the satisfaction of walking past him again and he was looking very sad and shocked. He had a look of total disbelief on his face, not to mention worry when this very big van driver got out to have a word with him. I nearly collapsed laughing. I did want to stay and gloat but I didn't. For about a week afterwards I'd smile every time I walked past that spot!'

RODNEY *Nicholas Lyndhurst*

Away from the cameras, Nick is nothing like the character he plays. Witty and articulate, he is good company and couldn't be more different from dopey Rodney. Like David Jason, he shuns the showbusiness party scene and likes his privacy, and when he's not working prefers to escape to his home by the sea in West Sussex. He loves the active life and he's a keen windsurfer, an advanced diver and has a private pilot's licence.

'It's not Rodney's sort of stuff at all,' says Nick. 'But I've always lived by the sea and loved it, and as a little boy I was always in love with anything that flew. I wanted to fly from way back when I was a kid. In fact at one stage, when I was much younger, I thought seriously about going into the Royal Air Force – until I saw what qualifications were required. I'd hate people to think, "He does these things because he's made a bit of money now and he's just showing off." I'd do these things whatever I did for a living.'

Nick says he and David became friends almost straight away when the show

MY FAVOURITE EPISODE

I've got more favourite moments than favourite episodes really. I love the Batman and Robin sequence from 'Heroes and Villains', the chandelier scene in 'A Touch of Glass', Grandad's war is hell speech from 'The Russians Are Coming' and all the stuff between Trigger and Rodney, like why he calls him Dave in 'Homesick' which was Rodney's first and last stand with Trig over him calling him Dave.

Nicholas Lyndhurst RODNEY

began. 'We hit it off from day one and I think that was down to luck and chemistry,' he says. 'I had been told that David might be a bit difficult to work with. I work with him fine so maybe I'm a bit difficult to work with as well. We've always got on well. We have never had any serious rows. Sure, we discuss things but I can't remember any problem other than something technical to do with filming. We give each other advice but we'd never tell each other what to do.

'*Only Fools* has always been a very happy show to work on and everyone gets on. I was nineteen when I started on it and thirty-five when I finished and that covered some very formative years and I do miss it and I always will miss it. I've had success with other things whilst I was doing *Only Fools* but it was always great to come back to it. Even now I've got this feeling that there should have been more episodes but now there can't be, and that's very sad.

'Seeing people on the streets who ask whether it's going to come back is a daily reminder of what I used to do for a living and probably will be for many years because a new generation is now starting to watch repeats and videos of older episodes and enjoying them. Lennard Pearce once said to me as we were walking past a shop, "Of course, I won't ever die now" and I said, "Why is that?" and he just pointed to a video recorder, which were quite new in homes then. That made him very happy and I often think of him saying that and I suppose he was right.'

Right: Nicholas Lyndhurst and Lennard Pearce share a joke in a break during the filming of 'Slow Bus to Chingford'.
Opposite: The Trotter brothers. The casting of the show is one of the key secrets of its success.

Could the props department have inside information about the future of the show? Maybe not, but they're paying £10 a week in storage charges to keep all the outfits from the series, so who knows?

Lennard Pearce
GRANDAD

Above and opposite: Lennard Pearce as Grandad Trotter. The role brought him the sort of fame he'd always wanted.

For an actor who had spent more than forty years in showbusiness, fame came late in life to Lennard Pearce. Yet becoming a household name as the Trotter boys' elderly grandad gave him a great deal of satisfaction and, according to friends, a new lease of life when he had previously been thinking about retirement.

Born in London in 1915, Lennard studied drama at the Royal Academy of Dramatic Art and was in the armed forces entertainment unit ENSA during the Second World War. Afterwards he spent most of his professional life in the theatre; in the early sixties he understudied Doolittle in the original West End production of *My Fair Lady* and played the part for more than 150 performances.

He joined the National Theatre under Sir Laurence Olivier in 1965 and appeared in a string of plays there, including *The Royal Hunt of the Sun*, *Much Ado About Nothing*, *Rosencrantz and Guildenstern are Dead* and *Tartuffe*. He was also a member of the Royal Shakespeare Company and played at many repertory theatres.

In 1975 he was Owl in *Winnie-the-Pooh* at the Phoenix Theatre in London and two years later he played Harper and Mr Witherspoon in a revival of the comedy thriller *Arsenic and Old Lace* at the Westminster Theatre. Leading television roles eluded him though, until he landed the part of Grandad in *Only Fools and Horses*, but he did appear in small roles in *Cathy Come Home*, *Take Three Girls*, *Dr Finlay's Casebook*, *Coronation Street*, *Crown Court* and *Minder*.

Oscar-winning actor Sir Anthony Hopkins appeared on stage with Lennard and has fond memories of him. 'He was a very nice man,' he recalls. 'A really gentle guy. I knew him at the National Theatre where he was playing a few small parts and I hadn't seen him for years until I saw him in *Only Fools and Horses* and it was nice to see him playing a major part in such a great series.'

…I didn't think John Sullivan could keep it up but I was wrong.

After being cast as Grandad, Lennard relished his work on the programme. 'I have never been in a hit series before and it's nice being recognised,' he told the *News of the World* during the transmission of the third series. He said he had been dubious about doing the third series. 'The first two were so well constructed I didn't think John Sullivan could keep it up but I was wrong. The standards are just as high and I aim to be around if there is a fourth series. It's not only a wonderful part but the script is tremendous. There's so much for us all to

Lennard Pearce GRANDAD

FACT FILE

NAME *Lennard Pearce*
OTHER TV WORK INCLUDES
Cathy Come Home, Take Three Girls, Dr Finlay's Casebook, Coronation Street, Crown Court, Minder and *Shroud for a Nightingale*

Above: Lennard Pearce with his screen grandsons, David Jason and Nicholas Lyndhurst. He loved the role which gave him recognition in later life and enjoyed being called 'Grandad' even away from the cameras.

The original 'Nelson Mandela House' which appears in the show's opening titles was Harlech Tower, Park Road East, Acton, in London, but since 1988 the block used for filming has been Whitemead House, Duckmore Road, Bristol.

get our teeth into.' Sadly, Lennard never lived to fulfil his wish and appear in the fourth series.

He had begun filming the series on location in December 1984 and had recorded scenes for the hilarious episode 'Hole in One', where Grandad falls into a pub cellar in order to gain compensation from the brewery. But, ten days into filming and before the episode had been completed, he suffered a heart attack and was rushed to hospital where, a few days later on 15 December, he had a second heart attack which this time proved fatal.

Even as he was recovering from the first attack, Lennard's mind was still on his acting. He fully expected to recover and was anxious to get back to filming the show as his agent at the time, Carole James, recalls. 'I remember going to see him in hospital after he'd had the first heart attack and he was in intensive care and he was sitting in bed surrounded by all the machinery,' she says.

'We started chatting and he said, "Darling, do you think you could get me the scripts in here because we've started filming and I want to be ready for when I get out." And that was the kind of professional he was. He wanted to prepare himself to carry on working. The job was very important to him and he didn't want to let people down. He loved going off to film the series on location.'

Nicholas Lyndhurst recalled at the time of Lennard's death, 'He was so thrilled at the reaction he got from the public. For the first time in his career he was being recognised in the street and approached by fans for autographs.'

Lennard, who never married, had been ill in 1980, the year before he was cast as Grandad in *Only Fools and Horses*. He nearly died and afterwards he had considered retiring from acting altogether. At the time of his illness he was appearing at the Bristol Old Vic. 'I lost my balance and kept falling asleep when I wasn't meant to,' he told the *Radio Times* in November 1983.

'I had to give up. It was hypertension. I was a workaholic and never took a holiday. I never relaxed. I have a different philosophy now and I always urge young people, if they are too tense, to get away and relax. It was many months before I could work again and I nearly gave up. And then this series gave me a new lease of life.' It also earned him more than his jobs in the theatre and, although his pay cheques from the series were not huge, they enabled him to treat his friends. 'I remember one Christmas he came in to the office with a very nice present for my assistant and me,' recalls Carole James. 'It obviously gave him pleasure to have money to spend like that.'

Carole recalls accompanying Lennard to a BBC Christmas party. 'He met several people he knew there, including Jan Francis, and then Lenny Henry came over,' she says. 'Lennard said to him, "I think you're wonderful, I'm a great fan of yours," and Lenny immediately said, "And I'm a great fan of yours too," and that really thrilled him because Lenny had been a big star for some time.'

GRANDAD *Lennard Pearce*

…After nearly fifty years in the business it was the first time he'd been recognised and he was absolutely thrilled…

John Sullivan remembers taking a phone call at home from Lennard. 'He phoned to say that he'd just got home from doing his weekly shopping at a super-market and some people had called him Grandad,' he recalls. 'After nearly fifty years in the business it was the first time he'd been recognised and he was absolutely thrilled, he really was. To me that was one of the saddest things about his death. He'd worked all his life in an attempt to really make it in the acting busi-ness and he finally made it for those brief few years, and that was a real high spot for him, and then fate took it away from him.'

'We were very fortunate that Nick, Lennard and I got on so well,' says David Jason. 'We'd always said if we ever started not getting on we'd just walk away from the series because it's hard enough working in comedy as it is. There is no point in trying to do it just for the money when you've got to work in an atmosphere where no one likes each other or doesn't talk to each other, so we ensured that we avoided any form of conflict. If we had anything to say about a scene then we would say it and we'd discuss it and work it out and when we'd decided who was right then that would be the way we'd play it.

'Lennard was great fun too because he was a man of great experience and when you had to say terrible things to him, like "shut up, you old git" and he looked hurt, you'd feel awful. But in real life it went straight over his head and he never took offence personally. He was just a lovely guy.'

'He's sorely missed to this day,' says Nick Lyndhurst. 'He knew exactly how to say his lines so perfectly. David and I would often have lots of lines and he'd be sitting there watching telly and then he'd just have one line and he'd bring the house down. We used to say: "You sod. We're giving you a twenty-minute lead-in to what you are going to say," and he just used to sit there with a fag in his mouth and say, "I know – but I'm old. I'm allowed." He was great. He loved people call-ing him Grandad and even signed my twenty-first birthday card "Grandad".

'I remember first meeting him at the BBC. He was quite dapper and I won-dered how this tidy man could be going to be our scruffy and smelly Grandad. But a bit of stubble and an old scarf and hat made a tremendous difference. He was also such an old giggler but he could get away with it by turning it into a wheeze or a cough. If you watch some episodes closely – like "Homesick" when he gave me a cigarette case and in the shelter in "The Russians Are Coming" – you can hear him wheeze, when he was actually giggling. He could laugh without shaking his shoulders but I can't do that.'

Ken MacDonald, who plays Nag's Head landlord Mike Fisher and knew Lennard from when they both appeared at the same theatre in Leatherhead, says, 'He was a lovely man and he couldn't believe it when he became a star in *Only Fools* because basically he'd retired after having a life in the theatre. Then suddenly his career was taking off in television and he was absolutely thrilled. It was so sad when he was taken from us so soon at a time when he was really enjoying what he was doing.'

Watching the episode 'Hole in One' brings back sad memories for Ken MacDonald, who plays Nag's Head landlord Mike Fisher, because in the shots of him looking up from the cellar which we see on screen, he was actually looking at Lennard Pearce. While some moments were reshot with Buster, Lennard's replace-ment, looking down at him, Ken's reaction shots are the originals he filmed with Lennard.

'Lennard told me he'd met Hitler once', recalls Nick Lyndhurst. 'He was on tour in Berlin in the late 30s and he was in a room at a theatre when Hitler and all his cronies came in, and he told me: "Knowing what I do now, what I wouldn't have given for a gun."'

Buster Merryfield
ALBERT

Above and opposite: Buster Merryfield as Uncle Albert.

This sounds like an outline for a novel: a man who always wanted to become a professional actor, but had to be content being in amateur shows because he'd vowed to his old mum that he'd stick with his secure job in a bank, retires and then lands a starring role in the nation's favourite TV show. Strange, but true. After all, that's just what happened to Buster Merryfield.

Born in Battersea, South London, Buster was the second child of packer Harry Merryfield and his wife Lily, a part-time waitress. Their first child, Irene, two years Buster's senior, died when she was eight. Harry and Lily were determined that Buster would have more opportunities than they had had, and encouraged him to get a professional job. They were delighted when, at seventeen, he was taken on as a junior clerk by National Westminster Bank.

He wasn't in the job long though. In fact Buster was just eighteen when war began to look likely, in the late summer of 1939. He immediately signed up to join the Territorial Army, along with many of his colleagues at the Lombard Street branch of Nat West bank. Uncle Albert's wartime service record is hazy to say the least – and no one is ever quite sure just how much is true. By contrast, Buster served his country with distinction during the war.

On 2 September 1939, the day before war was declared, he, along with thousands of other young men, was called up to active full-time duty. 'Day after day they'd been calling out all the reserves,' he recalls. 'As soon as they heard, people would down their pens and say "cheerio, mate" and they'd be off. Then it was my turn. Someone ran into the bank and said that the Territorial had been called out and everyone cheered and we all ran off and joined our units and I went off to mine in Fulham.'

Buster joined the Royal Artillery as a gunner (their equivalent of private) but soon gained promotion to lance-bombardier, then bombardier, and at the same time worked as a physical training instructor. Three years later he was offered the chance to train as an officer and he jumped at it.

His first posting as a newly commissioned lieutenant was in Windsor, where he and his men formed part of a troop manning four Bofors anti-aircraft guns positioned on the edge of town. He must have impressed his captain because, within weeks, he was given command of his own troop but this time on four Bofors positioned inside Windsor Castle. While the men slept in the stables, officers were allowed to sleep inside the castle itself, albeit on the library floor.

Buster Merryfield **ALBERT**

FACT FILE

NAME *Buster Merryfield*
DATE OF BIRTH *27.11.1920*
BORN *Battersea, London*
OTHER TV WORK INCLUDES
Hannah, The Citadel, Strangers and Brothers, The Third Age, The World of Paul McKenna, Shroud for a Nightingale and *A Tale of Four Ports*

HOW UNCLE ALBERT COULD HAVE BEEN AUNTIE DORIS

David Jason recalls that at one stage during the discussions on how to bring in a new, older character, it was briefly suggested that an old aunt should come to live with the boys at Nelson Mandela House. 'But as we talked about it we realised that it would never work.' says David. 'You couldn't bundle an old lady up into the back of the van and you couldn't say "Shut up, you old git" to a woman. You could get away with all that with a little old man but people wouldn't like it done to a woman so that idea went out of the window.'

Buster has written his autobiography called appropriately *During the War – and other Encounters*. It was published in 1996 by Summersdale.

Some time later Buster was sent by train to Glasgow where he and 2000 other men boarded the troop ship the *SS Almanzora*. 'We still had no idea what our final destination would be, even after we sailed,' he says. 'People would try to work out which direction we were heading by looking at the stars and some of them decided we were heading towards South America.'

Later Buster learned why trying to work out where they were heading was so difficult; the ship had been zigzagging in order to put German U-boats off their scent. Weeks later they arrived at their final destination, Durban in South Africa. It was there that Buster came face to face with the enemy when he was put in charge of a ship containing 1000 German prisoners of war before they were transported to Canada.

'There was only one German officer on the ship and the rest were troops,' Buster recalls. 'He had a cabin to himself and was guarded by two marines and I had to visit him twice a day. He told me with a smile that he'd escaped three times since his initial capture and he'd continue to keep trying. He didn't manage to.'

Weeks later Buster found himself aboard another ship which arrived in Bombay, India. That was followed by a five-day journey across India on a cramped train to Ranchi, which the British army used as a base from which to send men on to fighting units. Buster had to train newly arrived recruits in the art of jungle warfare. 'It was very physical,' he recalls. 'My job was to train people to live and survive in the jungle. We'd be left in the jungle for weeks and have to survive. One time I was left on my own and told to work out where to take the troops. It was exciting because you never knew what you might come up against, from snakes to tigers, and I enjoyed all that.

'One day I nearly died. I'd discovered that the quickest way to travel was along dried-up riverbeds because otherwise you'd have to cut your way through lots of jungle. On this particular day I was walking down a riverbed as wide as the Thames, with monkeys swinging in the trees and beautiful birds flying around and sitting in trees. I turned a corner and saw all these vultures picking at the carcass of a cow. For some reason I decided to fire my pistol to see them all fly away. They all flew up. Then they saw me and down they came – like the film *The Birds*.

…I was up to my waist in mud. I thought I was going to die.

'I ran up the bank at the side of the riverbed and they were chasing me, and when I got to the top of the riverbank I ran into the dark jungle, knowing they wouldn't follow. I ran through and ended up jumping into a tributary. But, because it was covered over by trees, the mud in the bottom of it was still wet and I sank straight down into it. I was soon up to my waist. I panicked. The birds were all gathered nearby and I was up to my waist in mud. I thought I was going to die. I thought, "No one will ever know what happened to me."

'I tried to move but every time I moved my legs I went down an inch. I was too far to reach anything to grab. I was sinking deeper and deeper. It was getting hopeless. I was miles from anywhere and there were no other soldiers nearby but I started to shout, which was a risk in itself because it would let tigers know where I was.

ALBERT *Buster Merryfield*

'I was there for about an hour and still sinking gradually. I was almost asleep and suddenly I heard a branch crack and I thought that was it: a tiger was going to finish me off. But I was lucky – it wasn't a tiger. It was a young Indian girl dressed in a sari. She just stood there at the top of the bank staring at me. Then she turned and ran through the woods. Half an hour later a lot of people came through the trees and they threw a rope and pulled me out and took me to their village.'

Afterwards Buster found himself back at his unit but soon fell sick with a range of illnesses, including malaria and dysentery. One illness – thought to have been caused by an allergy to a jungle plant – caused his face to swell up massively so that he couldn't even open his eyes, and he was sent back by train to Bombay. 'I was declared unfit for tropical service and put on the Australian hospital ship *HMS Wanganella* back to England,' he recalls.

Once recovered, he was ordered to take charge of a battery of Bofors guns on a clifftop in Kent tasked with shooting down the VI doodlebug flying bombs that were wreaking havoc in London. Buster's guns were the second line of defence, after the bigger ack-ack guns and before RAF fighters had a go, followed by the last line of defence in London, barrage balloons.

'I believe about eight out of ten were destroyed before they could do any damage,' he recalls. 'They'd reach us in waves of thirty or forty at a time and there were mid-air explosions every few seconds as the guns scored a direct hit. We were busy day and night with them and we slept in tents alongside our guns, always ready for action.'

In 1946 Buster was demobbed and resumed his career with Nat West Bank. He'd married in April 1942, and in 1947 he and his wife Iris had a daughter Karen. Buster wanted to become an actor but decided to stick with his bank job.

'I wanted to leave but my mum made me promise to stay there,' he remembers. 'She said that, with a wife to look after and a baby on the way, I'd be stupid to give it up. My parents hadn't had the opportunities that I had and I felt I owed it to them to stay in my secure job.'

Instead Buster threw himself into amateur dramatics, performing in dozens of shows with various theatre companies, before forming his own group which became known as The Merryfield Characters. With this company he directed more than forty plays, starring in every one of them and winning many awards. Meanwhile, his bank career flourished and by 1978 he became manager of the Thames Ditton branch.

It was while working at the bank that he grew his famous whiskers – much to the anger of his boss. 'I've had the beard on and off since the war,' he says. 'And I think I was one of the first people in the bank to have one. I grew it while I was working in the bank because I had to have it for a role I was playing. The day I turned up with about four days' stubble on, my manager sent for me and said, ''What's all this you've got?'' In those days, you see, there was never anyone in a

★★★ *Did you know?*

Buster isn't his real name – but he's vowed never to reveal his real Christian name.

In those days there was never anyone in a bank with a beard…and he said, 'Well, if you want to look like a ruddy gorilla'…

Buster Merryfield, when he was a bank manager at Thames Ditton, Surrey.

Buster Merryfield **ALBERT**

Below: Uncle Albert looks up at his nephews, Del and Rodney.
Opposite, top: Buster, the boxing champion with some of his trophies. Bottom: Buster at the piano on the pub set in 1990. In real life he is a gifted pianist.

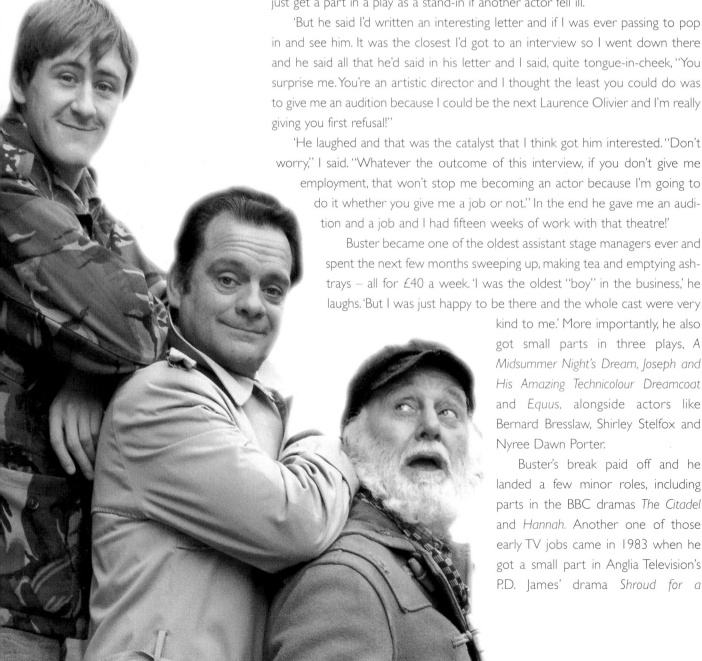

bank with a beard. I said, "I'm sorry, I'm growing this for a part that I'm playing," and he said, "Well if you want to look like a ruddy gorilla," and really gave me a wigging. But would you believe it, after a few months, all four cashiers on the counters had beards and I think they really did it to get at the manager because he told me off!'

Buster retired from his job at the bank at the age of fifty-seven. Feeling that his late mum would have been satisfied with his forty years with the bank, he decided to give acting a try full-time and he wrote off to countless theatres and companies trying to get work – to no avail. Even one of the more encouraging replies from Nicholas Young, artistic director at the Connaught Theatre, Worthing, indicated that he thought Buster's hopes were forlorn.

'He wrote back, saying that there was no way that a man of fifty-seven and an ex-bank manager could suddenly walk into rep,' he recalls. 'He explained that they only got two Equity cards per year and they gave them to drama students who helped out behind the scenes as assistant stage managers and who might just get a part in a play as a stand-in if another actor fell ill.

'But he said I'd written an interesting letter and if I was ever passing to pop in and see him. It was the closest I'd got to an interview so I went down there and he said all that he'd said in his letter and I said, quite tongue-in-cheek, "You surprise me. You're an artistic director and I thought the least you could do was to give me an audition because I could be the next Laurence Olivier and I'm really giving you first refusal!"

'He laughed and that was the catalyst that I think got him interested. "Don't worry," I said. "Whatever the outcome of this interview, if you don't give me employment, that won't stop me becoming an actor because I'm going to do it whether you give me a job or not." In the end he gave me an audition and a job and I had fifteen weeks of work with that theatre!'

Buster became one of the oldest assistant stage managers ever and spent the next few months sweeping up, making tea and emptying ashtrays – all for £40 a week. 'I was the oldest "boy" in the business,' he laughs. 'But I was just happy to be there and the whole cast were very kind to me.' More importantly, he also got small parts in three plays, *A Midsummer Night's Dream, Joseph and His Amazing Technicolour Dreamcoat* and *Equus,* alongside actors like Bernard Bresslaw, Shirley Stelfox and Nyree Dawn Porter.

Buster's break paid off and he landed a few minor roles, including parts in the BBC dramas *The Citadel* and *Hannah.* Another one of those early TV jobs came in 1983 when he got a small part in Anglia Television's P.D. James' drama *Shroud for a*

ALBERT *Buster Merryfield*

Nightingale, which starred Roy Marsden as Commander Adam Dalgliesh. By coincidence, while filming the drama, Buster met Lennard Pearce who also had a small role in the production and whose untimely death the following year would change Buster's life for ever.

'I was playing a pathologist and Lennard was playing the man on the gate of a big hospital. I had to drive up in a Rolls-Royce and stop at the gate and Lennard put his head out and I'd say who I was and he'd open the gate and I'd drive in and that was the only contact on screen that we had together. He was a nice fellow, rather quiet and very pleasant company, and we had lunch together. We talked a bit about what he'd done previously but we didn't talk much about *Only Fools and Horses*. Of course when I first went up for the part of Uncle Albert I was saddened to learn that he'd died.'

After he'd filmed his first two episodes of *Only Fools and Horses* Buster had no real idea that he was going to be in the show until it ended. 'I'd done the part of Uncle Albert in "Strained Relations" and "Hole in One" and I thought that was probably it. I'd helped them out at a difficult time and I'd enjoyed doing it and didn't think I'd done badly and hadn't let them down which was always my main concern. It wasn't until several episodes later that I actually felt I was in it for good.'

Buster loves playing Uncle Albert and is overjoyed by the response he gets from the series. 'The most pleasurable thing about playing Albert,' he says, 'is that I can walk down any street or get on any bus or train and people smile and go, "There's Uncle Albert", and that's magic.'

Only Fools and Horses viewers always see Uncle Albert pinching Del's brandy on screen, but off screen Buster never touches a drop. 'I'm teetotal,' he explains. 'And I don't smoke either. I wouldn't drink or smoke for the Queen. I've never had a drink in my life and I've never smoked in my life and this was largely due to my boxing career which I took up when I was about twelve.

'My gym master at school said, "If you ever want to be a champion then you should never smoke and never drink." Now I'm a pretty dedicated chap so I put the blinkers on and went for it and I wanted to be a champion. I'm pretty strongwilled so I've never touched a drop or smoked, nor have I even been tempted to since!

'I was a dedicated boxer and took it very seriously. My whole life was physical fitness. I'd never stay in at night, as I'd always be out running round the block. It all paid off though and I became Schoolboy Boxing Champion of Great Britain and used to knock everyone out. Later, during the war, I became Southern Command Army Boxing Champion in 1945.'

Buster can rarely go into a pub without a rum appearing on his table. '"All right, Albert," they go,' he says. 'It's very kind of them but I swap it for an orange juice!' He now lives in Dorset and is devoted to his family. He also spends much of his time working for local charities including the Royal National Lifeboat Institution. He's also still keen on keeping fit and goes swimming twice a week. He says, 'Swimming is great because it's one of those types of exercise that you can do in a short space of time and you feel marvellous afterwards. I don't want to prompt fate but I am very careful to look after myself.'

I've never had a drink in my life and I don't smoke either.

Roger Lloyd Pack
TRIGGER

Above: Roger Lloyd Pack with David Jason in the first series. The photograph opposite shows Roger (Trigger) in 1996.

RODNEY TO DEL:
Why d'they call him Trigger?
Does he carry a gun?
DEL TO RODNEY:
No, he looks like an 'orse!

From the first episode 'Big Brother'

Appearing as a builder in the West End play *Moving* in the spring of 1981 brought Roger Lloyd Pack a double helping of good fortune. Not only was his first son Spencer born while he was in it but it also led, by pure chance, to him landing a role that he would play for many years to come – that of dopey roadsweeper Trigger in *Only Fools and Horses*.

Producer Ray Butt had gone to see the play to see whether actor Billy Murray, who was appearing with Roger alongside Penelope Keith, Miranda Richardson, Richard Thorp and Peter Jeffrey, would be right for the role of Del. He decided against Billy but spotted Roger who he decided was perfect for the part of Trig. 'Ray called me in to see him and offered me this part of Trigger in this new series but he didn't know when it was going to start because he hadn't yet found the right person to play Del at that time,' Roger recalls. 'I was pleased because I knew it was good. It was a class above the rest.'

In the script for the first episode, Trigger is described as 'a local part-time villain. He is in his early thirties, tough, but none too bright. He is wearing grubby jeans, shortie wellingtons and a donkey jacket.' 'Over the years Trigger has refined down to his essential self,' says Roger. 'He was a bit sharper at the start but after a while Boycie took over the villainy aspect and over the years Trigger has become less and less involved in running the plot really and having anything to do with the action. He's just there!'

Roger has a big soft spot for Trigger. 'The impact of Trigger is not commensurate with the amount of time that he's actually on the screen yet he retains this incredible mythology about him and I'm told he's become a bit of a legend,' he says. 'I play him as if he thinks he's quite intelligent and he thinks that it's the rest of the world that's out of kilter with him. He's a bit of a dreamer and he's just in his own world really. A lot of people tell me that they know people like him.'

Roger loves playing him but admits he sometimes finds the response he gets from some people on the street, who assume he's as dim in real life as Trigger is on screen, a pain. 'You can imagine what it's like and it can be a drag but it goes with the territory,' he says. 'It's unavoidable but I deal with it as best I can. Some people are bloody rude and I swear at them or just ignore them. Most people shout "Alright, Dave" and then go off sniggering thinking they are the first to shout it at me.

'The upside of it is that most people are really nice and also that I earn a good living because of the high profile that *Only Fools* has given me. It also means I've been involved in some of the best comedy writing on television. It's also lovely to be able to play a character for 16 years because usually you only get to work on a character for as long as you do a play. It's also been extraordinary to have been in something that is so much part of the culture of the country.'

TRIGGER *Roger Lloyd Pack*

Some women too, it seems, have a thing about Trigger. 'They seem to be quite fond of him and I'm told some of them find him quite sexy,' laughs Roger. 'I think they like him because they want to mother him and they find him rather loyal, trusting and dependable. They also probably feel rather sorry for him and want to look after him. I've had ladies rush up to me on occasions and plant a kiss full on the lips so perhaps he's got more going for him than it first appears!'

Roger might be famous for playing the fool but in real life he's got a sharp mind and left upmarket private school Bedales in Hampshire with 'A' Levels in English, French and Latin, which would have allowed him to go to almost any university in the country. Instead though he chose to go to the Royal Academy of Dramatic Art to train as an actor, following in his father, Charles Lloyd Pack's footsteps. He had been a successful film and theatre actor, appearing in more than three dozen films.

'I hadn't always planned to be an actor,' he says. 'But I'd always messed around putting on shows as a youngster, acted at school and eventually I decided that was what I wanted to do for a living. My dad didn't particularly encourage or discourage me. It's like people going into a family business. You don't want your children to go into it just because you did; you want them to go into it because they really want to.'

Roger has made a considerable success of his career and is probably one of Britain's busiest actors. He lives in North London with his partner, writer Jehane Markham, and their three sons and also has a daughter, actress Emily Lloyd, from his first marriage. But despite his extensive list of other work, he thinks it will be for Trigger that he will always be best known. 'I think whatever I do, that when I die it will be a case of "Roger Lloyd Pack, best known for his portrayal of Trigger in *Only Fools and Horses*," ' he says.

'But I don't mind,' he adds. 'Writers are always remembered for their one popular play even if they've done lots of other work. Bob Hoskins and Maureen Lipman will probably be remembered for their BT ads despite all their other work. That's all down to the power of telly coming into people's homes. Sure I'd like be remembered for giving a haunting portrayal of Tartuffe or best known for playing King Lear at the Riverside Studios but only a few hundred people saw that. So I'm resigned to it and if Trigger has brought people pleasure then I don't really mind.'

FACT FILE

NAME *Roger Lloyd Pack*
DATE OF BIRTH *8.2.1944*
BORN *London*
OTHER TV WORK INCLUDES
Softly, Softly, UFO, The Survivors, The Professionals, Private Shultz, Boon, The Bill, The Chief, Inspector Morse, Selling Hitler, The Summer House, Lovejoy, 2 Point 4 Children and *Murder Most Horrid*

…I'm told he's become a bit of a legend.

BOYCIE: So you told them you were a road sweeper.
TRIGGER: No, I told them I was a bus inspector.
RODNEY: Why?
TRIGGER: To add a bit of glamour.
From the episode 'Dates'

★★★ *Did you know?*

Roger's father Charles, the son of a sewage engineer, added the 'Lloyd' to his name to make it sound posher to help him get acting work!

JUST WHY DOES TRIGGER CALL RODNEY, DAVE?

John Sullivan says, 'In the first episode Del says to Trigger, "You know my brother" and Trig says, "Yeah, of course, how are you doing, Dave." It was just a little gag on the fact that he obviously didn't know his name. Even after Rodney explains in "Homesick" that Dave isn't his name, Trig still gets it wrong. He's got it in his head that Del's brother is called Dave and in the end nothing Rodney or anyone can say will budge Trigger from the fact that his name is Dave! I've had letters from people telling me that there are Dave Clubs around now where people go round all calling each other Dave.'

John Challis
BOYCIE

...he'd really like to be one of the boys, but his innate sense of superiority won't allow him to...

Above: John Challis as Boycie in the showroom of his car dealership.

It's hard to imagine *Only Fools and Horses* without John Challis as dodgy second-hand car dealer Boycie – but it could have happened. Late in 1980, a few months before the show went into production, John was in America appearing in a string of plays. He enjoyed the experience so much that he nearly stayed. 'I thought America was the place to be at that time,' he recalls. 'But in the end I decided to come back, which is just as well, otherwise I'd never have got the part of Boycie.'

In April 1981 Ray Butt wrote to John Challis offering him the role of Boycie in the second episode of *Only Fools and Horses*, 'Go West Young Man', and enclosing a copy of the script. Ray knew John's work, as he'd previously cast him as a policeman, Inspector Colin Humphries, in an episode of *Citizen Smith* in 1979. 'I read the script and thought it was very funny,' John recalls. 'It made me laugh out loud, which is quite rare, and therefore I had no hesitation about taking the part.'

Writer John Sullivan had been so impressed with the character John had created that he told him that one day he'd find him a part in another series. Challis said, 'Yeah, yeah', and then two years later, true to Sullivan's word, the part of Boycie came up.

'It was only one day's filming,' John Challis remembers, 'and it was fun but I thought that was probably it. Then I came back to do one episode in the second series, two in the third and the rest, as they say, is history. Boycie is a great character to play because he's so pompous. He's got aspirations and would like to climb the social ladder so he pretends to be a bit superior.

'But the only thing he has over Del Boy and the others – well, up until they become millionaires in the last episode – is that he has money, however dubiously he has earned it. At the same time he's quite lonely, despite being married to Marlene and having little Tyler, and he'd really like to be one of the boys, but his innate sense of superiority won't allow him to fully be so.

'He sees himself as a bit of a lord of the manor and sees the others as underlings. He's got money and he likes to show it off a bit and he also feels that he's intellectually superior, whereas he's probably not at all... well, except perhaps in the case of Trigger!

'He's always thought of Del as a little ducker and diver who will never make a success of anything and never have any real money and will always be scrabbling about to earn a living. He sees him as low-life, albeit charming and lovely, but not really in his league. After all, Boycie's got a mock-Georgian house with an in-and-out gravel drive, and Del lives in a council flat.

'Of course all this goes out of the window when Del and Rodney find the Harrison watch and Boycie then suddenly finds that it has all been turned upside down and that they can actually afford the Rolls-Royce he used to tease them about having their picture taken next to.

'Boycie's voice comes from John Sullivan's lines. When I first read them I could

BOYCIE *John Challis*

tell the way he spoke,' says John. 'I could also imagine this guy called Gordon who I knew from a local pub, the St Margaret's Hotel in Twickenham, years ago, saying precisely the same sorts of things as Boycie came out with, so I used him as part of my idea for the character. He would come into the pub and always be on his own, and he'd have a little knowledge about practically everything and he'd bore everyone silly a lot of the time. He also said things with such utter certainty that people couldn't really refute what he said.

'Everybody nodded sagely at him and he always had this superior manner and was much derided because, although he always wore a suit it was never as neat as Boycie's. It was always stained and his white shirt always looked slightly grubby. He would also have a scruffy little white dog with him, which he adored, and he cried like a baby when it died.

'For a long time no one was ever quite sure what he did for a living. They'd say: "What do you actually do, Gordon?" and he'd say, "Well actually I can't really talk about it, suffice to say it's something to do with the electronics business." People then assumed that it must be something top secret, to do with rockets or something. It turned out that he was a travelling salesman selling video recorders and record players. He was a fantasist really but a riveting character who I sort of liked but thought was ridiculous as well.'

Gordon may have had the gift of the gab but it didn't work when it came to chatting up women. 'He loved women but they weren't very interested in him,' says John. 'One night we were out on the River Thames on a boat having a party and everyone was a bit drunk and Gordon suddenly declared to this girl how much he loved her.

'He then stripped off down to his underpants and leapt into the river. He thought he'd impress her by swimming across to the other side but he'd forgotten it was low tide and ended up hitting the bottom very hard and getting covered in mud. No one could believe what they'd seen and a few of us had to go and pull him out. He was covered in blood and fairly incoherent and we dressed him and he wandered off home. Everyone was rather concerned for him.'

Boycie might be a working-class boy made good – or bad, depending on your point of view – but John's upbringing is firmly middle-class. His father was a civil servant, his mum was a teacher and he went to Ottershaw School, a private school near Woking in Surrey. It was there that John got his first acting role at the age of eleven. 'I played Alison Elliot in *The Lady's Not for Burning* and very nice I looked too, in a long blonde wig and a posh dress,' he laughs. 'Then I graduated to playing older women and then, after my voice broke, I started playing men!'

Neither John's headmaster nor his parents thought acting was a very sensible or secure job so at eighteen he started work as a trainee estate agent in Surrey. 'I sat there for about six months and eventually got sacked because I wasn't doing any work at all and spent a lot of my time impersonating the partners and doing fake deals.' John's skill with voices helped him make Boycie one of *Only Fools and Horses'* best-loved characters – but his trademark laugh came about by accident. John recalls, 'I just did it one day and John Sullivan liked it. In the next script it said, "Boycie does one of his laughs", and from then on it became a regular thing.'

FACT FILE

NAME *John Challis*
DATE OF BIRTH *16.8.1942*
BORN *Bristol*
OTHER TV WORK INCLUDES
The Bill, Casualty, Doctor Who, Coronation Street, Wing and a Prayer, Soldier, Soldier and *The Sweeney*

MY FAVOURITE EPISODE 'The Sky's the Limit'. It was just a brilliant script.

John was once offered more than £100,000 to star as Boycie in a major advertising campaign but he turned it down.

★★★ *Did you know?*

Boycie's real surname is, of course, Boyce. He was rather embarrassed when his real Christian name Aubrey was revealed in the episode 'Sickness and Wealth' by medium Elsie Partridge.

Patrick Murray
MICKEY

FACT FILE

NAME *Patrick Murray*
DATE OF BIRTH *17.12.1956*
BORN *Greenwich, London*
OTHER TV WORK INCLUDES
*The Firm, Last Summer,
The Terracotta Horse, The
Bill, Keep It In The Family,
The Upper Hand* and *Hale
and Pace*

Mickey Pearce had been talked about in *Only Fools and Horses* for two years before John Sullivan decided to bring him into the series as a proper character. Producer Ray Butt spotted Patrick Murray in a television commercial for Pizza Hut playing a similar character and called him in. 'The guy I played was in a restaurant trying, and failing, to chat up these two girls,' recalls Patrick. 'It was quite funny but the ad got pulled by the company because apparently people were taking more notice of my character than the product!

'I saw Ray on the Friday and he asked me if I'd seen the programme and as I'm not a big TV watcher I hadn't. He told me about the character and I read a scene from "Healthy Competition" and Ray said: "Can you start on Monday?" I was delighted and two days later found myself in Bournemouth filming my first episode. I struck up an immediate rapport with Nick Lyndhurst and all the lads, and had a great time.

…He's always stitching Rodney up and Del is always threatening to clump him for it.

'Mickey is the sort of bloke who does a bit of what Del Boy does and is really a sort of understudy to him. Had he been Del's brother he would have been better at it than Rodney, who he sees as a bit of a gopher. Mickey is like Del in another way in that his antics always go wrong. Like Del, Mickey will try anything but he's not very trustworthy. He's always stitching Rodney up and Del is always threatening to clump him for it.'

In the 1989 episode 'Little Problems', Mickey and his pal Jevon are roughed up by the dreaded Driscoll Brothers and turn up at the Nag's Head in plaster casts. That wasn't in the original script but was added by John Sullivan after Pat had an accident that could have cost him his life. He fell over his dog at home and crashed through a pane of glass and cut his right arm very badly. He lost five pints of blood, had to have emergency neuro-surgery and was lucky not to lose his hand.

The first thing Pat did as soon as he came to the following morning was phone the *Only Fools and Horses* office at the BBC and speak to Production Manager Adrian Pegg. It was a Wednesday and he was supposed to be back with the team for rehearsals of 'Little Problems' the following Monday.

'I told him I didn't think I was going to be able to make it and that my arm was in a cast,' Pat recalls. 'He said, "Can you get around and can you talk?" and I said I could, and he said, "I'll have a word with John and I'll give you a call tomorrow."'

Adrian phoned back the following day and gave Pat the good news. John Sullivan had rewritten a section of his script and had incorporated the plaster casts into the storyline. 'I couldn't believe it,' he says. 'I'd been feeling very down

MICKEY *Patrick Murray*

in hospital, not just from the pain, and the idea of going back to work really lifted me. It made me feel better just knowing that they wanted me back on the Monday.

'The day I went back everyone had been down to the props room and had borrowed false plaster casts and when I arrived all their legs or arms were in

David Jason, Patrick Murray and Steven Woodcock in the episode 'Little Problems'. Pat's problem was very real: the arm in the cast was very badly injured and writer John Sullivan altered a section of the story to allow for it.

plaster. It was a nice gesture and really put a smile on my face and cheered me up because at the time, and through the recording of the episode, I was in acute pain as I filmed it. The doctors had said I'd never be able to use my hand again and although it was painful for a year afterwards I've got full use of it again now.'

Pat gets a great deal of public response from playing Mickey. 'Lots of people want to stop you for a chat and when I walk down the street I'm always getting tooted at by cars,' says Pat, who has three sons. 'The good thing about playing Mickey Pearce is that everyone loves *Only Fools and Horses* so the reaction is always a positive thing and people are always polite. I've met a lot of people who say they know someone who is just like Mickey but I've actually met more Rodneys than Mickeys! I've met more lanky wallies with nothing-between-the-ear expressions than anything else!'

Pat, the son of an Irish tunnel miner and a Spanish dancer, became an actor after spotting an advert for an actor's agency in the *Daily Mirror* when he was fifteen. Three days after he signed up with them he landed a part in a play, which then led to a string of other roles. He made a television commercial for electrical giant Zanussi which earned him that nickname for the next five years and then scooped a starring role in the acclaimed film *Scum*.

Pat is hoping that *Only Fools* will return one day. 'It's been great fun to do over the years and I'd love to do some more,' he says. 'I like Mickey really because I like tryers and he does try hard. He puts on his best suit and that says to me that he's having a go. He doesn't really want to stitch Rodney up particularly; it's just that he's just out for himself. That's the way of life where he comes from and so that's what he does.'

...he does try hard. He puts on his best suit and that says to me that he's having a go.

Kenneth MacDonald
MIKE

Above: Mike Fisher (Ken MacDonald) behind
the bar with one of Del's 'sophisticated'
cocktails in his left hand.
Opposite: Boycie confides in Mike. John Challis
and Ken MacDonald.

FACT FILE

NAME *Kenneth MacDonald*
DATE OF BIRTH *20.11.1950*
BORN *Manchester*
OTHER TV WORK INCLUDES
*Softly, Softly, Z Cars, It Ain't
Half Hot, Mum, The Thin
Blue Line, Silas Marner, No
Bananas, Brookside, Crocodile
Shoes, Moll Flanders* and
Touching Evil

He might be the butt of some of Del Boy Trotter's dodgier money-making schemes as Nag's Head landlord Mike Fisher, but actor Kenneth MacDonald isn't complaining. When he landed the part in 1983 he thought it was probably a one-episode role – he never dreamed he'd become one of the show's regulars and one of television's best-known pub landlords.

'I think that they were looking for a foil for Del Boy at the pub,' says Ken. 'John Sullivan wanted someone there who Del could flog his gear to, have a bit of banter with, and now and again stitch up. There had been several barmaids at the Nag's Head over the years but never a proper landlord who was there all the time.'

Once again it was Ray Butt who cast Ken in the role. 'I'd worked with Ray before, when he directed *It Ain't Half Hot, Mum* in which I played Gunner Nobby Clark, and he remembered me, and when he needed someone to play Mike I got the call,' says Ken. 'I was delighted because I'd always watched and enjoyed *Only Fools and Horses*. I didn't have many lines in my first episode, "Who's A Pretty Boy?", but I had a nice exchange with David Jason about doing up the pub and it was fun doing the show. I thought that was probably it and that I'd only be in the one episode. Then I went to the end-of-series party and got a hint that I might be back when John Sullivan came up to me and said he'd liked what I'd done and that hopefully there would be some more episodes for me in the next series. I thought, "Gosh, I might be back", and I went home elated.

…he still allows himself to be stitched up by Del because he's gullible…a real soft touch.

'Mike Fisher is a nice part to play because he's such a decent, reliable and big-hearted bloke. He's generous too, like when he paid for all the drink at the do at the flat after Grandad's funeral and, of course, my last line in the series in "Time On Our Hands" was "On the house, Del." He likes the Trotters and he's aware of what Del is like. But he still allows himself to be stitched up by Del because he's gullible. There's no question about that – he's a real soft touch. He's a good landlord though and runs a happy pub – and the punters must like it because it's usually pretty busy.'

Having one of the most familiar faces on television means that Ken is always being spotted by fans of the series. 'I get a tremendous response from *Only Fools and Horses*,' he says. 'Mike is your typical landlord and everybody's friend and confidant and people seem to like him. I'd played some nasty characters on television like George Webb in *Brookside*, but fortunately people seem to remember me most as Mike.

'They are always coming up to me or shouting across the street things like "Clean your pipes out Mike", "Put an umbrella in it, will you?" or "How's Del Boy?"

MIKE *Kenneth MacDonald*

and that familiarity is nice because you know the nation loves the show so much. Going into a pub is always amazing. The landlords usually say, "You should be round this side of the bar," and I've actually gone behind the bar and served a few pints on occasions just for fun.'

Ken will always remember filming the last episode of *Only Fools and Horses*. 'It was very, very sad because you just couldn't believe it would ever really come to an end,' he says. 'By the end everyone was in tears. There wasn't an actor who didn't shed a tear that day and most of the audience were in tears too. It was a grief we all shared and it felt a bit like a funeral although it was a happy event as well.'

Ken was born in Manchester, the son of Scottish heavyweight wrestling champion Bill MacDonald, who sadly died of kidney failure when Ken was just thirteen. 'Dad was only forty-three and his death hit me very hard,' he says. 'I still think about him now and just wish he could have seen me grow up and met my wife Sheila and our children William and Charlotte.'

Ken left school at eighteen to help support his mum Emily and took a job at a Kellogg's Cornflakes factory. 'I used to muck about during the night shift, performing *Hamlet* and other Shakespeare plays that I'd learned at school, and that earned me the nickname Hamlet,' he recalls. 'I'd also do daft things like fill a cornflakes packet full of free gifts and hardly any cornflakes. So a kid would open the packet up at breakfast and find loads of little Robin Hood figures. I used to think the kids would be delighted but their mums would have been rather less pleased.

'After about a year I'd had enough and I decided to go off and try my hand at acting. I knew I couldn't be stuck in a factory so I went to London and joined the National Youth Theatre. I was lucky enough to get a couple of telly parts very early on, in *Softly, Softly* and *Z Cars*, and then shortly afterwards did the pilot of *It Ain't Half Hot, Mum* which began in 1973 and ran for eight years.'

Ken met his wife Sheila while he was appearing in panto in Crewe in 1976. 'She was the costume designer and we met when she came over from college in Liverpool to measure me up for my outfit,' he recalls. 'It was love at first sight for me. As soon as I saw her, that was it. I knew she was the girl for me and I was right and we've been together ever since.'

★★★ *Did you know?*

Ken starred in classic BBC comedy series *It Ain't Half Hot, Mum* which ended the week before *Only Fools and Horses* began.

MY FAVOURITE MOMENT When Del and the others are playing Trivial Pursuit and he's asked what a female swan is called. Rodney tries to help him by waving a pen at him and Del says, 'Oh, it's a Bic!'

Del's favourite cocktail is a Pina Colada, complete with all the trimmings. Here Nag's Head landlord Mike Fisher alias Ken MacDonald, reveals his secret ingredients:

'Two and a half measures of dark rum, a tablespoon of white coconut mix (from supermarkets), a small bottle of pineapple juice, five or six ice cubes – put it all in a blender, mix, then pour into a glass. Put a quarter of a slice of pineapple on the rim of the glass, add a cherry on a cocktail stick and throw in a parasol and a straw. Lovely jubbly!'

Paul Barber
DENZIL

Denzil was conned by Del Boy the first time viewers saw him in *Only Fools and Horses* in the 1983 episode 'Who's A Pretty Boy?' and nothing much has changed over the years. However hard Del's lorry-driver school friend tries, he never seems quite able to keep out of trouble when Del Boy is around. That's probably down to Denzil's good nature and inability to say no and stick to it.

Take the time Del persuaded him to unload his consignment of dolls, which ended up nearly blowing the roof off Nelson Mandela House. Then there was the occasion when he had a breakdown after he kept seeing visions of Del and his little yellow van everywhere between London and Hull and even on the sea.

…it was non-racist, non-sexist and that was just up my street.

'Denzil is just a nice normal guy, who gets into trouble all the time with the help of Del Boy and Rodney,' says actor Paul Barber, who plays him. 'I love the scenes when we argue a lot because they are great fun to do. When I first played him, the character was already there. It was non-racist, non-sexist and that was just up my street. He's just a nice guy and that's his trouble. He always falls for it and then he knows he's landed himself in it.'

Like almost all of the show's main supporting characters, Paul was cast by Ray Butt and only thought he'd be in one episode. But writer John Sullivan saw the potential with Denzil and brought him back time and time again. 'It's like a family when we all get together,' he says. 'It's always a laugh.'

One of Paul's most memorable moments came when filming 'The Jolly Boys' Outing' episode. 'We all had to get into the pirate ship ride at the funfair and nobody wanted to go in it,' he recalls. 'The idea was that everyone would get in it and then Del would say, "Right lads" and lock the gate and start it, and everyone would come out feeling very sick.

'But hardly anyone wanted to do it so it ended up with just me, Patrick Murray and Nick Lyndhurst in there. Tony Dow, the director, told us to look as if we were having a fun time and we all laughed. Then the machine started to move and by the time we got to the top we weren't laughing any longer!'

Paul grew up in Liverpool and was brought up in care until he was eighteen after both his parents died before he was six. 'I was shipped around from foster-parents to foster-parents, foster-parents here, foster-parents there and I had a great time at school. Despite its ups and downs I loved my childhood and I treasure it.'

One of Paul's first jobs was at Lewis' department store in Liverpool. While he was there, he and a friend formed an *a cappella* band. One afternoon his friend spotted an advert in the local paper for auditions at the Liverpool Empire for parts in the musical *Hair*. 'I went along to keep him company but decided to audi-

Paul Barber as Del's mate, Denzil.

FACT FILE

NAME *Paul Barber*
BORN *Liverpool*
OTHER TV WORK INCLUDES
Lucky, The Brothers McGregor, Gangsters, The Front Line, Chancer, Needle, Brookside, The Boys From The Blackstuff, Tom Jones and *Casualty*

DENZIL *Paul Barber*

tion too,' he recalls. 'We sang, and the next day I had to go to Manchester to re-audition and I got a part – and my friend didn't.'

Paul ended up starring in the show alongside people like Paul Nicholas, Joan Armatrading, Floella Benjamin, Angela Bruce and Richard O'Brien. He was 21 when it finished and afterwards gained a part in the musical *Jesus Christ Superstar* followed by the lead role in a TV play called *Lucky*. Since then Paul has worked regularly and starred in the sitcom *The Brothers McGregor* and the hit series *Gangsters*.

Away from *Only Fools and Horses*, Paul is best known as Horse in the hit film *The Full Monty*. 'The weird thing is that for *Fools and Horses* I'm known all over Britain,' he says. 'But for *The Full Monty* I'm known across the world, which is quite something for a small part in a low budget movie!

'It really made me laugh when I first read the script,' says Paul, but he's not sure he can define just why it was such a huge success. 'It's a good solid story about working-class people with their backs against the wall and I think people from all walks of life saw a bit of themselves in the film.'

It's like a family when we all get together. It's always a laugh.

Denzil is literally driven mad by Del's yellow van in the 1985 Christmas special 'To Hull and Back'.

Sue Holderness
MARLENE

Sue Holderness as Marlene, wife of Boycie and very popular with all the lads in Peckham.

Do you remember Marlene? Oh yes, all the boys remember Marlene.

Sue Holderness joined the cast of *Only Fools and Horses* in 1984 to film one episode, 'Sleeping Dogs Lie', as Boycie's wife and that, as far as she was concerned, was that. She never expected that she'd be back the following year and from then on become a regular member of the team. She was cast after producer Ray Butt and director Susan Belbin spotted her in the TV sketch show *End of Part One*, a forerunner of *Not the Nine O'Clock News*, written by *One Foot in the Grave* creator David Renwick and *2 Point 4 Children* writer Andrew Marshall.

'Prior to that I'd really been known for playing middle-class or posh women on television,' she says. 'So playing downmarket Marlene made a nice change. I didn't audition for it, they just gave me the part and it was supposed to be one day's work.' Up until then Marlene had been referred to in the script – and so had her reputation. There had been gags along the lines of 'Do you remember Marlene? Oh yes, all the boys remember Marlene.'

'Marlene and Boycie fight but then they also get on quite well and I think she likes him really,' says Sue. 'It's just that Marlene also loves everybody else. She's much too sweet really to say no to men, and because of that she's become known as the Peckham bicycle. I think she's probably had flings at some stage with most of the regulars at the Nag's Head – but I doubt she can remember exactly who.

'I thought that one episode was it and then the following year John decided he liked the idea of seeing Marlene on screen and wrote her in again quite a lot,' she says. 'That was great for me because I like playing her. She's actually very sweet and quite daffy, although she can be quite shrewd with Boycie. She's also got much more money than sense.'

Marlene reappeared in the first episode of the following series, 'From Prussia with Love', in which Del tried to sell her and Boycie a newborn baby. John Sullivan had already worked out that Marlene and Boycie didn't have children and had been trying to start a family for years. In 'Sleeping Dogs Lie' it was clear that their dog Duke was really a baby substitute for Marlene, and in 'From Prussia with Love' Marlene's desperation to have a child was clear.

Later, in the episode 'Video Nasty', the couple discovered that it was actually Boycie who had the problem, with hospital tests showing that he had a low sperm count. 'That gave me one of my favourite lines,' says Sue. '"He's been firing more blanks than the Territorials!" and led to John Sullivan's infamous description of Boycie as a "Jaffa – seedless."

'Marlene was bloody angry when she found out that it was his problem because for the past twenty years she'd been blaming herself for not getting pregnant when actually it was him,' says Sue. 'Then later she managed to get pregnant and that changed their marriage too and she dotes on little Tyler.'

A character's desperate desire to have a baby isn't a subject most sitcom writers would risk trying to tackle, but John Sullivan bit the bullet and the

MARLENE *Sue Holderness*

poignancy of both Marlene's sadness and Boycie's embarrassment came through the laughter. For Sue it meant a bulging postbag of letters from women facing the same plight in real life. Ironically, though, Sue couldn't share their suffering very easily because when she filmed 'Sleeping Dogs Lie' she was actually three months pregnant with her first child.

'It was surprising to me just how many members of the public took it so seriously,' she says. 'Later they wrote to me asking for advice about what to do about infertility. That was very awkward for me to answer because by that stage I'd had two babies. So all the time I was playing this character who was desperate to have a child, I was in fact reproducing like mad. I found all that quite tragic because my situation was really the reverse.

'It was quite hard for me to communicate with these women because I'd experienced the joy of having children myself and that was after previously not being particularly maternal. Once you have them, you understand much more strongly how desperate it is for women who can't.'

Sue was still single in her mid-thirties and had begun to wonder whether she'd ever settle down and have a family. Then she met her husband, Mark Piper, and they decided to start a family soon after. 'I'd left it very late – I was thirty-six when I had my first child – because I'd been busy and had an exciting career and it wasn't until those hormones started churning at thirty-five that I thought I'd better get on with it.

'Prior to that I hadn't been maternal at all. If anybody had handed me a baby I'd have run away because babies used to scream as soon as I held them. I had no rapport with them and I didn't like them at all. Now, that's all changed and I'm a hopelessly besotted mother.'

Sue is frequently asked to open fêtes and start off charity events as Marlene which she does when she can, sometimes together with John Challis who plays her screen husband and who is a strong supporter of the wildlife charity Tusk. 'They want me to dress up as Marlene and so over the years I've bought various outfits in junk shops, including a wonderful leopard skin jacket which is just up Marlene's street. They are the sort of things I'd never wear out normally, but they are perfect for the character.'

Away from acting, Sue is a devoted mum to her children, Harriet, twelve, and eleven-year-old Freddie. The family live in Windsor, Berkshire, where her husband Mark is Executive Director of the Theatre Royal. 'I miss doing *Only Fools* because it is such fun and we are such a happy team,' says Sue, who also keeps busy by making corporate videos for clients like the Foreign Office, Marks and Spencer, and Rank. 'Not only that but it also fits in perfectly with family life. I hope we will do some more one day.'

As a child she studied dancing, and did her first acting at school. She caught the acting bug and after 'A' Levels she went to the Central School of Speech and Drama. 'From the first time I acted at school I knew that was what I wanted to do,' she says. 'My parents wanted me to go to university but I was hooked on acting and thankfully I've been able to make a career out of it and to this day I've never had more than three months without knowing what the next job is.'

FACT FILE

NAME *Sue Holderness*
DATE OF BIRTH *28.5.1949*
BORN *Hampstead, London*
OTHER TV WORK INCLUDES
The Sandbaggers, The New Avengers, End of Part One, Girls About Town, Canned Laughter, It Takes a Worried Man, The Cleopatras, Dear John and *You, Me and It*

She's actually very sweet and quite daffy, although she can be quite shrewd with Boycie. She's also got much more money than sense.

★★★*Did you know?*

At the same time as playing Marlene, Sue was also starring in another John Sullivan series, *Dear John*, in which she played Maggie, the wife of divorcee John's best friend.

Tessa Peake-Jones
RAQUEL

Tessa Peake-Jones as Raquel.
Opposite: Raquel with Del and son Damien.

...she had a heart of gold and then she met a similar man...

Veteran BBC newsreader Richard Whitmore appeared in two episodes of *Only Fools and Horses*, 'The Sky's the Limit' and 'Mother Nature's Son'.

Going shopping has never been the same for Tessa Peake-Jones since she appeared in *Only Fools and Horses* for the first time on Christmas Day 1988. The climax of the episode saw her character Raquel being revealed as a part-time kissagram girl who had been booked to peel off for Albert's birthday at the Nag's Head. Del was humiliated and their romance hit the rocks in a big way.

For Tessa, appearing in the episode had quite a dramatic impact on her life. 'I lived in the East End of London at the time and round there *Only Fools and Horses* is like the flagship programme. It's hugely popular. Straight after the episode was transmitted I got a lot of attention which I wasn't used to at all, and it wasn't always easy,' she says.

'For the first time in my career I got recognised a lot and people would stare at me in the bank and when I went to Safeways someone even said, "Are you going to take your clothes off!" In the episode I sang "Slow Boat to China" and when I walked into my local one night someone started playing it on the piano for a bit of fun.

'The main comment I got – and still do get – is: "Where's Del then?" People think that they are the first ones to have said it when in actual fact they are the nine hundredth! The great thing about *Only Fools and Horses,* though, is that all you ever get from people is how much they have enjoyed it. It's quite rare that the only feedback you get from the public about something is praise, and that's rather lovely and makes you feel very privileged.'

Tessa was booked to play Raquel in the autumn of 1988 and back then it was solely for one episode. 'John Sullivan had wanted to write more for a woman but I don't think he ever intended to match up Del with her long-term,' she says. 'It was a one-off Christmas special and in the end they split up and that was that. It was a great script and I had great fun doing it. I never expected to do any more.

'Comedy was quite a male-dominated area then and I thought the part of Raquel was fabulous. Suddenly John Sullivan, a man who wrote brilliantly for men but hadn't written much for women, had created this fab, well-rounded part for a woman. Raquel was a little bit lost and was trying to make enough money to keep herself going. She wanted to be an actress and she had a heart of gold and then she met a similar man, in a way. The script touched on things like loneliness and marital problems and seemed to me to have real depth.'

Four months later Tessa was filming another television series in Norfolk when a call came through from her agent, asking her if she would call *Only Fools and Horses* director Tony Dow. 'I spoke to Tony and he explained that John wanted Raquel to come into the series full-time and how did I feel about it,' she recalls. 'As you can imagine I was really chuffed but I had no idea I'd still be playing her years later.

RAQUEL *Tessa Peake-Jones*

'Over the years Raquel has developed as a character and grown as a person. When she and Del first met she really lacked confidence and Del gave her the boost she needed. Since then she's become tougher and tougher, probably partly due to living with him, and now she doesn't take any nonsense from him. Having a baby has probably made her stronger too.'

Tessa first saw an episode of *Only Fools and Horses* in 1985 when she watched the Christmas special 'To Hull and Back'. 'My Godmother, Auntie Renie, used to watch it, and it was her favourite programme in the world,' Tessa recalls. 'All my family had gone on for years about how good it was and I was a student at that time and never really caught much telly. Then I watched "To Hull and Back" and I thought it was hysterical. It was like this whole new world opened up to me and I suddenly became a huge fan.'

Tessa's parents divorced when she was a baby and she grew up in Harrow, Middlesex, where she was brought up by her mum and her Auntie Renie. When she was nine she began going to dancing classes. Later she started doing drama at school and then decided to give acting a try as a career. Encouraged by her drama teacher when she left school, she gained a place at the Central School of Speech and Drama in London.

She left after three years and gained her first television role in the drama series *Telford's Change*, before appearing with top playwright Alan Ayckbourn's theatre company in Scarborough for a year. Then she landed the starring role in a BBC adaptation of Iris Murdoch's *The Bell*. It was while acting in *Romeo and Juliet* at the Birmingham Repertory Theatre that Tessa and her partner Douglas Hodge met. They had the starring roles as Shakespeare's doomed lovers in the play and fell in love for real.

Only Fools and Horses was her biggest break. 'I've loved doing it and even though I came in much later than the others they were so welcoming and friendly that going back each year to film was like seeing members of your family again,' she says. 'It's also been great for my career and I know it has led to other work which is marvellous.'

FACT FILE

NAME *Tessa Peake-Jones*
DATE OF BIRTH *9.5.1957*
BORN *Hammersmith, London*
OTHER TV WORK INCLUDES
Telford's Change, The Bell, The Two Gentlemen of Verona, Pride and Prejudice, Up the Garden Path, So Haunt Me, The Demon Headmaster, Tom Jones and *Midsomer Murders*

Gwyneth Strong
CASSANDRA

Gwyneth Strong as Cassandra Trotter.

…I was able to learn from two of the best – David Jason and Nick Lyndhurst.

Gwyneth Strong went to audition for the part of Cassandra in *Only Fools and Horses* not really expecting to land the part. Four months earlier she'd had her first baby, Oscar, and she was feeling ready to work again. Going for interviews was a gentle way of getting going again. 'I really didn't think I'd get the part because I was so wrapped up in the baby world,' she says. 'I met Tony Dow and the interview went like a dream and then I got called back and this time met Producer Gareth Gwenlan. After that I walked from the BBC to my mum's house at Notting Hill and while I was there I got a call to say I'd got the part.

'I was delighted because I loved the show but back then I thought I was just going to be in one episode, "Yuppy Love", and because of that there was no pressure. My brief for Cassandra was pretty much as she is. Her dad is a working-class bloke made good and like him she's quite ambitious and got a good job in a bank, which has made her quite middle class. She was not the sort of girl that Rodney had been out with before.

'Rodney and Cassandra are mad about each other and that gets them through any crises they face. He's loyal and sensitive and I've seen surveys that say the character of Rodney is what most women adore. He's popular because mothers want to mother him and girls want to look after him and they love the fact he gets things wrong because he's not nasty at all.'

Despite being thrilled about getting the part Gwyneth was nervous. 'I was quite overawed when I started on it,' she admits. 'I mean, who wouldn't be? I was suddenly part of something that I had watched and enjoyed for years. Fortunately everyone was very welcoming. I'd also never done a sitcom before and rather naively thought it would be just the same as theatre acting of which I'd done quite a lot. That wasn't the case so I learnt on my feet very quickly and I was lucky because I was able to learn from two of the best – David Jason and Nick Lyndhurst.'

Some of Gwyneth's first scenes as Cassandra were romantic moments with Rodney. 'They were supposed to be a bit nervous and shy – and so were we for real!' she laughs. 'I think most actors are like that but they don't admit it. Over the years we've got to know each other better and have become much more relaxed with each other as have Rodney and Cassandra.'

After filming her first episode Gwyneth was asked back to do the next one, 'Danger UXD', and soon discovered she was to become a regular in the show. 'And by the end of that series Cassandra and Rodney got married,' she says. 'It was amazing that it all happened that fast and for me it was wonderful. It was quite a whirlwind.'

Gwyneth already knew that appearing in *Only Fools* would have quite an impact on her life – certainly in terms of public recognition. 'The Monday after my first episode went out I was banging my pram down the steps outside my house and I hadn't reached the bottom one when someone shouted: "Look, there's

CASSANDRA *Gwyneth Strong*

Cassandra!" and it has continued from then on. Since then I don't think I've walked down a street without someone shouting that or "Where's Rodney?" or "Oi plonker!", if they are really drunk.

'Usually you have to be in a show a while before you are recognised but *Only Fools* has such a high profile. It's quite good at parties though because I never have to say what I do for my living because so many people watch it. I've got lots of friends who are wonderful actors or actresses and do great work and it's awful at a party to say "I'm an actress" only for them to say: "Oh, have I seen you in anything?" which is really boring when you've been doing the job for 25 years.'

Gwyneth gets lots of fan mail from *Only Fools* fans, particularly teenage boys. 'If you're a teenage boy and it's not going easily for you then the idea of Cassandra being with Rodney I think gives you hope,' she says. 'I'd had fan mail before but not on that level.'

Admirers of *Only Fools and Horses* point to John Sullivan's interweaving of serious moments – like the hospital scene in 'Modern Men' after Cassandra's miscarriage – with humour. 'He's a genius,' she says. 'It's quite unique when he takes a subject like that and gives it everything it deserves in terms of emotional pain and also makes it funny. If you describe that, it sounds impossible, but John manages to do it.'

Gwyneth's favourite episode though is one of sheer comedy – 'The Unlucky Winner Is…' – when Rodney wins a foreign holiday in a painting competition. It was also one of the hardest to film with David and her having a long scene filmed in one take, interrupted by Rodney's return from a bout of skateboarding. 'It felt like it went on for about 20 minutes but it can't have been,' she says.

Gwyneth has been acting since the age of ten when she and a childhood friend Murray Dale, son of *Carry On* star Jim Dale, who lived round the corner, wrote to an agent enclosing a photograph of them together. It worked – and they both ended up getting acting work with Gwyneth gaining a small part just months later in the play *Live Like Pigs* at the prestigious Royal Court Theatre in London. 'I was so lucky,' she says. 'It was such a great place to start.' A year later she landed a part in the film *Nothing But The Night* with Peter Cushing, Christopher Lee and Diana Dors.

Her parents had been less than keen about her going into acting but nevertheless Gwyneth left school at sixteen determined to make a career in the profession and she hasn't looked back since. 'I've had quiet patches but if you are lucky no one really notices,' says Gwyneth, who has two children, Oscar and Lottie, by her former partner, actor Jesse Birdsall. 'Fortunately these days more often than not that's through choice because I try to avoid long tours away from home where you don't earn much money.'

Despite being watched by millions in *Only Fools and Horses* Gwyneth has managed to avoid being typecast and even appeared with her *Fools* co-star David Jason in his ITV drama *A Touch of Frost*. 'That was great,' she says. 'I played a senior officer to David's DI Frost who was investigating him and the hardest part of it was to be very dominant of him because that was a big role reversal from *Only Fools and Horses*.'

MY FAVOURITE EPISODE

It was in 'The Unlucky Winner Is…' when Del gives Rodney and Cassandra a list of things to do to get ready to go to Spain and his final instruction to Cassandra is: 'And there's just enough time to get your bikini line waxed.' I just found that so awful for someone to say that to you in a pub in front of everyone! I just kept laughing and when we came to actually shoot the scene just as I thought I had my laughter under control David squeezed my knee under the table because he knew that would make me laugh – and it did. I nearly knocked the whole table over and we had to do it again!

FACT FILE

NAME *Gwyneth Strong*
DATE OF BIRTH *2.12.1959*
BORN *East Ham, London*
OTHER TV WORK INCLUDES
Telford's Change, Shadows, Angels, It's a Lovely Day Tomorrow, Inside Out, King of the Ghetto, Shrinks, Living With Dinosaurs, From A Far Country, Paradise Postponed, Nice Town, Waiting On The Line, 99-1, The Missing Postman, A Touch of Frost and *Real Women*

PART
3

The First Series

After weeks of planning, work began on the first series of *Only Fools and Horses* on 6 May 1981. Then, just a few days into filming, the production team was hit by a big problem. On the morning of the third day of shooting producer Ray Butt, who had been working on the show since its conception, awoke at his West London flat in agony, having suffered a slipped disc during the night. As producer, Ray was not only the show's boss, but he was also due to direct the six episodes that were to make up the first series.

Writer, John Sullivan, recalls how he got the bad news. 'I was the first person Ray phoned,' he recalls. 'He was so worried about the show that he phoned me before he even rang a doctor or a hospital. There was this agonised voice on the line, obviously in great pain. With Ray off, we were in deep trouble. Our producer and director had been taken to hospital and all the actors were sitting around down in a market somewhere waiting to start filming, and wondering what the hell we were going to do.'

It was the last thing David Jason could have done with so early on, for although he was relishing getting into the character of Del Boy, he was nervous about it all. 'I think you are always a bit nervous when you first go into something because you don't really know the character or where you are going,' he says. 'You are desperately trying to settle down and for the first few days you are still finding your feet.

'Eventually it all starts to gel and then you start doing it instinctively and begin to feel you know what a character would or wouldn't do in a given situation. Like everyone else you are scrabbing round desperately trying to be funny.'

Ray's injury resulted in a three-week stay in Charing Cross Hospital in London. For the production it meant a major upheaval, and another director, Martin Shardlow, was rapidly called up to fill in and another senior producer in the comedy department Gareth Gwenlan, later to become the

Above: David Jason in the first series of Only Fools and Horses, *1981, outside the flats in Acton used for the exterior of the Trotters' home 'Nelson Mandela House'. Opposite: The Trotter brothers and Grandad inside their flat in the episode 'A Slow Bus to Chingford'.*

show's producer, stood in as producer during Ray's absence.

The first episode, 'Big Brother', was screened at 8.30p.m. on 8 September 1981 and was billed rather flatly in the *Radio Times* as the story of 'two brothers living with their grandad in a South London flat and existing off shady deals'. The episode cost around £28,000 to make (about average at the time for a sitcom) and was transmitted in the same week as the BBC began a six-part adaptation of John Wyndham's *The Day of the Triffids*; a new drama series *Blood Money*, starring Bernard Hepton and Michael Denison; and a fly-on-the-wall documentary series *Fighter Pilot*, which tracked the progress of new would-be RAF top guns.

It was sandwiched between a repeat of the American private eye drama *The Rockford Files* (starring James Garner) and *The Nine O'Clock News*, and was up against a documentary about new French President François Mitterrand on BBC2 and a drama, *The Flame Trees of Thika*, starring Hayley Mills and David Robb, on ITV. Its impact on television critics was negligible and few even bothered to review it, although one, Stephen Biscoe, writing in the *Yorkshire Post*, backed it from the start. In a review the day after transmission he said that Mary Whitehouse might not approve of the language used. 'But this viewer, on the other hand,' he wrote, 'will be watching it because he likes its earthy characters and therefore forgives them their earthy behaviour. There is, in fact, more than a touch of that earthiest of couples, Steptoe and Son, in this new series.'

The episode, in which Del tries to sell a batch of suitcases that don't open, attracted a respectable 9.2 million viewers but it's fair to say that it didn't set the world alight. 'We didn't really get any publicity and the show went out in a very bad slot,' says John Sullivan. 'I kept hearing about the BBC Publicity Department but to me it was something out of mythology. They never contacted us and therefore the

boys didn't do any interviews. The show just went out without that sort of promotion.'

Later on during transmission of the first series, John and David Jason complained about how the show was being treated inside the BBC. 'In the BBC Television Centre foyer each month were displays of massive photographs from different departments,' John remembers. One particular month it focused on comedy and they were all up there: *L for Lester* (starring Brian Murphy), *To the Manor Born* and lots of others, but no *Fools and Horses*.

'So we made enquiries, wondering if we'd missed it, and we were told there was one up on the sixth floor of BBC Television Centre which was the sort of place only executives go to for a bit of lunch sometimes. We definitely felt then that we were a bit of an embarrassment to them and they wanted to hide us away. We ended up having a meeting with John Howard Davis about it and he said he'd get it moved to somewhere a little more noticeable. It was nothing you could put your finger on but we just had this feeling that we were the black sheep of the family.'

'We felt desperately unloved for a good couple of years,' says Nick Lyndhurst.

The second episode, 'Go West Young Man', sees Del trying his hand at the second-hand car business after cadging

an old banger from Boycie (Boycie's first appearance in the show). Del sells the clapped-out Ford Cortina GT convertible to a mouthy Australian, played by actor Nick Stringer (who was to return in the episode 'Who Wants To Be a Millionaire' in series five, as Del's old pal Jumbo Mills).

Filming on location at a council estate in North Acton, North-West London, was a worry for producer Ray Butt. After all, the script called for Rodney to drive the car at high speed and nearly run Del over. Keeping the public away from filming was no problem but Nicholas Lyndhurst hadn't passed his driving test and therefore wasn't allowed on public roads. 'But I needn't have worried,' recalls Ray. 'Technically we weren't on a public road where we filmed it but even so I told Nick not to go too fast because I was going to undercrank the film – which meant it would come out looking like it had been speeded up.

'He came round the corner and it looked unbelievable. The tyres were screaming and black smoke was pouring out the back (because we'd put smoke canisters under it at the back and the car was on two wheels). He did it far faster than I'd asked him. Even though Nick hadn't passed his test he was still a superb driver.'

Nick recalls, 'In the script the car was supposed to have spongy brakes but I made damn sure they worked because

I had to stop just before a parapet and if I'd not stopped I'd have had a 40-foot drop!'

'Cash and Curry' sees Del getting embroiled in a deal with two Indian businessmen – and at one stage he kicks a burly minder between the legs. Del then delivers one of David Jason's favourite lines. David says, 'The businessman goes on about having a big house and lots of land and then Del says, "Yeah, and he's got a couple of acres an' all, hasn't he!" It's a brilliant line. You can't go wrong with stuff like that. We always tried to play it straight because the jokes are there in the script. I always used to say, "Don't put a joke on a joke," then it works better.'

In 'The Second Time Around' Del meets up with his old fiancée Pauline Harris, played by Jill Baker (who coincidentally also appeared with David Jason in 1998 as a gynaecologist in his ITV drama *March in Windy City*). Rodney has bad memories of how she dumped Del and he's not enthusias-

Above: Nicholas Lyndhurst and David Jason in the episode 'Cash and Curry'.
Opposite: The brothers in their nuclear fallout shelter, the sixth episode in the first series – 'The Russians Are Coming'.

tic about them getting together again, particularly when he hears that both her previous husbands died. 'I remember how she treated you when you was engaged,' Rodney tells Del, when he accuses him of being hostile to her. 'I may have only been a little nipper, Del, but I remember how she screwed you up.'

Soon after, Del announces that he and Pauline are going to get married and she moves into the flat, where she causes uproar by serving Rodney and Grandad corned beef while she and Del have best steak, hiding Grandad's false teeth, and suggesting they put him in an old folks' home. When she starts talking about Del having life insurance, Rodney and Grandad decide to leave home. Fortunately Del realises before it's too late that she's really only after his money. The trio flee the flat for five days. When they return they find she's gone, but not before running up a huge phone bill: she's left it off the hook but connected to the speaking clock – in America.

Del's entrepreneurial flair takes a new turn in 'A Slow Bus to Chingford' when he starts Trotter's Ethnic Tours. He decides that tourists want something new. 'Your average tourist gets fed up seeing the same old places – the Houses of Parliament, Buck House, the National Gallery,' he tells Grandad and Rodney. 'Once you've seen one Rubens you've seen them all – this is where a dynamic person like me steps in.'

Rodney meanwhile is far from happy with his new job as a night watchman, particularly with the impact it has on his romance with Janice, not to mention his traffic warden's uniform. Del's £17 ethnic tours fail to catch on – but that's perhaps not too surprising when the itinerary includes the Lee Valley Viaduct, the glory of Lower Edmonton at dusk, a walkabout in Croydon, the birthplace of Sherlock Holmes, and the summit of Mount Pleasant. It might have helped, though, if Grandad had actually sent out the advertising handbills, as he was supposed to do, but he's got a good excuse: 'It wasn't me, Del Boy, it was me brain.'

With US–Soviet relations taking a turn for the worse in the early eighties, the timing of 'The Russians Are Coming' was very appropriate. In this episode, Del buys a pile of old bricks which Rodney discovers is actually a prefabricated nuclear shelter. Del's all for selling it but politically-aware Rodders reckons World War Three is just round the corner and wants to build it. 'It only takes one little rumble in the Middle East and them missiles are gonna start flying,' says Rodney. 'And what have we got in this country to combat the might of the Soviet Union? Three jump jets and a strongly worded letter to the Russian Ambassador.'

Getting to the shelter when the four-minute warning goes off is a problem, but not as hard as it would be if they built it in Grandad's preferred location – the New Forest. In the end they decide to put it up closer to home – on the roof of Nelson Mandela House. There Del offers his theory about the younger generation not having had the chance of going off to war. This angers Grandad who launches into an unexpectedly profound speech about war in general and treatment of the young men who were injured in the First World War. After the armistice, he recalls, 'As the nation celebrated, they were hidden away in big grey buildings, far from the public gaze.' Then he adds, 'They promised us homes fit for heroes, they give us heroes fit for homes.'

The first festive episode, 'Christmas Crackers', which was added on to the six-part series as an extra, takes place on Christmas Day in the Trotters' flat but was actually screened on 28 December. It sees Grandad cooking the Christmas dinner and Del and Rodney complaining about it. The episode isn't a classic but nevertheless has some fine moments, such as Del trying to cut the turkey with an electric carving knife minus its plug, and some great gags, like Del insisting they can't go out and leave Grandad at home – and then the old man himself going out.

The fact that it was totally studio-based, and that most of the action took place in the flat, brought home what Christmas is really like for a very close-knit family. There's the boredom, the arguments and the reliance on watching television. And when Rodney complains that he's bored, as many youngsters do on Christmas Day once present-opening is over, Del tells him, 'Everyone's bored. Christmas is a religious festival. It's meant to be boring.'

Traditionally the BBC has always prided itself on nurturing programmes even if they aren't instant hits. They would normally commission a second series, even if the first wasn't a major success, simply because someone had a hunch that it might take off. However, the viewing figures for the first series of Only Fools and Horses were disappointing – averaging 7.7 million – and clearly someone senior at the BBC thought it didn't have much potential and didn't deserve to be re-commissioned for a second series.

'After the first series finished I had a meeting with John Howard Davis and he asked me what I was doing next because at that stage I was under a contract with the BBC,' John Sullivan recalls. 'I definitely got the feeling, although he never actually said it, that they'd probably rather I went off and came up with something else. That was a bit of a shock because at that stage the BBC had this policy whereby they'd give something a second chance, unless the writer or principal actors didn't want to do any more. The way John was talking to me, saying things like "I liked that other idea of yours," I felt I was being steered towards forgetting Fools and Horses and doing something different instead.'

However, Ray Butt still thought the show could work and John had another strong ally in David Jason who was solidly behind it. 'David and I had many meetings, drinks and dinners and he was very, very supportive,' remembers John. 'He was really eager for it to work.'

'I had total faith in it,' David says. 'I could see that it was very funny, there was no question about that. One problem we had though was the title, which no one understood, and the fact that it didn't have anyone in it. I mean, it had Nick, Lennard and me, but it didn't have anybody in it who was so well known that people would want to switch it on just to see what they were doing. For whatever reason, people weren't tuning in and we weren't really building an audience.'

At a further meeting with John Howard Davis, John Sullivan insisted that he really wanted to give it another go. John Howard Davis agreed to give the show a second run – and at the same time it was decided to dump the original theme tune in favour of one written by John Sullivan that explained the show's title. During transmission of the first series the BBC had been bombarded by letters from viewers wanting to know what Only Fools and Horses meant. The new title tune would explain it all. In any case, John Sullivan had always been unhappy with the show's original music, a typical seventies-style sitcom theme tune.

'The script had described the music as Chas and Dave-style rockney,' he says. 'What we got was Ronnie Hazlehurst's version of that and, to be honest, I didn't like it that much. My version had already been written for the first series and I thought they'd use it but for some reason Ray had decided to go with Ronnie's. No one was very happy about it, including the cast, so between series one and series two it was changed to my version, which is the one people are now familiar with.

'I'd written the theme music for the closing credits on Citizen Smith and Over the Moon and just got into the habit of doing them. I wasn't supposed to do the singing on the Fools and Horses theme because Chas and Dave were going to do it. Then they had a number one hit called "Ain't No Pleasing You" and they became very busy and couldn't do it. That was a bit of a choker because if they'd done our theme that might have gone to number one too. I'd recorded it originally just to get the tune so Ray said to me, "You do it". I wasn't keen and had to be persuaded with lager! Going into a studio and singing with a band was not really my kind of thing.'

Car hire boss Martyn Scott from Milton Keynes bought an old Reliant van for £60 and turned it into a wedding car.

WHY A THREE-WHEELED VAN?

John Sullivan gave Del a three-wheeled van to drive as a chink in his armour. 'I had this smart, confident little guy with the gift of the gab who cared about his appearance a great deal and then had this silly vehicle,' says John. 'It's a real contradiction but it's all he can afford. Outwardly he tries to project this image that he's doing very well in life and then he walks outside and there's the truth.

'I thought he'd need something practical to carry his gear round in so that ruled out something like a Capri. Reliants are cheap to run and you only need a motorcycle licence to drive one.' And amazingly, even though the van is so key to the show, and instantly recognisable, John says, 'It was kind of a last minute thought. I had to give him something to drive and it could have been an old transit van and I suddenly thought, "I'll give him a three-wheeled van."

'I got the New York – Paris – Peckham idea on the side of the van from a packet of Dunhill cigarettes except theirs says London – Paris – New York. Del would have seen it and been slightly in awe of it and

therefore impressed and stuck it on his van.'

Only Fools and Horses has done wonders for Reliant, the British-owned car manufacturer that makes the three-wheeled vehicles. Del's van is actually a Reliant Regal Supervan III and that particular model hasn't been made for 30 years. 'That model is a classic car and now a collectors' item and they are very rare,' says Samantha Heynes, Reliant's Company Secretary. '*Only Fools and Horses* did the company the world of good by putting it on the map. Traditionally January is a very quiet month in the motor industry but it wasn't for us. After the last three episodes of the series were screened our sales increased tremendously.'

Although the Tamworth-based company, which has 80 employees, doesn't make the exact model that Del drives any more it does still make a full range of cars and vans and they can be bought in yellow, although Nightfire red is the most popular choice. They cost around £5500 but, for people who don't want to buy a full-sized version, then Lledo, the die-cast model car makers, sell a 1:43

scale replica for just £9.99. Since it was launched in November 1997 around 200,000 of the model have been sold, making it the company's biggest-selling vehicle.

Dentist Peter Nelson is certain the van's helped attract visitors to his Cars of the Stars museum at Keswick in the Lake District. One of the BBC's original vans used on the show takes pride of place there alongside a host of original film and TV vehicles including two 21-foot Batmobiles, James Bond's Aston Martin and Lotus and Chitty Chitty Bang Bang. Most of them cost thousands of pounds but, quite appropriately, he snapped up the Reliant for a knock-down price of £995.

Peter reckons it accounts for a big percentage of his visitors. 'It makes people smile when they see it,' he says. 'And it's still the best value-for-money vehicle I've bought. Not only that but the BBC have borrowed it back and their hire fees meant I got half the £995 back! I could have a million-pound Bugatti here but it still wouldn't attract as many visitors as Del Boy's van!'

Designing the Trotters

THE CLOTHES

Creating the look for the characters in *Only Fools and Horses* has involved the writer, the cast, the producer and the various costume designers who worked on the show over the years. The woman responsible for the outfits used for the first series, which then set the tone throughout the programme's history, was costume designer Phoebe De Gaye.

'*Only Fools and Horses* was my first design job at the BBC,' recalls Phoebe, who has since gone on to design costumes for films like *Tom and Viv*, *Carry On Columbus* and TV series like *The Sculptress* and *Lorna Doone*. 'I was allocated to the show and went off to meet Ray Butt and then I met the actors.'

Phoebe got her inspiration for Del's gear by going to car boot sales and looking at people not unlike Del Boy. 'I remember one guy struck me,' she remembers. 'He was a real jack-the-lad type, with a paunch and white shoes and pushed-up hair. I thought Del ought to have permed hair like footballer Charlie George but I couldn't persuade David to go for that!'

Once she had some ideas, Phoebe made some rough sketches which she then presented to the production team. They approved them and, with only a very small budget to spend, she then set about gathering what she needed. Del's costumes needed a little more variety, so she took David Jason shopping in London's Oxford Street to find the stuff for Del Boy.

'I had this terrible old mini at the time which I drove him in, and when the engine got going all these fumes started drifting up through the floor – it was quite like the Trotter van in that respect!' she recalls. 'We went to lots of different shops and I got David to try on all these horrible cheap suits. After looking around for a while we finally bought the suit in a really cheap and cheerful shop.

'I bought some horrible, tight, brightly coloured Gabicci shirts from their warehouse in Edgware. They were very fashionable at the time and were made of fine, silky material. One of the ones I got was red with a black suede pocket on it. It was disgusting! The sheepskin coat we ended up buying was memorable, too, because it was made of lots of pieces of sheepskin and had lots of horrible seams.

'Things would be bought at the sort of places that the Trotters themselves would have shopped at,' says Phoebe. 'And all Del's rings and his bracelet were fake gold and came from Chapel Street Market, as did his chain with his initial on, which I've still got somewhere in my kit, although I've absolutely no idea why!'

In the early days Rodney was rarely seen without his green camouflage combat jacket which came from the BBC Costume Department, and Phoebe added a Yasser Arafat-type headscarf which she bought at Shepherd's Bush Market.

'Rodney always had a grungy look well before grunge became fashionable!' she says.

'I soon got rid of that scarf though,' laughs Nick Lyndhurst. 'Purely because it kept getting in the way.'

Grandad's costume was very straightforward. 'The idea with Grandad was that he never took his hat off even when he went in the bath,' she says. 'Nor did he really ever get dressed properly. He would almost always have part of his

ONLY FOOLS AND HORSES – PILOT
DEL.

soft leather casual jkt

beer belly

trashy jewellery watches, neck chains etc

tis tight here and here

hair carefully blow dried over ears and dyed

suspicion of built up heels – otherwise feet teeny in proportion to bulk up above, and fashion con...

pale libe sc

pyjamas on under anything else he might be wearing – and his clothes would never be very clean. To get that crusty effect, I'd make it dirty with Vaseline, a bit of make-up and even real food.'

Robin Stubbs took over as costume designer on the show in 1986 and was responsible for getting Del's costume together for his new yuppy image in the sixth series. Del's new, more upmarket suits were bought from Austin Reed in London's Regent Street and cost about £200 each, though trying them on was far from easy. 'We always had to be discreet when we went for them,' says Robin. 'Because if David is recognised he gets mobbed.'

After Del smartened up his act, everything else came from high street stores. His ties came from Tie-Rack, his raincoat came from Dickins and Jones in Regent Street, and his shirts came from Austin Reed and Marks and Spencer. His jewellery was just as worthless as before though, even if it looked like it cost hundreds of pounds. 'We usually replaced it for each series,' says Robin, 'because it was so cheap and the gold paint wore off. It was the sort of stuff Del Boy would sell himself!' It came from cheap jewellery stores in London's Soho and 'cost just a few pence'. His rings with D on them cost just 50 pence each, but Del's necklace with D on it was actually worth something! Robin had it specially made and it was worth around £70 – more than all the rest put together.

☆

THE HOME AND POSSESSIONS

John Sullivan's original script for the first episode of *Only Fools and Horses* gave clear guidance on how the Trotters' flat should look. It read: 'The room should reflect their styles of business. Nothing is permanent. The settee and two armchairs are from three separate suites. (The other pieces being used as make-weights in various past swops.)

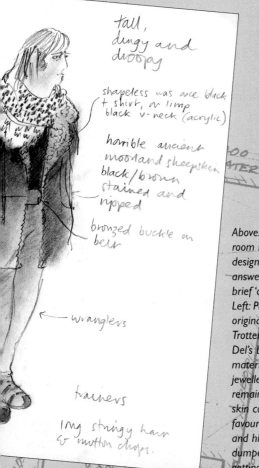

tall,
dingy and
droopy

shapeless was once black
+ shirt, or limp
black v-neck (acrylic)

horrible ancient
moorland sheepskin
black/brown
stained and
ripped

bronzed buckle on
belt

← wranglers

trainers

long stringy hair
& mutton chops.

Above: The set of the main room in the Trotters' flat – designer Tony Snoaden's answer to John Sullivan's brief 'clean but gaudy'. Left: Phoebe De Gaye's original sketches for the Trotter brothers' clothes. Del's beer belly never materialised but the trashy jewellery and tight jeans remained. Rodney's sheepskin coat was dropped in favour of a combat jacket and his PLO scarf was later dumped because it kept getting in the way.

'There are three TV sets, one colour, one black and white and the other has its back off awaiting repair.

'There are a couple of stereo music centres standing one on top of the other. Various video games, talking chess game etc litter the room.

'Their phone is one of the ornate 1920s types with separate ear-piece (on an alabaster base).

'The decor is clean but gaudy. Dozens of clashing patterns. It should look like a bad trip.'

That gave designer Tony Snoaden a clear idea as to how he should turn Sullivan's brief into reality. For inspiration about the actual layout of the flat he visited two different blocks of council flats, one near Kew Bridge in South-West London and another in North Acton in North-West London. There, he drew up plans for the set that would become one of the most familiar flats in Britain.

Cheap wallpaper was chosen from books in the BBC Design Department's sample room as was poor-quality carpet. Both were then ordered from the manufacturer.

Tony then went out with Props Buyer Chris Ferriday and chose the props that would litter the flat. They scoured specialist firms that sell or hire bits and pieces for TV shows and came back with everything from Del's ice bucket to reproduction paintings and from a tacky wrought-iron guitar to ornaments. They also looked round Del's fictional stomping ground, like markets, to pick up oddments.

'We were looking for the sort of things that people like the Trotters would have in their living room,' says Tony Snoaden. 'I had quite a lot of freedom to dot things around, like leaving an old tyre in a doorway, and that was because Del thought he could sell almost anything and therefore would have all sorts of stuff just hanging around.'

Each episode would feature different boxes of junk and reflect Del's latest line, but some things like the old chairs, Del's cocktail bar and telephone would remain constant. 'It had to have a constancy about it but we'd still add things each week depending on what Del was selling,' says Tony. 'Even in much more recent episodes I've spotted things that we had during my time on the show.'

More than a decade later, designing the sets for *Only Fools* fell to Donal Woods, whose first episode was the 1992 Christmas special 'Mother Nature's Son'. He inherited the main sets – the flat, Rodney and Cassandra's pad and the Nag's Head interior from a string of different designers who had gone before him.

Each time a new series or special was filmed the set would be rebuilt from scratch because it's cheaper to do that than store old sets. 'Each designer would keep detailed records of what they'd used in the way of props and wallpaper and carpets so we could follow on from that,' explains Donal.

'The wallpaper might change each year depending whether we could get it. In the end we had real trouble getting the same old cheap stuff we used because it had gone out of fashion, and Fads, the company we got it from, scoured the country and found us their last four rolls.

'Some of the props – things like the bar, the wall lights and the drapes – have stayed the same for years and then we'd add things for each episode. The stuff that Del was selling would be John Sullivan's ideas. He'd write something in and we'd have to find them or make them and get boxes specially printed with the details of the contents on the sides.'

The most difficult prop that Donal has had to find was a watch to play the Harrison timepiece for the final episode. 'It needed to look right so it took a lot of research,' he says. 'In the end we made three of them to be used for different scenes. We had one that could open, one that could be thrown around, and a nice one that could be used in the auction scene at Sotheby's. They were only shells made of brass but they cost a total of about £1000.

'The best thing about working on the show,' says Donal, 'is that because it is so popular, people and companies are really keen to help. Wherever you go people have heard of it. For instance when we filmed at Sotheby's for the final episode they couldn't have been more helpful. They got in early a whole set of seriously valuable Old Master paintings to decorate their gallery for us, brought in their telephone dealers and got porters in for us.

'Then, of course, we put the Trotters' van outside. When you think about it – this is one of the major auction houses in the world and you want to put a three-wheeled Reliant van outside their building. If it was any other show they'd probably tell you to get lost. But they even took down scaffolding for us for a day so we could film it there. No one would normally do that.'

The Second Series

The second series went into production in April 1982, the same month that Argentina invaded the Falkland Islands in the South Atlantic and Britain dispatched a large task force to retake them. The opening episode, 'The Long Legs of the Law', sees Rodney committing a cardinal sin according to Del's rule book, by going on a date with a policewoman, played by actress Kate Saunders, who went on to become a journalist on the *Sunday Times* and latterly a successful novelist. 'Rodney dating a policewoman was like a poison chalice to Del,' says David Jason. 'You couldn't really bring anyone in the police round to the flat because there were always one or two things in there that he wouldn't want them to see.'

In 'Ashes to Ashes' Del tries to sell Trigger's gran's antique urn – but comes a cropper when he and Rodney discover that it contains the remains of Trigger's grandad. They try all sorts of methods of disposal: scattering them

Above: David Jason during the second series of Only Fools and Horses, *1982.*
Below: Kate Saunders and Nicholas Lyndhurst in 'The Long Legs of the Law', the episode where, to Del's alarm, Rodney dated a policewoman.

on a bowling green, dumping them in the River Thames, even adding them to a cement mixer – until the ashes finally accidentally disappear up the vacuum pump of a road-sweeping lorry.

David Jason recalls, 'Nick and I had to rush up to the bloke in the cab and say, "Stop, you've just sucked up our urn." Then the driver would say, "Oh my God! What, was he a little kitten?" The cameraman was in the cab looking down at us, and every time we said it he just fell about laughing. The camera would then shake and we'd have to do it all again. When that happened we'd crease up. We ended up doing it about six times and in the end he had to give it to his assistant to do. It was very funny.'

Nick Lyndhurst hasn't forgotten being out on the Thames in a small rowing boat for one scene in the episode. 'It was high tide and it was very rough out there,' he explains. 'David had to row very hard to keep

Above: The Trotter brothers and the remains of Trigger's grandad from the episode 'Ashes to Ashes'.

up with it and we were nearly swamped. I doubt they'd let us do it these days.'

In 'A Losing Streak' Del and Boycie play a high-stakes game of poker which was inspired by John Sullivan's own knowledge of the game. 'I'd been to all-night card sessions, even though I was no big player myself,' he says. 'What fascinated me was how friends fell out in games and not just over money. A game would be like a duel and people took it very seriously and would sometimes accuse friends of cheating. My father was a big gambler and that was why I never gambled, because as a kid I saw how much money you could lose and the rows it would cause at home. I remember one night he came home drunk after a game of cards. With him was a greyhound he'd bought off some guy in a pub. The next night he took it over the common. He threw a tennis ball and the dog zoomed off after it and got the ball and carried on. He never saw him again. He came home and I remember him saying, "I tell you what, he was bloody fast so he was still a good buy."'

'No Greater Love' demonstrates the real bond between Del and Rodney. In this episode Rodney falls for an older woman called Irene, while selling clothes door-to-door. Del does his best to dissuade Rodney from continuing with the relationship, reminding him that she's got a dodgy husband, Tommy MacKay, who's about to be released from jail. Although Rodney takes no notice it's Del who ends up suffering the wrath of Tommy, played by David Daker (who later found fame as Michael Elphick's pal in the ITV drama *Boon*). He catches up with Del on a dark night and mistakenly thinks he's Rodney. But, instead of saving himself from a beating, Del keeps quiet and takes a vicious assault on his brother's behalf. 'That episode showed the strength of John's writing,' says David Jason, 'because he wasn't frightened of having a serious scene like that.'

In 'The Yellow Peril' Del sends Rodney off to decorate a Chinese restaurant with yellow paint and the pair later decide to spruce up their mum's ornate gravestone. Only afterwards do they realise that the paint they've used is actually luminous. 'It looked really gaudy,' says Nick Lyndhurst. 'We filmed the scene in a park and the tombstone was made of fibreglass and, to make it glow, the electricians had put lights inside it. It was so bright that traffic nearby kept slowing down to see what it was. We were lucky that we didn't cause an accident.'

Location filming for a whole series is always done in one or two blocks, before any interior studio recordings take place. This makes planning easier for the production team and cuts out the need to keep transporting cast and crew back to locations. Right from the start of filming, David Jason and Nicholas Lyndhurst got on well so it came as a bit of a shock to the production team, during their first week on location for a new series, to hear the pair having a blazing row in their caravan or winnebago, which was used as a mobile green room (the place where actors wait before they are called on to a set).

As they lined up to get their lunch, the crew could hear cutlery and plates flying about, along with insults. They listened in horror – it seemed that their stars were falling out in a big way. Suddenly the caravan door burst open and Nicholas stormed out, shouting: 'Don't you speak to me like that' at David, who responded by telling him rather bluntly to 'piss off and don't come back!' before shouting after him, 'Go on – bleat to the bloody production crew.'

I'm not bloody working with him again.

It was every director's nightmare and it happened to be the first day as director for Mandie Fletcher, who had previously worked on the show as first assistant director and would later have great success as director of the hit series *Blackadder*. She and the crew stood around mortified. Someone approached Nick Lyndhurst to try to find out just what had gone wrong and why the pair had had such an enormous bust-up. All they could get out of him was 'I'm not bloody working with him again.' The production team, including Tony Dow who had joined the crew as a trainee assistant floor manager and would later become the

---

HOW DID DEL END UP WITH A COMPANY CALLED TIT?

Something that has always fascinated David Jason is John Sullivan's ability to hide gags, as it were, for them to be exploited later. Says David, 'For example, did he do the TIT gag first or did he invent Trotters Independent Traders and then afterwards realise that the initials spelt TIT?

'It was an accident,' says John Sullivan. 'I had the name Trotters Independent Traders and I put it on the van and suddenly I looked at it and thought, "Shit, the abbreviation spells TIT!" and wondered if anyone else had noticed. I pointed it out to Ray Butt and he just said, "Great!" I'd love to say it was a deliberate idea from the start but it wasn't, it was a pure accident.' ·

---

show's director, were going spare. How could they produce a series when the two stars wouldn't speak to each other?

It was lunchtime and phone calls were made to Television Centre and then to writer John Sullivan who got on well with both men. Could he come down and have a chat with them and see if he could smooth things over? Eventually David came out of the caravan to get his lunch and still the two of them wouldn't speak to each other. Throughout the afternoon they would only converse through other people and the unit's morale was plummeting.

What the crew didn't know was that the whole thing was an elaborate hoax that David and Nick had come up with for a bit of fun. At the end of the very tense afternoon the pair collapsed into fits of laughter during the 4 o'clock tea break and there was relief all round – mixed with a little anger. John Sullivan recalls, 'I got a phone call asking me to come out to where they were filming which was quite a way out from my home. I was told that there was a big problem between David and Nick because they weren't talking to each other and saying they wouldn't work together again. So I was just about to get in my car and drive down there when I got another call from one of the production team thankfully explaining that it was just David and Nick mucking about. That call was quite a relief and saved me a bit of petrol too!'

David explains, 'We were a bit bored and Nick had said, "Why don't we have a pretend row – that will wind everyone up." We thought it would be a bit of a wheeze to have these two actors who suddenly appear to be unable to abide each other. So we started the shouting and stuff and we could see out of the window that everyone could hear and they were all looking a bit panicked. We could see out but they couldn't see in. After Nick had stormed out and I'd gone to get lunch I could see they all thought it was real. Their faces were white! I said, "I don't want to talk to him. I won't have him in the same caravan." In the end we both started laughing but it had gone on for a few hours by

Opposite: To the cast's disappointment Studland Bay, near Bournemouth, substituted for Spain in the episode 'It Never Rains…'.

Del and single mum Heather (Rosalind Lloyd) in the episode 'Diamonds Are For Heather'.

Despite the two Christmas episodes, the future for *Only Fools and Horses* was not looking good. The viewing figures for 'A Touch of Glass' had gone up to 10.2 million (the highest ever for the show at that time), but, overall, despite a series-on-series increase, they remained relatively poor, with an average of 8.85 million. These days that figure would be considered quite reasonable but, back in 1982, there were only three terrestrial TV channels, with Channel Four becoming the fourth on 2 November, during the run of series two.

There was no competition from the satellite and cable companies, as there is now, and domestic videos were still some years away. The *Only Fools and Horses* viewing figures were being compared unfavourably with those of the other big hits of the time, like *The Two Ronnies*, *Last of the Summer Wine* and *Dallas*, which all regularly attracted around 16 million viewers. Comedies like *Hi-De-Hi!* and, ironically, *Open All Hours*, still featuring David Jason alongside Ronnie Barker, were also being watched by about 14 million people every week.

For John Sullivan it was a time of great disappointment. He felt that the show still hadn't received the backing it needed from the BBC. 'I'd hoped they would have thrown their weight behind it more,' he says. 'But it hadn't happened and we'd still had no publicity. I wanted David and Nick to go on chat shows to let people know we were out there but we didn't get any noticeable support. The viewing figures did improve slightly but they didn't really take off. I was disappointed it hadn't really worked out and began thinking about what I could come up with next.

'I'd tried one pilot script after series three of *Citizen Smith* called *Dear Old Pals,* about the Pals' Regiments during the First World War, with the idea of Ronnie Barker and David Jason starring in it. It was about two old boys who'd been in the First World War together, after being born in the same street, and growing up afterwards and now living in a very modern world. But Jimmy Gilbert didn't seem to like it and that was quite a disappointment.'

Then, on 5 July 1983, a repeat run of the second series of *Only Fools* began and something changed. It wasn't screened in a noticeably better slot, going out at 7.45p.m. after a new lifestyle show called *Looking Good, Feeling Fit*. But even though the repeats were screened during the summer, when fewer people tend to watch television, they peaked at a respectable 7.7 million. That fact, combined with an episode-on-episode rise of the original run of the second series, suggested to BBC executives that they perhaps ought not to axe the programme after all. Perhaps, against the odds, the previously dead-in-the-water show was showing signs of life. Head of Comedy John Howard Davis decided to put his neck on the line and commission a third series.

'I picked up the paper and glanced at the TV ratings and there was *Fools and Horses* at number five and then it went up to two or three,' recalls John Sullivan. 'And I had no real idea why. It was as if the public had finally noticed the show. If that hadn't happened we would have been dead. There was no way a third series would have been commissioned.'

John got called into John Howard Davis's office and asked if he had seen the ratings and would he be willing to write a third series. Smiling to himself, he agreed. The BBC later improved the offer – and added a fourth series. 'As you can imagine I was delighted,' says John, 'and very relieved from my own financial point of view. Up until that point I'd been getting increasingly convinced that I'd have to come up with something new. I remember David, Ray and I chatting about it and thinking, "About bloody time – they've realised this thing they've got here is quite strong." We felt we'd proved a point, particularly because, prior to that, we thought we were down and dead.'

The success of the repeat of series two gave John Sullivan's confidence a great boost. 'If you are from a working-class background and you are fortunate enough to crack this business, until you've actually had that success, you are writing for your money,' he says. 'You write scared almost and you worry about every idea you get, and you tend to think that some of them are just too outrageous, and that can make you think of holding back and doing a nice script that doesn't offend, because your money relies on it.

'It meant I could take the shackles off a bit and open up. Not long after, I wrote *Just Good Friends* and I felt myself doing better and the fear I had had began to disappear, along with any inhibitions I had with my writing.'

The BBC began to take note of just what a valuable product they had in *Only Fools and Horses* and just what a talent they had in John Sullivan. His next project *Just Good Friends* was instantly commissioned for a full series and became a hugely popular show, starring Paul Nicholas and Jan Francis as Vince and Penny, long-time lovers who never really got it together properly.

THE *ONLY FOOLS AND HORSES* STAGE SHOW THAT NEVER WAS

The success of stage versions of comedies like *Dad's Army*, *Are You Being Served?* and later *Bread* and *'Allo 'Allo!* led the *Only Fools and Horses* team to consider doing a version of the show to be put on either in the West End or at one of the big regional theatres for a summer season in 1988. Producer and writer David Croft had done well with his shows on stage, which he co-wrote with Jimmy Perry and later Jeremy Lloyd and they were known to be a great way of making money.

'None of us were making much money in those days and it was a case of what could we do to make some more money?' recalls Ray Butt. 'I suggested to John that we cobble three or four scripts together but John didn't want to do that. He liked the idea but the theatre wasn't a medium he had any experience of and he was always busy and by that stage was writing both *Just Good Friends* and *Only Fools and Horses* and he was always behind with them. David, Nick and Buster were all keen but we just never got it together.'

'It would have been very successful financially,' says David. 'But I've never done anything for money. It's always been the work first, then I try to discuss money afterwards. I think it would have worked brilliantly but I was getting to the point where people were beginning to only think of me as Del Boy and that was beginning to worry me, as much as I was enjoying playing him.

'I needed some space to do other things and I felt that if we went and did a summer season or a West End season we'd be doing it every night and we'd be doing it more for money than anything. It was a bit of everything really. When it started to be quite heavily mooted, before it went any further I personally was pouring cold water on the idea but maybe everybody else was too. Or maybe if everyone had really gone for it then I would have been sucked along with it.'

The Third Series

Location filming on the third series began on Friday 2 September 1983 for scenes for the first episode 'Homesick'. This story sees Grandad having a health scare and the Trotters trying to get a new council bungalow to save the old fella from walking up twelve flights of stairs (because the lifts have broken). Rodney's new position as chairman of the local housing committee helps him persuade the council that Grandad is a deserving case, and, with the assistance of council official Miss Mackenzie, they are offered a new home.

Lennard Pearce has some priceless moments in the episode, with the best one coming as Grandad lies in bed looking very poorly after collapsing on the lounge floor. He calls Rodney over, and shows him an old cigarette case with a big dent which he says he wants to leave to Rodney, explaining that his grandad had

Below: Del and Rodney concerned about Grandad's health in 'Homesick'.
Opposite: Del and the axeman (Christopher Malcolm) in the classic 'Friday the 14th'.

it with him during his army service in the Boer War: 'One night my grandad was on sentry duty, standing there alone in the middle of Africa, when suddenly a sniper fired at him. The bullet was aiming straight for my grandad's heart but he had that cigarette case in his breast pocket and the bullet hit that instead.'

'Jeez. It saved his life,' exclaims Rodney incredulously.

'Well not really,' says Grandad. 'See, the bullet ricocheted up his nose and blew his brains out!'

For Lennard, filming this episode reminded him of his own real-life health scare a few years before, as he told the *News of the World* in December 1983. 'I had a supposed deathbed scene in that episode,' he said. 'It brought back memories of my time in hospital when I wasn't playing it for laughs.'

In the next episode, 'Healthy Competition', Rodney leaves Trotters Independent Traders to set up with Mickey Pearce, but Mickey jets off to Spain for a holiday using their company capital. Rodney's too embarrassed to admit to Del that he's been ripped off and tells him that Mickey has gone there to look into setting up a self-catering holiday division.

Del can't quite see how they can do this on just £200 and Rodney says, 'We're starting in a small way', to which Grandad pipes up with the line: 'What have you got? A Wendy house?' The line brought the house down and the laughter from the studio audience was so loud and long it almost brought filming to a halt.

'It got a huge laugh and both Nick and I could barely get the next lines out,' David recalls. 'It just floored us. It stopped Nick and I in our tracks.

'When we got to the end of the episode people were still talking about it. Just for fun I said to the studio audience, "I'm going to resign. That's it. I don't want to be in this show any more. Do you realise that Nick Lyndhurst and myself have spent twenty minutes in this show working our socks off? Lennard Pearce hasn't said a bloody word in the whole show and he just says "Wendy house" and it gets the biggest laugh I've ever heard.

'Old Lennard was chuckling away. He really enjoyed it.' From then on any line in the script that the cast thought would get a big laugh would be given a Wendy rating.

As David Jason explains: 'If it got the biggest laugh of the show then it would be termed a Wendy. A sub-Wendy would be just below that; a mini-Wendy would be an average laugh. When someone got a line we thought would bring the house down, then we'd say, "Look out, Wendy alert!"'

Shades of Hammer Horror films came to *Only Fools* in the guise of the classic episode 'Friday the 14th' in which Del borrows Boycie's West Country holiday cottage as a base from which to do a spot of poaching. The gags come thick and fast when the Trotters are stopped by a policeman who they think is after them on suspicion of poaching. Of course, they deny all knowledge, despite the fact that the roof is packed with fishing rods.

One scene sadly didn't make it to the screen due to the episode over-running. It saw the Trotters enjoying lunch at a country pub and meeting an old country yokel, played by actor Michael Bilton. Nevertheless it has been tracked down and is included on page 99, along with a scene from 'The Jolly Boys' Outing' (page 128), which would also have featured Michael Bilton, and one from the show's very last episode, 'Time on Our Hands' (page 142).

Even when he's left alone with the mad axeman Del seizes the opportunity to capitalise on his situation when his captor challenges him to a game of snooker, to be played on an imaginary table. The madman, we discover, hates winning – and wants Del to beat him, so ever-sharp Del Boy decides to play the game for cash.

'That was just brilliant,' laughs David Jason. 'The whole script had some great lines in it but that ending was just fantastic.'

Clearly people at home thought the same. That episode attracted 9.7 million but, even more significantly, the following week's episode was watched by 10.6 million – a week-on-week gain of close to a million. *Only Fools and Horses* was becoming a show that people would watch and then talk about down the pub with their friends and that sort of word-of-mouth praise can add tens of thousands to the ratings. The winter of 1983 saw it beginning to become a 'don't miss' programme and, from that week on, it has never once attracted less than 10 million viewers.

Del's hopes for a fishing weekend are dashed in 'Friday the 14th'. This episode was watched by nearly 10 million people and since then it has never had a smaller audience.

'Yesterday Never Comes' sees Del apparently scoring with posh antique dealer Miranda Davenport, played by Juliet Hammond. What he doesn't know, though, is that she's really only interested in a painting he's got hanging on the wall at the flat. The episode features one of Del's most cringe-making chat-up lines, when he slaps her on the bottom and says, 'Fancy a curry?'

'Of course we didn't know that she only said yes because she was after his picture,' says David Jason. 'And Rodney nearly faints with shock when Del tries this approach with her and it works – or, rather, it seems to at the time.'

Nick Lyndhurst can't forget the time a party of Finnish directors came to see how the BBC made comedy shows. 'They came to a studio recording and didn't understand the gags at all,' he recalls. 'They had an interpreter but, because of that, their laughter came through fifteen seconds after the British audience. There was a whole row of them and it was quite disruptive to our timing and in the end we asked them to move further back so we couldn't hear them.'

'May The Force Be With You' saw the first appearance of Jim Broadbent as Detective Inspector Roy Slater, who turns up at the Nag's Head like a bad penny looking for trouble and Del Boy in particular. Ray Butt had been keen to use Jim ever since he'd had to turn down the part of Del. 'I was very pleased to play Slater,' says Jim, who has gone on to become a hugely accomplished star with roles in films like *Bullets Over Broadway*, *The Borrowers* and *Life is Sweet*, and on television in *Blackadder*, *Wide-Eyed and Legless*, and most recently in BBC1's *The Peter Principle*. 'It was a nice role for me.'

Despite his other successes, there's some irony in the fact that the public remember him most from *Only Fools and Horses*. 'Whenever I'm spotted they say, "All right, how's Del Boy?"' he laughs. But he has no regrets about turning the job down. 'I never really took it as an offer at the time because

In 'Who's a Pretty Boy?' the Trotters attempt to decorate Denzil's place, to the consternation of his wife Corinne (Eva Mottley).

I was busy working,' he says. 'And if I'd done it I'd only have done two or three series because I like to constantly move on and do different things.'

'Wanted' is one of those episodes in which John Sullivan demonstrates his extraordinary ability to weave comedy and pathos together. The plot sees Del winding Rodney up to believe that a woman he helped in the street has accused him of being a pervert. Del, as is par for the course, takes the joke too far, telling Rodney that he's been dubbed the Peckham Pouncer and that vigilantes are after him. Poor Rodney decides to go on the run. The denouement comes when Rodney is found by Del hiding at the top of Nelson Mandela House. In an emotional scene Del admits that it was all a huge tease and Rodney agrees to come home. But,

unusually, it is Rodney who comes off best – with the last joke being on Del. He's been drinking from the tower block's water tank all day, only to find that Rodney has peed in it. 'It was Rodney's turn to win,' says David Jason.

'Who's a Pretty Boy?' rounded off the third series and saw the first appearance of Paul Barber as Denzil and Kenneth MacDonald as new Nag's Head landlord Mike Fisher. In the episode Del cons Denzil into allowing the Trotters to decorate his lounge, after warning him off using Brendan, the local Irish painter and decorator, played by David Jackson (best known as Gan in the BBC science-fiction series *Blake's Seven*).

Denzil's plan is very much against the wishes of his wife

Corinne, played by Eva Mottley, who according to the story still hasn't forgiven Del for the disastrous catering he arranged for their wedding reception. As she says in the script, 'What was it we were supposed to have, Del? Lobster vol-au-vent, game pie, kidneys with saffron rice, beef and anchovy savouries… and what did we end up with? Pie and chips all round!'

Meanwhile, a Trotter from another generation shows it's not just Del who can pull a fast one… Grandad proves he's not as daft as he looks when he buys a canary for £45 and charges Del £50 for it. But it's Del who ends up smiling at the end by roping landlord Mike Fisher into a con on the brewery.

Del offers to decorate the pub for £2000 when Brendan has said he'll do it for £1000. Del then tells Mike why he should plump for the higher offer. 'Because of all the advantages it has to offer, like my specialised profit-sharing scheme,' he says. 'Let me explain how it works. The £2000 would be dispersed thus: there would be £500 for vous and £500 for ve.'

To which Mike replies, 'What, you mean I get 500 quid?'

'Oh yes,' says Del.

'And what happens to the thousand that's left over,' says Mike.

'We give that to the Irishman and let him do the job,' Del explains.

Sadly the episode was to be the only appearance in the show for Corinne, although John Sullivan had planned to bring both her and Denzil back in later episodes. But tragically actress Eva Mottley, who played her, died of a drugs overdose on St Valentine's Day 1985.

Barbados-born Eva, who was just thirty-one, had found fame as Bella in the hit ITV drama *Widows* but had later left the series suddenly after a row with producers.

'Her death was a great shock and suicide is so terrible,' says Ray Butt. 'She was a very vivacious lady and great fun to have around, and didn't seem to have a care in the world.

Peter Woodthorpe, cast as the boys' Dad, Reg Trotter, in 'Thicker Than Water' because of his likeness to David Jason.

I'm sure she would have been back in the show at some later date because she and Denzil were good characters and nice people and there was a lot of scope with them.'

'It was a terrible shame,' recalls David Jason. 'Eva was lovely and was going to be a good team player and Denzil and Corinne would have worked well in the future as a couple. She was obviously the one with the get-up-and-go in that relationship and he was the hen-pecked husband. She was very strong and would take no nonsense from Del Boy and had him completely sussed. Del knew this and he was all slimy and creepy-crawly with her, trying to get on her good side, to no avail.'

Christmas 1983 saw the transmission of the first Christmas Day special of the programme, 'Thicker Than Water', and the only appearance of the Trotter boys' father Reg, played by actor Peter Woodthorpe. Woodthorpe had been cast by Ray Butt because of his likeness to David Jason, something David himself was never quite convinced about. 'I couldn't see a likeness at all,' he says. 'But then others did think he looked like me. To me he just looked like himself!'

In this story Del is out when Reg turns up at the flat and is furious on his return, when he finds him in his (Del's) favourite seat, smoking one of his best cigars. Reg then proceeds to cause a family rift by revealing that he is suffering from a hereditary illness and then calling into question Del's paternity after he and Rodney receive the results of blood tests.

'I never brought Reg back, because he'd turned up and blotted his copybook so badly that I couldn't see Del ever accepting him again,' says John Sullivan.

'It was good having Reg Trotter come into the series because it showed what a total shit he was,' says David Jason. 'The character had left them and their mother and he was a real rotten bastard and it was good to remind people of that.'

☆ MISSING SCENE ☆

This scene comes from the 1983 episode 'Friday the 14th' and was filmed but cut because of lack of time. It immediately preceded the scene where the Trotters were stopped by the police. Michael Bilton played the old yokel.

SCENE 2A. FILM. EXT. DAY. A COUNTRY PUB/VILLAGE GREEN.
THIS IS ONE OF THOSE IDYLLIC SCENES STRAIGHT OFF A POSTCARD.
OUTSIDE THE OLD PUB WE HAVE A COUPLE OF TABLES AND CHAIRS, THE VAN IS PARKED CLOSE BY.
AT ONE OF THE TABLES WE HAVE AN OLD RUSTIC TYPE PUFFING ON A PIPE.
AT THE OTHER TABLE SIT DEL AND GRANDAD. DEL IS STILL WEARING HIS CAMEL-HAIR COAT, ETC.

DEL: (Lighting a cigar) This is what it's all about annit, Grandad eh? This is yer *real* England!

GRANDAD: It's lovely annit? And it's so clean an' all!

DEL: And I'll tell you what shall I? Because the people out here have *respect* for their environment! (He throws his empty cigar packet away) Men went away in the war and fought and died for this!

GRANDAD: I know – I almost did!

DEL: You almost died?

GRANDAD: No. I almost went away and fought for it!

DEL: Oh yeah!!… I love this life! This is what nature intended. Freshly baked bread, beer from the wood and honest food straight from God's good earth!
ROD EXITS FROM PUB CARRYING A TRAY OF DRINKS (PINTS).

ROD: (To Del) They've never heard of a Pina Colada and they don't do pizzas!

DEL: Don't do pizzas? Stone me – what sort of a dead and alive hole is this?

ROD: (Thinking this might offend the yokel) Sshh!!… (To the yokel) Morning.

YOKEL: (Staring into distance) Af'rnoon!

ROD: (Checks his watch, taps it) This deep sea diver's watch still ain't working right!

DEL: Leave off Rodney. (Indicates yokel) He's tryna tell the time by the sun!

ROD: But you can tell the time by the sun!

GRANDAD: But it's hardly bloody TIM is it!!

DEL: He's right an all! (To yokel) Lovely weather for a bit of sheep-shearing eh?

YOKEL: Oh arr, fine weather! Soon be turning though!

DEL: Will it?

YOKEL: You mark my words sir, before the night's out there'll be a storm the likes of which you've never seen before! There'll be thunder that'll wake the dead from their sleep. Rain and flooding and a wind a'howling so fierce you'd think it came from the mouth of Satan himself!!
DEL AND ROD LOOK AT EACH OTHER AND REACT.

GRANDAD: Still, it'll be good for the flowers won't it!
DEL GIVES HIM A DAMNING LOOK.

ROD: How do you country people know these things? Is it because the cows are all laying down, or can you tell by the clouds?

YOKEL: (Turns to face Rod, we see he has an ear-piece which is connected to a radio) No, I just heard the forecast on Radio 4!
ROD REACTS.

DEL: Come on, drink up!

The Fourth Series

100

As if to reflect the series' hugely increased popularity, in April 1984 *Only Fools* won the Television and Radio Industries Club Top Situation Comedy Award. Location filming began for the fourth series in early December 1984, at a pub just off Ladbroke Grove in West London for the episode 'Hole in One'. In it Del and Rodney are so strapped for cash that Grandad decides to 'accidentally' fall down into a pub cellar and then claim compensation from the brewery.

The following Sunday, filming moved to the Magistrates Court at Kingston for scenes when Grandad and the boys go to court to win compensation for his injury and he's later exposed as having pulled the same trick quite a number of times before. Shooting ended around lunchtime and the cast and crew went their separate ways.

Ray Butt jocularly asked Lennard Pearce, 'When are you with me again, you lazy old sod?'

'He said, "Next Sunday,"' Ray recalls. 'I said, "I'm buggered if I'm paying you for a whole week when I'm not seeing you because we're all still working!" and he laughed and I told him to take care and that I'd see him the next Sunday.'

It was to be the last time they saw each other. Lennard suffered a heart attack on the Wednesday and was rushed to the Whittington Hospital at Highgate, North London. Lennard's landlady phoned John Sullivan to tell him the bad news. 'Jan Francis (who knew him well) and I went up to see him,' John recalls. 'He had lots of wires going into him and he showed us what he said was a life support machine. It was just a small box and I thought he'd got it wrong because I thought they were these big things.'

John took with him a lucky charm pig just like Trotter, the pink china one that took pride of place in the control box during studio recordings of the series. It had been bought by Ray Butt's secretary Penny Thompson and, after she'd showed it to Lennard Pearce before a studio recording and he'd gone on to have a really good show, he'd always go and touch the pig for good luck before a recording.

'I couldn't find the original Trotter,' John recalls. 'So I bought another one that I called Son of Trotter and took that along for him.'

At around 8a.m. on Sunday 16 December, the day Lennard was due back on location for his next block of filming, Ray Butt received a phone call at home from Lennard's agent Carole James, telling him that he had died.

'We were due to start at 9a.m. and I had to go up there and tell them that Lennard had died,' he recalls, clearly still moved by the memory. 'Everyone was absolutely gutted and there were lots of tears.

'To most people – cast and crew – Lennard was Grandad. They all called him Grandad and hardly anyone called him Lennard and he loved that. So we cancelled filming. No one was in a mood to work that day. It was a very sad time.'

David Jason and Nick Lyndhurst were in make-up when Ray came and told them the dreadful news. 'That was it,' he says. 'We all just went home. We couldn't even think about working that day, it was just too upsetting.'

...I stood facing a shop window and cried my eyes out.

'Ray came into make-up and stood in the doorway and just shook his head gently and then walked out again,' remembers Nick Lyndhurst. 'He didn't say anything and he didn't need to. We knew. Lennard had been on our minds all the time since he'd suffered his first heart attack. No one had been thinking about much else all week. David and I followed Ray out and it started snowing really heavily just for a few minutes, and I stood facing a shop window and cried my eyes out. After a while we went back to our trailer and I remember David very gently swearing under his breath every so often. We were both very upset.'

John Sullivan recalls, 'Apparently a few days after Jan and I visited him they took him off the machine and he had another massive heart attack. Without the support of the machine he couldn't live. My wife Sharon took the call from Ray saying that Lennard had died, and she was in tears. We were devastated because he was such a lovely old man and such a kind man and was always sending things for the kids.

'He was like a third grandad to our kids. It got very confusing for them at school and I think they thought someone had married twice because both the boys had Grandad John, Grandad Charlie and Grandad Trotter. The boys thought they had three grandads too, because they'd get presents from all three, and Lennard would just sign the card "Lots of love from Grandad" and they'd say "Which one?" and we'd say, "That's from Grandad Trotter".'

The following day, Ray Butt went to his office at BBC Television Centre and had meetings with John Sullivan,

*Opposite: The end of an era.
Lennard Pearce died during the filming of
the first episode of series four.*

manager turned actor being right for the show was correct.

'There was coffee, cakes and sandwiches and we chatted and David asked me what I'd been doing, work-wise, and asked me about the pantomime I was appearing in,' Buster remembers.

'We didn't talk about *Only Fools and Horses*. We were chatting about general things and nothing in particular and it was all sort of geared towards seeing if we spoke the same language. Again I read a bit of script, just a page I seem to recall, but this time with David and Nick playing their proper roles, and after that it was time for me to once again head back to Windsor and the panto.'

...Once people get to know you, you might find it alters your life...

Again, Ray Butt walked Buster to the lift and told him that he'd call him later that day. 'He was very nice and considerate,' says Buster. 'He gave me some encouragement and said, "You did very well Buster. Before you go back, there's something I'd like to tell you. If you get this part – and I repeat *if* – you will become famous and I say that because you must tell your wife. Once people get to know you, you might find it alters your life and her life as well. It could disrupt your normal way of life and you ought to be aware of that before deciding what to do." He said he'd ring me later.'

With Buster back in the car and on the way to Windsor, Ray and the others began discussing the pros and cons of casting a completely unknown and relatively inexperienced actor in a top-rated sitcom.

'David and Nick weren't 100 per cent happy and I think that was mainly because they were still thinking about Lennard,' says Ray Butt. 'It was the same for all of us really. I had all the same emotions as them but the job had to be done and the show had to go on. It was as simple as that. We had to make it work. Buster had read OK and he looked the part. Nevertheless it was a terrible gamble. But I thought we could mould him and get away with it, and it really was desperation time.'

As he waited for the call at the Theatre Royal, Windsor, Buster tried not to build up his hopes too much. 'I'm not a stupid fellow and I knew they might just turn round and say, "Sorry, you're not quite the chap for us." I'd had auditions before, and then afterwards they'd say that I wasn't tall enough, or fat enough or whatever, so

I was quite used to the way the business worked.

'Nevertheless, when one of the girls at the theatre came up to me during the matinée and said, "Can you phone the BBC back?" I was shaking. I thought, "This is going to be the answer, one way or the other." So I phoned Ray back and he thanked me for coming up again and I was thinking, "Please get to the point!" Then he said, "We'd like you to join us." I couldn't believe it!

'He said, "We're filming tomorrow." I thought, "Oh Lord." Ray then added, "And we will need you on set for filming at 7.30a.m. We'll send a car for you. Is 6a.m. all right?" I'd thought I wouldn't be needed for a few weeks and by then I'd have finished in the panto. But I was wrong, so for the next fortnight I'd start at 6a.m. filming *Only Fools and Horses*, and then go and do the panto and finish at 10p.m. at night.'

The following morning Buster found himself on location outside a pub, which was doubling as the Nag's Head, to start filming the story 'Hole in One', the episode the team had been shooting when Lennard Pearce died.

'When I arrived they were all ready to start filming,' Buster recalls. 'Ray came out and said, "You better go over to the costume van and get yourself some gear for Albert's costume."

'We knew he was an old sailor so we were sort of looking for stuff that would suit him. There was a costume designer there who suggested this old peaked cap, and we spotted a duffel coat so I put that on and tracked down an old pair of cords. Everything was done in a great hurry and not much research went into it. We were just trying to pick something suitable for that day.

'We topped it off with a scarf, mainly because it was so cold. When I arrived on set I had no idea what I was going to be doing. Of course it turned out that I was filming what would be my second episode but I had no script as such – just a sheet of paper with my four or five lines on it. I wasn't that nervous because it wasn't like being in the theatre where, once you leave the wings, you are on your own. I'd done a small bit of telly beforehand and I knew if something went wrong then we could cut and do it again. My first scene was where Del speaks to Mike, the Nag's Head landlord, who is down in the pub's cellar. Albert has a word with Mike, and Del then drags him away when he mentions a dodgy deep-fat fryer that Del

Opposite, top: Filming the episode 'Hole in One'. Below: Refilming the scenes which featured Lennard Pearce, replacing Grandad with Uncle Albert – Buster Merryfield.

THE ONLY FOOLS AND HORSES STORY

106

has sold Mike. That was pretty much it, and then I had to dash off and get back to Windsor for the afternoon's matinée performance of the panto. It was quite hectic.'

Buster's first day had gone quite well. He'd enjoyed it but worried unnecessarily about lines he'd got wrong, even though no one else was unhappy with his performance. He still had no idea that he was to become a regular member of the team; nor did John Sullivan who was really writing the series on the hoof. The more he could see Buster was capable of, the more lines he'd give him.

Two weeks later, on Sunday 27 January, Buster was wondering whether he'd taken on more than he could cope with, and starting to doubt his own ability. It was the studio recording of the episode 'It's Only Rock and Roll'.

Recorded in the vast TC6 studio at BBC Television Centre in front of a live audience including his family it was a daunting experience for Buster. Despite his vast experience of amateur theatre, he'd never faced anything like this before. 'I was dreading it,' he admits. 'I was frightened to death because I knew there would be an audience of two or three hundred people. I was very apprehensive because I'd never done a recording in front of an audience before.

'I was so keen not to get it wrong. I remember I made my entrance at a particular point and I forgot my lines. I felt terrible. I never usually forget my lines and, compared to some of my big theatre parts, I had relatively little to say. We did it again a couple of times and I got it right but I still went back to my dressing room and sat there thinking, "You fool. You've blown it!" I thought that forgetting your lines was the most serious thing in the world.

'I was really panicked. I felt terrible and I didn't think they'd want me. I was so inexperienced myself and I held people in television in such esteem that I thought that they never dried up. I was very intimidated by it all, and all the cameras moving about, but I had to go back on again and do my next scene and I must have been ashen.

'I was terribly nervous and I was probably shaking a bit and I think they noticed how worried I was. I said a line and got it right and David Jason as Del answered me and he got his words wrong. He forgot his line and he was saying, "What's the line? What's the line?" All the audience started laughing and he said, "What are you lot laughin' at? You didn't pay to come in, you're getting it for nuffink aren't ya? What do you expect?"'

For Buster it was a moment that helped enormously.

Now he could see that even seasoned performers like David Jason could fluff their lines and that perhaps it wasn't such a great sin after all.

It wasn't until after the recording had finished that Buster realised that perhaps David's 'gaffe' hadn't been quite so spontaneous. 'I reckon he saw how nervous I was, and did it deliberately to put me at ease. I never knew for sure but I think that's what happened – and that's the kind of man he is. Of course now I realise that getting lines wrong is a regular thing that can happen to anyone but at the time I had no idea. It was a necessary thing to experience and now I don't worry about it.'

Days after shooting his first scenes for 'Hole in One', Buster was filming exterior shots for his second episode, 'Strained Relations', although it was screened first as episode two of the series. It was the episode that dealt with Grandad's funeral and was the hardest script John Sullivan has ever had to write. Having just lost a much-loved friend and colleague, he had spent the Christmas break reworking the next series. To his credit, John decided to tackle Lennard Pearce's death directly and kill off the character of Grandad. Not only that but he chose to include the funeral in an episode, rather than just refer to it.

'It was a terrifying idea,' says Ray Butt. 'To open a comedy show with a funeral would normally, to use a terrible pun, be death. But John was brilliant. He engineered it so well.'

With consummate skill Sullivan wrote a script that, to this day, remains one of his best. Not surprisingly, the funeral scene wasn't littered with jokes. It was dark and gloomy, much the way the cast and crew felt at the time. But Sullivan knew he couldn't make the whole script downbeat, so he broke the mood with a gag which was a master stroke.

Rodney drops Grandad's trilby hat into the grave before it's filled in by the grave diggers. As far as Del and Rodney and the viewers are concerned, that's that – until the vicar sets off for home and asks if anyone has seen his hat. This was a typical Sullivan twist which lightened the moment completely and lifted the gloom.

'You had all the pathos and all the sadness, which is an important element of comedy, and then he pricked it by the fact that Del and Rodney had thrown the wrong hat into the grave,' says Ray Butt. 'It was a brilliant idea by John Sullivan and he engineered it so well and put it in exactly the right position, and it lifted the whole episode.'

David Jason agrees. 'It's a tribute to the brilliance of Sullivan's writing that he could handle something as delicate as a death in the family with such skill that one minute you are laughing and the next minute you are crying.'

Nevertheless there were problems during rehearsals of 'Strained Relations'. The episode could not be squeezed into thirty minutes and kept running at thirty-five, even after pages of script had been dumped.

'Whatever we did, it would not run to time,' John recalls. 'And we were already down to just the bones of the thing. Everyone was very fed up – and still upset over Lennard's death. I asked Gareth Gwenlan for an extra five minutes and he said it was impossible because they couldn't shave five minutes off the preceding programme, *Top of the Pops*, or the following one, *The Nine O'Clock News*.'

In the end John stormed out of the rehearsal room. He needed to cool off. The pressure had finally got to him. When he saw John leaving, Ray Butt jumped out of a kitchen window – the quickest route – and chased after him before he could drive off. The men talked but there was no row. After all, they were on the same side and were both under great strain. Back home John called his agent to talk about the problem. Calls were then made to the BBC.

Minutes later, BBC1 boss Michael Grade was on the phone telling Sullivan, 'You've got your extra five minutes. I'm telling *Top of the Pops* they'll have to lose a bloody record.'

Back at rehearsals the following day, the relief was huge, and amazingly the next run-through ran to just thirty minutes.

'It just picked up,' John says. 'Perhaps it was because the pressure was off but in the end I had to ring Michael Grade back and tell him that we didn't need the extra five minutes and we even put some cut material back in!'

For the production team and the cast, though, these were the hardest days of filming they'd ever experienced. Just a fortnight before, they'd buried Lennard Pearce for real. Now they were at a cemetery in Acton, filming his character's burial.

'I can't think of anything worse than that day,' confesses Ray Butt. 'It really was hard.'

'It was a bitterly cold day and all our thoughts were with Lennard,' says Ken MacDonald.

'It was a very difficult time…' David Jason recalls. 'Yet we still had a few laughs because that was the best way to get through. Someone, and I can't remember who it was, which

is probably just as well, said, "Lennard must feel lucky," and I said, "Why?" and they said, "Well he's the only man I know who has been buried twice!"'

Indeed, Lennard Pearce's real funeral wasn't without laughter, and that's something that, by all accounts, he would have wanted. John Sullivan was sitting directly behind David Jason and, seconds after the vicar announced hymn number 187, John saw David's pew begin to shake. David was having a fit of the giggles. David turned round to show John that the page was missing from his hymnbook and the two men smiled. 'John realised why I was laughing,' David recalls. 'We were both thinking the same thing: "Had Del Boy supplied the hymnbooks?"'

'All our emotions were so stirred up and suddenly something like that happens and you do see the funny side of it. It wasn't an insult to where we were, or to Lennard's memory. And I think Lennard would have seen the joke in it too.'

'Strained Relations' also featured an exchange between Del and Rodney that must be one of the best sitcom scenes ever written. It comes when grief-stricken Rodney asks him how he can have got over Grandad's death so quickly. Of course, he hasn't.

'Get over it? What a plonker you really are, Rodney. Get over it? I haven't even started yet. I ain't even started, Bruv. And do you know why? Because I don't know how to. That's why. I've survived all my life with a smile and a prayer. I'm Del Boy, ain't I. Good old Del Boy – he's got more bounce than Zebedee. "Ere pal, what you drinkin"? "Go on Darlin', you 'ave one for luck." That's me, that's Del Boy, isn't it? Nothing ever upsets Del Boy. I've always played the tough guy. I didn't want to but I had to, and I've played it for so long now that I don't know how to be anything else. I don't even know how to…oh it don't matter. Bloody families, I'm finished with them. What do they do to you, eh? They drag you down and then they break your bloody heart.'

'John Sullivan has written so many great scenes in *Only Fools and Horses*,' says David Jason. 'But that is certainly one of the best, as far as I'm concerned. He's just brilliant at expressing real emotion in his characters. We put all our energy into that episode in Lennard's memory. We were all a bit sensitive at the time for an episode or two. And it was hard for Buster too, as the new boy, as he didn't know any of us, but we got over it and formed a new and happy relationship with Buster. Joining the show like he did must

have been very hard for him and we tried to give him as much support as we possibly could and tried to make him feel relaxed.

'We didn't want him to feel like an outsider and he responded to that. It was potentially very dangerous to bring someone new in like that but, bless him, he rose to the occasion. He made the character his own quite brilliantly and Uncle Albert was very different to Grandad and that gave John a chance to exploit Buster's way of carrying on which gave John fresh ideas.'

After 'Hole in One' came 'It's Only Rock and Roll'. This episode sees Del deciding to go into music management and taking on Rodney and his mates' band, which he dubs 'A Bunch of Wallies'. Not surprisingly everything goes wrong, with Del getting bookings in the most inappropriate places. Sadly for Rodney, it's only once he quits the group (after rowing with them over Del) that they have a big hit with 'Boys Will Be Boys' and get to appear on *Top of the Pops*.

Actor and writer Daniel Peacock, who played psychotic singer Mental Mickey, had a great time filming it. 'I was twenty-six at the time and being on *Only Fools and Horses* and *Top of the Pops* was a double coup,' he says. 'I thought they'd just build a set for the *Top of the Pops* appearance but I was wrong. We rehearsed the song we had to sing, "Boys Will Be Boys", for a couple of hours and then we were whisked over to the actual *Top of the Pops* studio to record it while they were filming the real show. It was great. We were up there in front of all these screaming girls and Radio One DJ Mike Read introduced us.'

'Sleeping Dogs Lie' includes the first appearance of Sue Holderness as Boycie's wife Marlene in the episode in which the pair go on holiday, leaving their new dog Duke in the less-than-safe hands of the Trotter family. The dog falls ill and it is later discovered that Albert has mistakenly taken Duke's vitamin pills instead of his own sleeping pills, and vice versa. The climax of the episode sees Del and Rodney mischievously calling 'Here boy…' to Albert.

The day after it was transmitted Buster was walking along the road at Clapham Junction, South London, and was spotted by some fans. 'I heard someone call out "Albert, Albert" and I looked over the road between the buses and saw three shabbily dressed chaps in their twenties smiling away. Suddenly they got in a line and shouted, "Here boy, here boy!" They copied just what had been on the programme. It was lovely and it made me laugh.'

Nick Lyndhurst had a lucky escape during filming. For one scene he had to carry the dog and then fall over with it on top of him, and Duke got a little bit frisky. 'They cut just in time, otherwise in another few seconds it would have become a very different show!' he says. 'It was only crafty footwork that got the dog off me in the end!'

'Watching the Girls Go By' focuses on Rodney's continuing lack of pulling-power. When Mickey Pearce teases him about not being able to bring a girl to a party at the Nag's Head, Rodney ends up betting him that he'll have a girl on his arm that night. Egged on by Del, the bet gets as high as a 'round fifty'. Rodney is in a fix and Del decides to buy the bet off him. He's now got an interest in Rodney's success and gives his old friend Yvonne, a stripper and would-be

'It's Only Rock and Roll'. Daniel Peacock, David Thewlis and Marcus Francis with Nicholas Lyndhurst and David Jason.

singer, £20 to go on the date with Rodney. Everything goes wrong when Yvonne gets drunk and takes her clothes off and Rodney is humiliated. But it's Del who ends up most upset, when it turns out that Rodney's bet with Mickey was for 50 pence, not 50 quid!

The final episode of the series, 'As One Door Closes', was inspired by an article John Sullivan read in *The Sunday Times* about changes in Britain's climate. 'It said some famous butterfly that had never been seen here before had been spotted and a big cash reward was being offered by a collector to whoever caught one alive,' he recalls. 'If Del had read the article it was just the sort of thing he'd have gone for.' In the last scene Del catches the butterfly, only to have his hands slapped by Denzil – with obvious results.

In rehearsals Paul Barber suggested he did the scene on roller skates – an idea he soon regretted. 'I couldn't skate at the time and then had to spend two weeks going round my local park trying to learn how to,' he recalls. 'But I did get to keep the skates after we finished the episode!'

David Thewlis, one of the lads in the band in 'It's Only Rock and Roll' has gone on to become a big star in films like *Big Lebowski*, *Seven Years in Tibet* and *Dragonheart*.

Christmas 1985 saw the first ever feature-length special, 'To Hull and Back'. The previous Christmas, the BBC had had a big ratings success with a ninety-minute episode of John Sullivan's comedy *Just Good Friends*. The fourth series of *Only Fools and Horses* had also been a big success, despite the upheaval over the loss of Lennard Pearce and the introduction of Buster Merryfield as Albert.

So, in April 1985, BBC1 bosses decided to follow the previous Christmas hit and commission a festive feature-length episode. As John Sullivan started working on the script, producer Ray Butt set about budgeting for it. It was then that they hit a major snag which nearly sank the production.

'I prepared the budget, which was a normal procedure, and put it in to my manager,' recalls Ray Butt. 'He said, "We can't afford that," and I said, "Well if you can't afford that, then you ain't gonna get it, mate. It's as simple as that, because that's what it's going to cost."'

John Sullivan's script had the Trotters hiring a fishing boat and travelling to Amsterdam on a very dubious diamond-smuggling expedition arranged by Boycie and his shady business contact Abdul (played by actor Tony Anholt), while being chased by Detective Inspector Roy Slater (again played by Jim Broadbent).

By the time the episode was screened on Christmas Day Tony Anholt would have become a big star and very familiar to television viewers as ruthless tycoon Charles Frere in the BBC sex and sailing drama *Howards' Way*.

'The foreign filming made it expensive and it was to be a six-week shoot, all on film, and shot in late summer,' says Ray. 'I told my manager, "If I spent that much last year then, with adding a bit on for inflation, it's going to come to at least that much, and for less than that I can't do it."'

'He said, "We just haven't got that sort of money."'

Some five weeks later Ray Butt, who was directing and producing a series of *Just Good Friends* at the same time, went to the Montreux Television Festival in Switzerland. At a dinner Ray found himself sitting next to Michael Grade, a high-flying television executive, who had recently joined the Corporation as Controller of BBC1. The two men hadn't met before, although Butt knew Grade was a fan of *Just Good Friends*, and they introduced themselves to each other. 'He asked me how it was going and what was the news on *Fools*,' Ray recalls.

'I said, "Well frankly, mate, we've got this great idea but the firm tell me

it's too dear." He said, "Well tell me about it." So I did, and told him how much we needed, and he said, "You've got it. If you've got a problem then ring me."' Grade's high-level intervention saved the show – or at the very least gave Ray Butt the money he needed. Grade added almost £250,000, taking the budget to around £850,000.

By August 1985 the BBC had discovered that ITV's big Christmas Day hope was a feature-length episode of its hit drama *Minder*, called *Minder on the Orient Express*. Michael Grade moved quickly and revealed that he would be putting on the *Only Fools and Horses* special in direct competition, and the press began billing it as a Minder versus Del Boy clash. In the *Daily Mirror* Tony Purnell pointed out that it would be viewers who would suffer and quoted an unnamed BBC source as saying that 'It's another case of the viewer losing out yet again'.

'Millions of fans will be forced on Christmas Night to choose between lovable London rogues George Cole and Dennis Waterman and equally lovable London rogues David Jason and Nicholas Lyndhurst,' Purnell wrote.

The *Daily Express* said it presented an 'agonising choice' for viewers and called on both the BBC and ITV to repeat the shows early in the New Year to give viewers a chance to see the one they had missed. The paper decided that Michael Grade's move was connected to the BBC's loss of its popular American drama *Dallas* to the ITV company Thames, which made *Minder*, and it said he was still smarting at its loss.

It quoted him as saying, 'We are in direct competition with ITV. That's the way it is and always will be.'

We will be funnier and better… no doubt about that, my son.

In early December, even David Jason joined in the friendly rivalry when asked who would pull in more viewers. 'It's got to be us, innit?' he was quoted as telling the *Daily Mirror*. 'We will be funnier and better… no doubt about that, my son. I will put my feet up with the rest of the country.

'Poor Arfur will have to make do with *Minder*, along with his three regular fans.'

George Cole, who played wheeler-dealer Arthur Daley in *Minder*, hit back, 'There is already talk of an ITV blackout. Obviously Del Boy is behind it because he's so worried.' Joking apart, the two actors clearly felt sad that the

Opposite: The old sea dog awaits his orders to sail. Buster Merryfield as Uncle Albert goes back to sea in 'To Hull and Back'.

viewers would have to choose which to watch, with David Jason saying that TV bosses who engineered the clash are 'buggers, aren't they. It's bound to cause rows in families up and down the country… There is nothing we can do about it, I guess.'

George Cole said, 'It's a shame. We must have a similar following and not everyone has got a video to record one of them for later viewing. Millions of fans will be disappointed.'

Nevertheless the viewers made their choice and the BBC gave ITV a thorough pasting in the ratings, with 16.9 million tuning in to watch *Only Fools and Horses* compared to a few million less for *Minder*. It was a great confidence boost for John Sullivan, a second-in-a-row Christmas hit for Ray Butt, a tribute to the acting of the cast, and a successful gamble for Michael Grade.

Only Fools and Horses…as much a part of the British Christmas Day as the Queen's Speech.

'It proved to be money well spent,' says Ray Butt. Its success set a trend for the next eleven years, when, with the exception of 1994 and 1995, *Only Fools and Horses* would dominate seasonal TV and become almost as much a part of the British Christmas Day as the Queen's Speech. For David Jason, Nick Lyndhurst and Buster Merryfield, along with Ray Butt and his production team, it made some tough days filming on the North Sea seem worthwhile.

'We shot a lot of it at sea on this terrible old 90-foot boat and travelled up and down the Yorkshire coast,' Ray Butt recalls. 'At the start we were ferried out to the boat that was moored off Spurn Head. I was one of the last to arrive as usual and as I got alongside, Buster and Nick were waving and they said, "Christ, Ray, have you got a problem. David is in the aft cabin and he's feeling terrible."

'There was a bit if a swell and it had always been a worry to me how everyone would react to filming at sea. We had about a five- or six-day shoot to do on this boat at sea and David feeling really lousy was all I needed. I climbed aboard and said, "Right, I'll go and see how he is," and I walked down to this stinking old cabin and there was David laid up on one of the bunks. He looked terrible.

'I said, "All right, mate?" and he just groaned. I said, "Is there anything I can

get you?" and he groaned again. Then he burst out laughing – he couldn't keep it up. It was a wind-up and I'd fallen for it hook, line and sinker. I shouted a few rude words at him and said, "Get out of that bloody bunk – or I'll throw you over the side of the boat!" It was very funny – and I found out that one of the make-up girls had got at him to make him look so poorly!'

Ironically it wasn't the cast who were affected by sea-sickness. Instead Ray found his crew strength massively depleted as, one by one, they fell ill. 'The weather wasn't that bad but we had quite high seas,' he recalls. 'The boat did roll a bit and there was one time when the whole of the costume department were sick and one make-up girl was having to do the lot – costumes and make-up.

'All the sparks [electricians] were gone, Tony Dow was holding the lamps, and the poor cameraman was having a horrible time trying to film the actors with the whole background going up and down. He had to keep stopping and was as sick as a dog. I think in the end, of the eighteen or so crew we had aboard, only about four of us were still operational, plus, fortunately, the actors.' Ray, a keen sailor, adds, 'I loved it though. It was great fun.'

Buster Merryfield also loved being at sea, despite being quite seasick. Albert, being an old sea dog, was – rather worryingly – in charge of the boat. Buster had no such trouble. 'I was on the helm and I found it quite easy,' he remembers. 'And the real skipper was there, just out of sight of the camera, in case I got anything wrong.'

One of the most memorable moments in the episode is when Del calls to a man working on a gas rig and asks directions to Holland. The scene lasts only a few seconds on screen but took nearly a day to film. 'We actually shot it on a British Gas rig in the North Sea,' recalls Ray Butt. 'It was a six-hour sail to get there, then we shot it quite quickly. Tony Dow was on the boat with a camera looking up at the rig and I'd gone out to the rig by helicopter with another camera looking back at the boat.

'It was all controlled by walkie-talkies and we did it all in about six takes, then they had a six-hour trip back to Hull. But, although they had the longer journey, they had the last laugh on me because, before they'd left port, they'd filled the boat up with booze and on the way back they had a bit of a party and got absolutely plastered, whereas on the gas rig there was no booze at all

Opposite top: Del is happy on the seven seas but Rodney doesn't feel too good. Opposite: The old fishing boat Inge *which played a major role in 'To Hull and Back'.*

and I was sat there waiting for a helicopter! But it was a good gag and worth doing and it's something everyone seems to remember.'

Christmas week 1985 also saw the screening of a special spoof film on BBC1's *Breakfast Time* in which Consumer Editor Lynn Faulds Wood did a Roger Cook-style door-stepping report on Del Boy. In the short Cinderella-type sketch Lynn confronted Del over his sale of a pumpkin, which was supposed to have turned into a coach, and four white mice, which were supposed to have become horses.

'It was a lot of fun and I remember thinking David was very attractive!' says Lynn, who went on to present the BBC's *Watchdog* programme. 'Del was supposed to be outraged that I could have possibly thought that he was selling dodgy merchandise.'

The Fifth Series

Four months later, in April 1986, the team were back together for a new series, with 'From Prussia With Love' being the first episode and featuring actress Erika Hoffman as German au pair Anna who has been sacked from her job and thrown out by her employers after falling pregnant. Del senses there is cash to be made and takes Anna in, so that he can then sell her baby to childless Boycie and Marlene.

The episode brings the Boycie and Marlene infertility storyline, hinted at in 'Sleeping Dogs Lie', to the fore, and actually ends rather poignantly, once again demonstrating Sullivan's ability to mix comedy with serious subjects. For Sue Holderness, who made her second appearance as Marlene in the episode, it remains a favourite.

'It was very touching,' she says. 'It was as if everything Marlene had longed for in her life was going to come true and it was going to be perfect. And it was very sad when it all went wrong. As an actress it was very rewarding to work on the episode because Marlene went through a great deal of emotion – having a baby had been the overriding thing in her life since she was sixteen. Then she'd got the chance of having one and then it was taken away again. It was beautifully written – as good as any Chekhov or Shakespeare play.'

Below: Del thinks there's money to be made from German au pair Anna's (Erika Hoffman) unwanted baby in 'From Prussia With Love'. Opposite: Del arranges a 'miracle' to make some money in 'The Miracle of Peckham'.

A good deal of fun was had by David Jason and Nick Lyndhurst while filming the next episode, 'The Miracle of Peckham', in which Del fleeces a string of gullible journalists after conning them into paying him large wodges of cash to film a statue of the Virgin Mary apparently weeping.

John Sullivan recalls arriving on the set near a church in Bermondsey, South London, to find David waiting for him. Herding John into his caravan, the mischievous star explained what he and Nick were up to. 'We've convinced Buster that you are writing an episode where there is a flashback sequence to when Albert was thirty,' David told him. 'And we've told him he's going to have to shave his beard off!'

'Now that beard is Buster's trademark,' says John. 'Not to mention his fortune when it comes to the pantomime season. So I was lumbered with the task of breaking this "news" to Buster. He was sitting in the make-up van and, as I walked between David's caravan and where Buster was, I had to make up a tale of what it was I was actually writing and why he had to shave his beard off.

'Now David and Nick are good at keeping straight faces in such circumstances but I can't. So I'm standing there telling him and Buster is taking it

very seriously and saying, "Couldn't we just sort of brown it and trim it?" I was saying, "No mate, it's got to come off. The make-up people have said to me they can make you look so much younger and that's how it's got to be. Buster looked quite sad about it and I thought, "This is getting cruel."

'Then I looked out of the window and outside were David and Nick laughing and in the end I just broke down into fits of laughter. I couldn't keep it going and Buster was mightily relieved. And it didn't take him long to work out who the perpetrators were. After all, he didn't have to look far with them two around!'

You could get a false one while your one grows back…

'Nick and I had got bored waiting to start filming so we came up with this idea,' smiles David Jason. 'Buster got quite worried about it but, being such a professional, he was prepared to do it. We said to him, "It's all right, you could get a false one while your one grows back," and he said, "No, it takes years" and we said, "Well, you could get a false one for years."'

'The Longest Night' includes a guest appearance by actor Vas Blackwood as Lennox, who's been hired to pull off a fake robbery at a supermarket by the debt-ridden manager and aggrieved security boss. He gets into the manager's office after getting caught shoplifting, an idea that came from a real event.

'A friend of mine heard about this bloke in prison who got to the manager's office and the store safe by deliberately getting caught shoplifting,' says John Sullivan. 'He then pulled a gun on them and told them to open the safe. I liked the idea of that for a story but I needed to take the sting out of it. I didn't want to show somebody with a real gun and so I came up with the idea of the three men being in league and the Trotters became their witnesses – with the extra twist that Lennox was late and the safe was on a time switch because his mum had bought him a dodgy watch from Del.'

'Tea for Three' sees Rodney and Del fighting over the same girl, Trigger's pretty niece Lisa (played by Gerry Cowper). Del has been bragging about his exploits as a paratrooper and Rodney decides to stitch him up – and make him live up to his boasting – when he is offered the chance to go hang-gliding. David Jason, an enthusiastic glider pilot, was keen to do his own stunts as Del took to the skies, over Butser Hill in Hampshire.

'I wanted to do it,' he says. 'But they wouldn't let me, for insurance reasons, so they got a stunt man instead. I could see their point of view because when you are filming a series you'd be in real trouble if your leading man broke his leg or something because it would delay filming.'

In 'Video Nasty' Rodney gets a grant from the local council to make a community film and Del then tries to earn money by selling endorsements on it. This idea was inspired by the largesse of the Greater London Council. 'Ken Livingstone had given out money to various art

Above: 'The Longest Night'. Lennox (Vas Blackwood) with Del Boy. Opposite: 'Tea for Three'. Top, David Jason filming the paragliding close-ups for the episode. Bottom, Rodney has spent too long on the sun bed but like Del he is still keen to impress Trig's niece Lisa (Gerry Cowper).

classes to make minority films and the papers and people were complaining that it was a waste of money,' explains John Sullivan. 'Rodney is a bit arty and it would have been right up his street.'

The episode also revealed Boycie's infertility problems and Del dubbed him 'Jaffa' because he was 'seedless'. That led to a number of complaints to John Sullivan from viewers who thought it was insensitive. 'They came from people trying to have babies who had the same problem and I wrote back, apologising and explaining that it was mainly aimed at making Boycie uncomfortable and not to hurt anyone,' he recalls.

The week John was about to begin writing the final episode of the fifth series he and his wife had dinner with David Jason and his girlfriend at the Caprice restaurant in London. During the evening it became clear that David felt five series was enough and wanted the series they were working on to be his last. John went home saddened but understood David's desire to pursue other acting avenues.

After discussing the situation with Head of Comedy Gareth Gwenlan he went away and wrote 'Who Wants to be a Millionaire'. In it Del is offered the chance to go to Australia with his old friend Jumbo Mills (played by Nick Stringer), and takes it, leaving Rodney behind because he is refused the right to emigrate, due to his minor drugs conviction.

'The last scene was to have seen Del flying out of the country and Rodney walking out of the airport looking a bit lost,' John recalls. Contingency plans would then have seen the programme continue with the new title *Hot Rod*, without Del but with the option of him coming back at a later date. '*Hot Rod* would have featured Rodney trying to continue the business but being constantly stitched up by people like Mickey Pearce and all the others. I never wrote that ending though, because in the meantime David changed his mind and talk of him leaving the show was forgotten and we started discussing the next series. By then I was too far into the episode so I just changed the ending so that Del says no to Jumbo's offer.'

Filming for 'A Royal Flush', the 1986 Christmas special, was interrupted when David Jason lost his voice for three days and shortly afterwards Nick Lyndhurst came down with a bout of flu. Filming had begun during the second week of November, in Salisbury, Wiltshire, and the episode centred on Rodney's blossoming romance with Sloane ranger Victoria, daughter of the Duke of Malebury, supposedly a cousin to the Queen. Before they've even had their first date at the opera, at the Theatre Royal, Drury Lane, Del can see pound signs and is already planning to marry Rodney off.

The entrance, foyer and bar scenes were shot at the actual Theatre Royal but, for the lengthy auditorium scenes and shots of the performance, the production moved from Salisbury to the Opera House at Buxton, Derbyshire. 'If I'd used the interior of the Theatre Royal, Drury Lane, it's such a big house that I would have needed thousands of extras, whereas Buxton is quite small in comparison,' says Ray Butt. 'Even so, I couldn't afford to fill it completely but still hired 200 people for it. I also hired the Kent Opera Company, with their scenery and orchestra, and it all cost an awful lot of money. But it was a very funny scene, so it was worth it.'

The delays in filming led to there being no time to run the tape in front of a studio audience to add a laughter track, nor was there time to add music to the soundtrack. The interior shots of the flat were filmed on a set built at

Elstree Studios, and there was even a contingency plan at one stage to do the final scene at the flat live on Christmas Day. Despite all this, the episode was only just finished in time, with Ray Butt and Tony Dow finishing off the editing in the early hours of Christmas Day. 'I went to sleep on the floor of the edit room,' Ray recalls.

The result was an entertaining episode with some fine moments, like the unforgettable shot when we see Rodney dressed up as a toff, but which somehow has a slightly incomplete feel. It is generally conceded, though, that the dinner scene at Victoria's father's stately home isn't up to the usual standard. Del, it seems, turns from being mischievous towards Rodney to being almost nasty.

It's something Ray Butt takes the blame for. 'I think that scene ruined Del's regard in the public eye,' he says. 'It was the one scene I wasn't happy with. I think that David went a bit over the top. That was my fault because I should have spotted it and brought him down. In retrospect I wasn't happy with it. I think Del turned too nasty and lost his warmth. Del's a villain, fine. But, like Bilko, there's warmth there and you've got to maintain that.'

John Sullivan was away in Paris, on location with his other hit show *Just Good Friends*, while the dinner scene was being filmed, something he now regrets. 'I wish to God I'd been on *Only Fools* instead,' he says. 'It was written for laughs not drama, and I wanted David to be Del as a jolly drunk rather than a morose drunk, which is what he ended up looking like. Not having a studio audience didn't help matters either.'

'Perhaps that scene wasn't as good as it could have been but the episode itself was fine,' says David Jason. 'Some people think it was a weak episode, but I just think of bits like Del turning up at the clay pigeon shoot with a gun he's borrowed from 'Iggy' Iggins, the bank robber. That was classic.'

As if the actors weren't busy enough filming 'A Royal Flush', in October 1986 a request came through asking the three stars if they would appear in the Royal Variety Show, which was to be staged at the Theatre Royal, Drury Lane, on 24 November.

'That was horrendously difficult,' recalls David Jason. 'They asked us to do it and we thought we'd take something out of one of the episodes, but they wanted something original. So John went away and wrote this great long script that lasted about twenty-five minutes when it should have been three!' The story had the trio supposedly making a delivery of dodgy booze to a pal of Del's called Chunky Lewis, who ran a nightclub in London's West End. They'd take a wrong turning and end up walking on stage at the Palladium during the show.

The script arrived in Salisbury where they were filming and it was only then that the cast understood just what they had taken on. David recalls, 'We got the running order of the show and realised that everyone else who was appearing either had an act – like Bruce Forsyth does – or were from a West End musical and had a singing or dancing routine. That meant they were really well rehearsed and knew their stuff backwards – except for us.

'We were the only people to appear who had never tried their material in front of an audience before and it was going out live. That started to hit home. From then on, every night after we finished filming, for about a week beforehand, we would get back to our hotel and the three of us would rehearse it over and over again. And, as it got nearer, we worried and we worried and we worried.

'We took out all sorts of insurance, like learning each other's parts and learning it backwards, because if one of us forgot our lines no one could help us but ourselves because you couldn't have a prompt. We'd be out there on our own and if anybody dried up no one would be able to give us a cue. We were ready to help each other out if one of us went wrong but we were still very worried about it.

'Then we finally got in the car to go to Drury Lane and on the way we rehearsed it and then fell into silence. We all felt sick with nerves. We were told to wait at the theatre over the road because we weren't on till the second half. There were all these singers and dancers there, getting excited about the show, and all we were feeling was very, very nervous. We fancied a drink but we couldn't have one because we needed our wits about us.'

…we'll get ourselves locked up in the Tower for this!

Another worry was the line David had to deliver to the Royal Box, which would be occupied by the Queen Mother and the Duchess of York. 'I'd said to John Sullivan, "Christ, we'll get ourselves locked up in the Tower for this!"' remembers David.

John Sullivan says, 'When I wrote about Chunky I didn't know the Duchess of York was going to be there. It was

before she'd joined Weightwatchers and in those days she had a few pounds on her. I was watching at home and thought "Oh God" when I saw she was in the Royal Box.'

'We didn't even know if anyone was going to laugh because, although we knew it was funny, we'd never tried it out on an audience,' says David. 'Comedy has this weird trick that it can play on you, in that the line you thought they'd laugh at they don't, and then they go mad about another one and catch you out. As soon as we walked on, we got a huge round of applause, which was great and made us feel welcome, and then we got our first laugh and it gave us a bit of confidence, but really you are on a knife edge because you can't afford to fail.

'The Royal gag was very funny. Nick looks up to the Royal Box, while Del is looking elsewhere, and he sees the Royal Family and starts scraping and bowing and I say, "What's the matter with you?" and then Del looks up to this box and, dazzled by the lights, says, "Chunky, is that you?"'

The line brought the house down – and provoked an instant reaction from the Queen Mum, as David recalls. 'She started to do the Royal wave,' he laughs. 'I couldn't believe it. Everybody fell about. Bless her cotton socks, perhaps she'd been on the gin and tonics by then, but for whatever reason she did it!'

After the show, along with all the other performers the trio were presented to the Queen Mother – and it was Buster who was singled out for unusual Royal attention. 'She spoke to David and Nick and then when she got to me she put her hand out to my beard and said, "So it's real then!" and I just said, "Yes Ma'am!" which was all I could think of saying at the time.'

Afterwards David and Nick had to be taken by car back to Salisbury for filming the next day but they got their driver to stop at an off-licence on the way back to buy a bottle of Famous Grouse whisky. 'And between London and Salisbury we did the whole bottle,' recalls Nick. 'It was a great way to let off steam!'

'The Frog's Legacy' was the 1987 Christmas special and will always stick in Ray Butt's memory, not only as his last episode on the show but also because his father Bill died during the filming. 'It was incredibly difficult,' he recalls. 'I got a phone call on the Friday evening as we wrapped, and I had to go and tell my mother. And then the next morning we were filming a funeral scene where Rodney gets a job as a pallbearer.'

The episode was being shot in Ipswich in East Anglia, and by coincidence the company hired to provide the funeral cortège for the programme came from Colchester. 'My father died in a hospice in Colchester and I said to the undertaker, "By the way, I've got another job for you next Wednesday or Thursday," and he said, "What, more filming?" and I said, "No, my old man died last night, can you bury him for me?"

'He didn't believe me at first and then he did, and he buried my dad for me. That was hard but not as hard as Lennard Pearce's death because I was so hyped up with work that my father's death didn't hit me for another six months.'

Shortly after filming 'The Frog's Legacy', Ray Butt left the BBC for a new post with ITV. 'I was offered a job at Central as Controller of Comedy, which sounded interesting but ended up as a disaster. It was so small after the world I was used to working in.

'It was like playing for Liverpool then joining a team in Division Three – it was a different league. Although I was head of comedy, you're really head of nothing. Head of Pencils was more important!'

Tony Dow took over as director, a choice that was very popular with Ray Butt. Tony had been with the show since the first series, when he joined Ray's team midway through, as a trainee assistant floor manager.

'I always thought he had a lot of talent,' says Ray. 'That's why, when I was leaving, I backed him to take over as director. Gareth Gwenlan, who was then Head of Comedy, was a bit nervous because Tony wasn't that experienced. But I knew he could do it because he'd filmed bits for me unofficially and he had a great rapport with the actors. He also worked hard, knew the game very well and he was a very quick learner.'

Tony Dow was joined by. Gareth Gwenlan who took over as producer, while also remaining Head of Comedy, and a new era for *Only Fools and Horses* was underway, building on the old strengths and adding a new element – longer episodes. John Sullivan had always wanted to do longer episodes. In fact his episodes always over-ran and had to be cut back, with huge chunks ending up on the cutting room floor or torn out during rehearsals.

When he was producer, Ray Butt had gone to the then Controller of BBC I Alan Hart and tried to persuade him to let it become a 45-minute or preferably a 50-minute show. 'But he turned the idea down, on the grounds that "it would dilute the comedy,"' Ray recalls. 'They should have gone to a 50-minute slot much earlier. We had to cut and throw a lot of good stuff away because of the time restriction because John always over-wrote. But John's a very astute writer and he managed to use some cut material again in other episodes.'

John talked over his frustration at being restricted to writing just 30 minutes with David Jason, who was in full agreement. Between them they decided to launch a joint campaign to lengthen the show. David remembers, 'We would always cut what we thought was the weakest…and what would tend to go would be very good jokes, good situations and the emotional stuff. All that would go because you couldn't cut into the actual narrative.

…but that's other writers, that is not John Sullivan.

'We wanted to do them longer but all the hierarchy would say was "That's impossible because situation comedy is 30 minutes." I'd say, "Yes, but that's other writers, that is not John Sullivan." They said that they could cut any sitcom into 30 minutes and that that was standard BBC format. I said, "I know you can cut it to 30 minutes and I have seen some of your cutting and you end up with bloody rubbish." It all started to get a bit heated. I got so frustrated, I said to John afterwards, "It's sacrilege – and all for the sake of people saying that you have to write to a set 30 minutes."

'The trouble with John at this time was that he was gaining so much strength with the characters and was enjoying them so much that when you asked him to write 30 minutes you'd end up with a 40-minute script or more, and then we'd have to cut it about. John and I went out for dinner one night and had a meeting, and he was really getting upset because he could just see all this stuff being thrown away. Some of it he would retain and use again but a lot of it was just apposite to that particular episode and would be wasted. In the end we decided that we'd tell them that we wouldn't do any more unless we could do 40 minutes. We agreed it – and we both meant it.'

New producer Gareth Gwenlan, a pragmatic, astute man, wasn't against Sullivan's proposal in principle. However he had a major problem, in that studio time was already booked and the episodes had to be produced and finished in a week. Getting a half-hour episode made in a week, with just one day in the studio, was the standard form, although most directors or producers would have been grateful for more time. Filming a 40-minute episode in that timescale was considered close to impossible, and Gareth Gwenlan told John Sullivan so. On top of that, the cast had been contracted to appear in 30-minute shows and any increase in the episode running time would lead to a big increase in the series budget. Nevertheless Gareth went to see his boss Michael Grade, Controller of BBC 1, and said he wanted to give Sullivan an extra five minutes for his episodes by way of a compromise.

'Michael said that, from the point of view of finding a transmission slot for 35 minutes, it wasn't too much of a problem,' Gareth recalls. 'There would be a problem with a show of that length for overseas sales, but *Only Fools and Horses* doesn't sell, which in those days it didn't. Both John Sullivan and the series were held in very high regard and Michael said, ''Tell him to do 35 minutes.'' So I told John he could have the extra five minutes and what happened? The first script came in and it was an hour long. I said, ''John…'' and he said, ''What about 50…'' I said, ''Listen, I'm sure the Controller would be delighted with 50 minutes but we are in deep shit. We have got six Sundays in the studio to record them and no one has recorded a 50-minute show in one day.'''

A massive 40 per cent increase in the show's budget had to be found, and location filming, which always took place in one whole block for the series prior to the weekly studio recording, was extended so that each episode would have more film inserts, leaving less to be done in the studio. That was fine for the first three episodes of the series, which had large chunks already written for location recording on film, but the last three episodes were almost totally studio-based. 'It was a seriously difficult thing to do and it nearly bloody killed all of us,' Gareth recalls.

…Nick and I nearly died. We had to work almost 24 hours a day.

David Jason, partly responsible for the new heavy workload, laughs now and says, 'We really shot ourselves in the foot! Nick and I nearly died. We had to work almost 24 hours a day. We stopped to sleep. I'd get up at 6 a.m. and try

Uncle Albert has mentioned his old skipper Captain Kenworthy a few times in the series. He's named after leading showbusiness journalist Christopher Kenworthy – the first man to write about *Only Fools and Horses* in 1981 and a friend of John Sullivan.

to learn my script, rehearse all day, come back and look at the next day's script, and then go to bed early to be up, and so on. We were absolutely dead after we'd done the studio recording on the Sunday. After we'd done the last one someone piped up and said, ''You've proved that a 50-minute show can be done in seven days, so you'll be able to do it again next time.'' I said, ''Over my dead body,'' and I nearly was a dead body. We said, ''Never again – unless we get more time,'' and when it came to doing the next series everything was redesigned and we had ten days to rehearse and film them in, which was much more sensible.'

The other major change for the programme-makers at that time was the decision to move location filming from London to Bristol. 'During the early part of the eighties, filming in London was always difficult,' says Gareth Gwenlan. 'One by one, the markets became impossible to use and didn't want to know because filming was too disruptive for them.

'It also became increasingly impossible to film with Nick and David on the streets of London because they would just get mobbed. We knew we needed to move out to a provincial city and someone suggested Bristol. So Tony Dow, John Sullivan and I went down for a recce. Architecturally it had everything we needed, in terms of the pubs, houses, a market, and most importantly we found the right block of flats.

'We talked to the residents' association who were, and still are (the last time we used it), absolutely fantastic and, although it's not exactly the same as the original block in North Acton, London, that we used in the opening titles, it was just what we needed.

It would be dangerous to film at North Acton now. I spent half a day there in 1996, filming a commercial for Rover cars in New Zealand with David and John Challis, and we had to have the police with us all the time. The back of Acton is like the drug capital of the UK. It is not pleasant and you could never film there at night because things would probably get nicked. In Bristol it's very different. The police are very co-operative and the people are very nice, and the only thing we have to do to make it look a little more like London is to take a couple of red London buses down to put in the background in various scenes.'

The Sixth Series

Filming of 'Dates' began promptly on the morning of Monday 7 November. 'Dates' was the 1988 Christmas special but was filmed as the first part of series six or 'F' as it was known by the production team. 'I decided to do "Dates" because I felt Del had to start meeting more mature women,' says John Sullivan. 'I couldn't keep having him chasing twenty-year-olds, so I brought Raquel in, although when I wrote it I hadn't planned to bring her back the following year. For me "Dates" was a try-out for Del to have a more mature relationship, because I knew that it had to come.'

The first 50-minute episode, 'Yuppy Love', sees the first appearance of Gwyneth Strong as Cassandra and also features Del adopting his new image. The film *Wall Street,* starring Michael Douglas as ruthless stock market trader Gordon Gekko, has clearly had an impact on Del who now wears the standard City garb of striped shirt, brightly coloured braces and, of course, the obligatory filofax.

…we got rid of the camel-hair coat and smartened up his image…but we kept the yellow van.

'Del always thought he was a trend-setter and of course he'd always get the trends wrong,' says John Sullivan. 'Yuppies were the big thing at the time so Del moved into that image. I also saw the film *Wall Street* and I knew that if Del had seen it then it would have had a big impact on his life and he'd be straight out the following day to buy a pair of red braces and a smart shirt. So we got rid of the camel-hair coat and smartened up his image, giving him a green mac, an aluminium briefcase and a mobile phone, but we kept the yellow van.'

In 'Dates', Charles, the restaurant maître d', is played by Nicholas Courtney who is best known for his role as the Brigadier in the cult BBC series *Doctor Who.*

Above: From the episode 'Yuppy Love'. One of the most famous and memorable scenes from Only Fools and Horses *when Del leans on the bar and discovers that it's not there any more.*
Opposite: Tessa Peake-Jones joins the cast as Del's computer-date, Raquel. Location filming for 'Dates' at Waterloo station.

Rodney, too, tries to better himself by attending evening classes, and it is at one of these that he meets Cassandra. Of course, things rarely go smoothly for Rodney and he's humiliated when she finds his name written in his coat – kindly put in by Del as a joke. The episode features one of the show's most famous moments when Del leans on a bar flap in a yuppy wine bar without noticing that the barman has opened the flap. The resultant fall humiliates Del, who has been trying to impress two girls with his spiel about being a high-flying trader.

It looks so easy on screen but the scene took lots of planning. 'John Sullivan was in a wine bar and he saw this bloke lean on the bar and it wasn't there because they'd lifted the flap up,' David Jason recalls. 'He just recovered himself and looked round to see if anyone had seen. We both thought it was really funny and agreed Del should do it in a scene but I said, "He's got to fall right over."

'It took a long time to set up and we distracted the audience's attention with two girls so they didn't particularly notice the barman lifting up the flap. It was planted there but it wasn't made obvious. The actual fall was very difficult to do because, if you fall like I did, it's a comic fall, not a real fall, which is what makes it funny. The trouble is though, when you do it your instinctive reaction is to try to break your fall with your hand and look where you are falling.

'It's hard to do, because you have to ignore all the danger signals that your brain is giving you. But it was worth it because everyone loved it and it's one of those moments that people always talk about. Thank goodness we got it right first time so that I only had to do it once on camera and I landed on a small crash mat out of sight.'

Rodney meanwhile makes progress with Cassandra but is too ashamed to admit that he lives in a lowly block of council flats, on a rundown estate. Instead he convinces her that he lives in an upmarket suburb, and when she gives him a lift he gets her to drop him off outside someone else's home. Once again, it was one of John Sullivan's real life experiences that inspired the scene.

I remembered a road…which had some nice big detached houses… so I told her I lived there.

Years ago, before he met his wife, John was at a party in London and met a girl he quite fancied. At the end of the evening she offered him a lift home in her car, as she was going to pass through South London where he lived. 'She was a friend of a friend and she lived in Ewell, a nice place just outside London, whereas I was living in a rough terraced street,' he recalls. 'Her dad was a stockbroker and she mentioned they had a swimming pool…by contrast I was going to take her back to the Bronx! I didn't want her to see where I lived, because I was hoping to see her again and didn't want to put her off. I remembered a road near my old school called Clarence Avenue which had some nice big detached houses, and there was one there that particularly impressed me so I told her I lived there. We said goodnight and she drove off and then I had to walk two miles back to my real home. It started to rain very heavily and by the time I got home I was soaked. Not only that but I never saw her again, so it was all in vain anyway!'

Del's eagerness to make a few quid goes very wrong in 'Danger UXD', when the Trotters discover that the faulty dolls Del has persuaded Denzil to give them are more the type for weirdos than children. The inspiration for this episode came from an incident at a party, when a friend of John's had his room filled with dozens of inflatable dolls as a joke. 'They looked so stupid,' laughs John, 'that I had to put them in a story and I was also amused by the thought of: "How the hell do you get rid of them all?"' The end of the episode sees the dolls exploding and this sequence was filmed on a disused part of Bristol Docks.

Nick Lyndhurst recalls, 'It was a bloody big bang and we all got showered with dirt.'

Another explosion had been planned for an early episode, though it never reached the screen. In the proposed story, Del is trying to sell a damaged radio which has lots of wires protruding from it. He leaves the van with the radio in the back, along with Rodney (who is sleeping off a hangover), outside a government building, while he goes off in search of Boycie. A security guard spots the wires, thinks it is a car bomb and calls out the army bomb disposal squad who seal off the street and, using a robot device, do a controlled explosion on the van, blow-

Below: Most of the regulars –
Boycie, Del, Mike, Trigger and Rodney – team
up to make a packet on a deal with a retired
jeweller in the episode 'Chain Gang'.

THE ONLY FOOLS AND HORSES STORY

ing it to pieces. Del was to have come back and found his van blown apart and no sign of Rodney except his boots. Later he discovers that Rodney had changed into his trainers and gone off to get a pint before the security alert.

According to John, 'Ray Butt pointed out that if we blew up the van there was no way Del would go and buy another one that was identical and we'd lose the van that was giving everyone so many laughs because by then it had become the Trotters' trademark, so we abandoned the idea.'

The inflatable dolls used in 'Danger UXD' led to a number of viewers complaining to the BBC and a few days after the Sunday night transmission David and Nick took a break from rehearsing the next episode to go on live daytime TV to respond to the criticism. One woman had asked how she was supposed to explain what the dolls were to her seven-year-old daughter.

'We were happy to go on and defend the episode,' says Nick. 'The dolls in the show had been specially adapted by our special effects people so that they weren't that explicit.'

The next episode, 'Chain Gang', was a classic ensemble piece, in which all the supporting cast got plenty to do. It also saw the team make a brief return to London for location filming. 'It came about because I wondered what would happen if someone had a heart attack when they'd just taken your money for a deal,' says John Sullivan. 'You couldn't grab it from them, nor could you follow the ambulance because they'd dash through red lights. I just developed it from there and made it into a scam.'

'The Unlucky Winner is…' sees Rodney winning a trip abroad in an art competition. He's delighted, until he remembers that he never actually entered one, and it's only later that Del reveals that he sent his entry in, in the under-fourteen category. Rodney is furious, and is a less than enthusiastic member of the 'groovy gang' which all the winners are enrolled into. The classic moment in the episode comes when Rodney – all six foot two of him – is seen for the first time in his skateboard gear, being chased by a youngster who has a crush on him.

In the next episode, 'Sickness and Wealth', Del has stomach pains and eventually goes to the doctor but he discovers that his old male doctor has left. Instead there is a new woman doctor at his local surgery who he outrages when she asks him to strip to the waist and he strips from the waist down. However, when he's told he needs to go to hospital for tests the viewer sees his vulnerable side when

he insists that Rodney must go with him.

Del's illness is a mystery but he mistakenly thinks he's got AIDS. It turns out it's all down to too many curries and Pina Coladas. Once again, the episode gave John Sullivan a chance to show his ability to combine pathos with comedy. At the time AIDS awareness campaigns were running non-stop and there was a great deal of misinformation circulating in terms of how people could be infected. In this episode Del reckons he might have caught it because he once had a gay hairdresser, allowing John Sullivan to make an important point but not in a preachy, politically correct way.

'Little Problems' saw Rodney finally tie the knot and marry Cassandra. It was an episode that David Jason found very moving. 'It was a very emotional one because we realised that Rodney had become a man and that was quite an eye-opener for Del, and for me too because Nick and I had been together for years. It was the Simply Red song "Holding Back the Years" that got me, and I shed a few tears for real when that started during rehearsals. By the time we came to film it, though, the tears were gone and my eyes were dry again.'

Back in early 1988, leading film and stage actor Anthony Hopkins had told Terry Wogan on his BBC1 chat show how much he loved *Only Fools and Horses* and how he'd love to appear in it. John Sullivan happened to be watching and decided to create a character for him, in the hope that he'd be available when it came to filming it.

John had mentioned the terrifying hard men, the Driscoll Brothers, before in scripts and he now decided to bring them into the show as characters, with the elder one, Danny, an ideal cameo role for Anthony Hopkins. 'Unfortunately when we got to film it he wasn't free. He was in America filming some movie called *The Silence of the Lambs*!

'And after that we never heard of him again, did we?' John jokes. 'He could have come with us and become famous!'

Of course Anthony's performance in *The Silence of the Lambs* earned him a Best Actor Oscar and confirmed his place as one of the world's biggest stars.

'By then I had the Driscolls in the script so we got another good actor, Roy Marsden, in to play the part instead and he was brilliant, as was Christopher Ryan who played his little brother Tony,' adds John.

'Little Problems' could have been the last episode of the series and it would have gone out on a terrific high. The 50-minute episodes had gained an average of 16.7 million viewers and everyone seemed to be talking about the series. John Sullivan was getting letters practically every day from desperate pub landlords. They were going spare because their takings were falling on Sunday nights because so many people were staying in to watch the show. 'They'd write and ask me not to make it so funny,' he remembers.

'And some of them decided that if you couldn't beat them then it was time to join them, so they moved their televisions into their bars!'

On 1 May 1989, a little over two months after the show went off air, production began on that year's Christmas special 'The Jolly Boys' Outing'. In this story, Del had organised a day trip to Margate, Kent, for the regulars at the Nag's Head.

One unforgettable moment comes when a car radio –

no need to guess who supplied it – ignites the fuel tank in the coach and causes a massive explosion which blows up the vehicle. Normally vehicles for filming are supplied by specialist hire companies but none of them would have been too pleased to have their coach brought back on a lorry as a mass of burnt-out metal. So the production team bought their own for the Del Trotter-style knockdown price of £2,000. However the coach had to be completely safe and pass its MOT before it could be used on the roads for the scenes of the group travelling to Margate.

For the explosion scene a BBC visual effects team got to work and placed tanks containing hundreds of gallons of petrol all the way along in the luggage compartments. Three cameras were used to film the shot so that it was covered from different angles, and everyone in the cast and crew was moved back to a safe distance of about 400 yards. Fire-fighters from the Kent Fire Brigade also stood by, ready to extinguish the flames.

'We knew that we could do the explosion two or three times if the flames were put out quickly,' says producer Gareth Gwenlan. 'If you look carefully on the tape you can see there are about six different shots of the explosion all cut together very quickly.'

Gareth was closer because, along with director Tony Dow and cameraman Alec Curtis, he was behind one of the cameras, about 100 yards from the coach, and felt the blast. 'I wasn't blown over but I was certainly blown back,' he recalls. 'Then the fire brigade went in, put it out, and a while later we did it all again.'

While filming, it became apparent that the show was in the running to scoop a BBC award as British children's favourite comedy show but the schedule was too tight for the cast to be given time off to attend the awards. Later the team learned that the show had in fact won and a helicopter was sent to pick up David Jason, Nick Lyndhurst and Buster Merryfield. 'It was wonderful,' recalls Buster. 'The heli-

Above: Denzil and Albert in the episode 'The Jolly Boys' Outing'.
Opposite: 'Little Problems'. Rodney and Cassandra tie the knot.
Inset opposite: Denis Lill who plays Alan Parry, Cassandra's father and Rodney's boss. Denis became a regular cast member from 1989.

copter waited for us to finish filming and then flew back into London along the route of the Thames before landing at Westland Heliport, which meant I was able to fly over my old school in Battersea. I thought, "If only my mum could see me now!"'

Nick had worked with the pilot before and decided to play a trick on Buster before the flight. 'I told him to come in and introduce himself to Buster and David and say to me, "Have you done the pre-flight briefing, Nick?" David was in on the joke and I told Buster that I was going to do the passenger briefing, because the pilot was busy. I went on about straps and things and explained that, in the event of engine failure or needing to ditch, because of the rotor blades, you have to keep you hands over your head and we ought to practise it. I told him to pretend that the winnebago door was the helicopter door, so he should open the door, shout "1000, 2000, 3000 – check" and jump with his hands on his head and run away as fast as he could, and he did it and we got a lovely Polaroid of him doing it!'

Back in Ramsgate, where the team were staying, John Sullivan spotted a shower cap in his hotel room, and, due to the close proximity of Dover and the number of French visitors who stayed there, it also had the words 'shower cap' in French. The translation, 'Bonnet de douche', seemed to be the sort of thing Del would say for a toast. At dinner that night he tried it out on the cast and crew and then added it to the script, and another bit of *Only Fools and Horses* mythology was born.

Actor Graham Cole, who plays PC Tony Stamp in ITV's *The Bill,* played a customs officer in the freeze-frame sequence in 'It Never Rains…'. Nula Cornwell, who used to play Sun Hill Detective Constable Viv Martella, played Nag's Head barmaid Maureen in five episodes of *Only Fools and Horses.*

☆ MISSING SCENE ☆

This scene comes from the 1989 Christmas special 'The Jolly Boys' Outing' and was recorded but cut from the final episode because of lack of time. It follows the scene where the Trotters find a room at the Villa Bella. Arthur and Betty were played by Michael Bilton and Fanny Carby.

THE TROTTERS FOLLOW INGA UPSTAIRS.
MRS CRESWELL FOLLOWS THEM.
DEL LOOKS INTO THE SEMPRINI ROOM AT A SAD-FACED COUPLE (ARTHUR AND BETTY) FROM OOP NORTH.

DEL: Are you guests or has she hired you to cheer the place up.
ARTHUR: No we're guests.
BETTY: Guests, aye.
DEL: This place is no Club Med, is it?
ARTHUR: It's really 'orrible here. The food's awful.
BETTY: Awful food.
ARTHUR: And not much of it either.
BETTY: No. She only allows you one jacket potato a day.
DEL: Well you never know, she might give you an extra lump of custard with yer afters.
ARTHUR: Well she hasn't previous years.
BETTY: No.
ARTHUR: Aye.
DEL: Well, stay lucky
DEL ASCENDS STAIRS.

THE FANS

Only Fools and Horses has always appealed to a complete cross-section of people. It straddles the social and age divide in a way few other programmes are able to and repeats of old episodes are constantly bringing a new generation of fans to it. Famous fans include Oscar-winner Sir Anthony Hopkins, rock stars Sir Paul McCartney and Tom Jones, industrialist Sir John Harvey-Jones and tycoon Richard Branson.

Even members of the Royal Family are known to be fans of the programme, and Her Majesty Queen Elizabeth The Queen Mother was certainly familiar enough with the characters to join in the fun at the 1986 Royal Variety Show. Advance tapes of Christmas specials have regularly been requested and sent to Buckingham Palace and as Nick Lyndhurst says, 'I guess they must have liked them because they never gave them back!'

The programme also has a thriving fan club run by Perry Aghajanoff from Chingford, East London who works in the fashion trade. Formed in 1993, The *Only Fools and Horses* Appreciation Society now has more than 1500 members worldwide including Croatia, Argentina and Thailand. Its newsletter *Hookie Street* is published four times a year and the group's annual general meeting takes place at a pub called the Nag's Head.

'I got into the series right from the off in 1981,' says Perry. 'One of the reasons I like it is because of the British mentality of loving a loser and Del is the eternal loser. The show is infinitely watchable and however many times you see the same episode it's still funny. I've probably seen every episode about 50 times and I still enjoy them as much, however many times I've seen them.'

Perry drives a Ford Escort for everyday use but he's also got no fewer than ten yellow Trotter vans. 'I've bought some of them for just £30,' he says, 'and members of the fan club put New York – Paris, and then the name of where they live, on the side of theirs.' He's also got a collection of *Only Fools* memorabilia that is second to none including Trigger's inflatable dolphin as used in 'The Jolly Boys' Outing', scripts and a signed photograph of Lennard Pearce.

☆The *Only Fools and Horses* Appreciation Society, PO Box 92, Romford, Essex RM6 9DN

The Seventh Series

The 1990 Christmas special 'Rodney Come Home' was filmed as the first episode of the seventh series, or series 'G'. Following on from the end of 'The Jolly Boys' Outing', it saw John Sullivan concentrating on the faltering relationship between Rodney and Cassandra. 'It was quite a downbeat episode but that was down to John moving the characters on a couple of gear changes,' explains Gareth Gwenlan. 'The episodes that followed were only possible because we'd done "Rodney Come Home". John and I had long conversations about it because it wasn't a conventional episode but it was very pivotal to what happened afterwards.'

It had been filmed in Bristol in October 1990 and by that stage Gareth Gwenlan had relinquished his post as Head of Comedy in order to spend more time making programmes as a producer. It was the biggest Christmas Day show with 17.97 million viewers, followed closely by Steven Spielberg's hit film *ET* which got 17.5 million. ITV's best shot, a Ken Dodd special, didn't even make the top ten.

The critics, too, seemed to like the domestic drama brought about by Rodney's tempestuous marriage to Cassandra, and Del's rollercoaster relationship with Raquel. *Today*'s Pam Francis said, 'Rather than keep the Trotter brothers in a time warp, their creator John Sullivan has taken the risk of moving them on with the times. By doing so, and getting Rodders hitched, he's been able to tackle relevant issues.'

The *Daily Mail* agreed. 'John Sullivan clearly still loves the show and thanks to his fertile imagination it's far from running out of steam,' wrote TV critic Marcus Berkmann. 'He's kept the series alive but it's lost none of its energy and pace.'

The next episode, 'The Sky's the Limit', went out just five days after the Christmas Day show. In it Boycie's new satellite dish gets stolen and Del buys it back for him – for

Above: Rodney's marriage hits problems and Del comforts Cassandra in 'Rodney Come Home'.

a profit. Or so he thinks, until he actually discovers that he's got the air traffic control radar from the main runway at Heathrow Airport and that planes are now homing in on Nelson Mandela House.

'They say never work with children or animals and during the filming of that episode we had to do both,' recalls John Challis. 'We were filming at the house we use for Boycie and Marlene's mock Tudor home and Boycie was messing about with this huge satellite dish which he didn't really know how to operate. At the same time as trying to control it, Duke the dog was bounding about all over the lawn, and we had the little lad who plays Tyler there in the pram, dressed in a replica of what Marlene was wearing.

'The Great Dane playing Duke was actually quite lazy and didn't do that much bounding around and his trainer was trying desperately to get him to move rather than just loll around. Then the sound people needed some slobbering noises from the dog so the guy with the boom microphone knelt down to record them, and it saw the furry cover on the microphone and leapt on it and savaged it which reduced everyone to hysterics.'

'The Chance of a Lunchtime' saw Raquel deciding that there was more to life than clearing up after the Trotters at Nelson Mandela House and deciding to go back to acting. 'That episode was a turning point for Raquel because she got an audition to join a theatre company and then she got offered a part in a tour but she had to turn it down because she'd discovered that she was pregnant,' says Tessa Peake-Jones.

'Stage Fright' guest-starred Philip Pope as singing dustman Tony Angelino. In a hilarious scene, where the cast can be seen almost laughing for real, we learn that he can't pronounce his Rs and therefore has to sing 'Cwying' and the 'Gween Gween Gwass of Home'. Philip is a multi-talented performer. In addition to acting in shows like *Blackadder, Drop the Dead Donkey* and *Underworld,* he's also a brilliant musician and one of the country's top programme theme tune writers with dozens of credits to his name – including the infamous '*Spitting Image Chicken Song*'.

Tessa Peake-Jones spoke to director Tony Dow shortly after getting the script for the episode and seeing that she'd have to sing as Raquel. 'But I don't really sing,' she explained. 'And Tony said, "Well she's not meant to be good!" and I thought, "Oh thanks!" I had sung and danced to get my Equity card but I'd never put myself forward as a professional singer.

'It was a bit nerve-racking in the night-club where we filmed it because a lot of the supporting artists that were there were club acts themselves. I was very. aware of singing "Crying" rather badly in front of an audience who were sitting there being paid to look fairly bored and who *were* rather bored. They'd seen everything shot loads of times so I was very aware of their critical eyes but I just had to get on with it. I started very nervously and hit none of the right notes but I think I got better as the day went on. I did hit a couple of bum notes though, which Tony had to cut away from when it came to editing. He disguised them by cutting to Del and Rodney at the bar and turning my singing down and their voices up. I was just too out of tune and Tony said, "There are a couple of times I just can't hide it!"'

'The Class of '62' saw the return and final appearance of Jim Broadbent as Roy Slater, who viewers discovered had just been released from prison where he had been serving his sentence for diamond-smuggling revealed in 'To Hull and Back'. More surprising was the revelation that Slater was in fact Raquel's much referred to but never identified ex-husband.

Philip Pope, who played Tony Angelino, the singing dustman in the episode 'Stage Fright'.

'I'd never met Jim before,' says Tessa Peake-Jones. 'He was great fun though, and I know that the others felt that it was like another old boy and member of the team back. There was a school reunion in the story and it was a bit like a school reunion for the boys too!'

'He Ain't Heavy, He's My Uncle' saw the team return to filming in London for scenes shot all over the City and nearby Docklands, when Albert goes missing and Del and Rodney try to track him down. 'That was no problem to shoot because the City is deserted at weekends,' says Gareth Gwenlan. The soundtrack for the scene was Paul and Linda McCartney's 1971 single, 'Uncle Albert', which had been a number one hit in the United States. John Sullivan remembered it and it fitted in perfectly with the mood of the episode. For Buster Merryfield, in particular, it was quite an emotional experience. 'I found it very moving filming the scene where Albert had returned to the place where he'd lived as a boy,' he says. 'I could easily have cried. Not many people can write scripts like John Sullivan.'

Hands up who's had a baby in the last hour…

The hospital scenes in 'Three Men, a Woman and a Baby' were filmed at a recently closed ward at West Middlesex Hospital at Hillingdon, which has also been used for filming births in *Waiting for God* and most recently *Roger, Roger.* However, the ward below was still open, and that made finding a newborn baby to play Del and Raquel's child Damien very easy. 'When we were ready to film it, we went down and said, "Hands up who's had a baby in the last hour who's prepared to lend it to the BBC?"' recalls Gareth Gwenlan. 'I think the mum was thrilled that her baby was going to appear on the telly.'

Felix Bowness, who played Fred the jockey in the classic BBC comedy series *Hi-De-Hi!,* was a regular warm-up man who entertained the studio audiences before recordings of *Only Fools and Horses.*

Above left: The return of Jim Broadbent as Roy Slater in 'The Class of '62'.
Right: Del and Raquel and the imminent arrival of a son and heir in 'Three Men, a Woman and a Baby'.

Tessa Peake-Jones asked a midwife for advice because she hadn't yet had any children. 'I didn't have a bloomin' clue at the time how you did it,' she laughs. 'So she sat David, Nick, Buster and myself down in a room and showed us a video of a woman giving birth. We'd all just had a cooked breakfast and we all felt sick at the end of it because it went into very graphic detail.

'I remember at one point looking at the others. There was Buster, this man in his seventies, with his mouth just wide open in amazement watching this baby coming out, David was going "Oh my God" and obviously being put off for life, Nick was speechless and I'm sure wanted to vomit, and I was just thinking "I can't do that!" The woman looked in such pain and terror and was making horrible noises. That lasted half an hour and then I went into the ward and sat on the bed and did what the woman did in the film – well almost. I knew John didn't want me to hold back so I put in lots of screams.

'I was tired at the end of the day but it was just acting and it was less than a year later that I gave birth to my own daughter Mollie for real. I didn't scream half as much because I didn't have the breath to do it but, like Raquel, I did have a male midwife called Paul who was lovely.'

Inspiration for many of the hilarious lines during the birth sequence came from John Sullivan's own experiences when his wife Sharon gave birth to their children. In the script Raquel says to Del, 'Don't you ever come near me again, Trotter' and John says, 'Sharon had said that to me and then she asked to hold my hand and she dug her nails in and I said "ahh" and she said, "Now you know what it bloody well feels like!" So I used that too.'

He gives me the ammunition and I fire the gun.

A month after the 1991 series ended, David Jason scooped a BAFTA Best Light Entertainment Performance Award for his work in the series, after unbelievably missing out five times previously despite being nominated. At the glittering awards ceremony – the British equivalent of the American Oscars – David generously paid tribute to John Sullivan, saying, 'He gives me the ammunition and I fire the gun.

'I was very pleased,' says David. 'I'd been nominated every year and was always being pipped at the post. I started getting used to it and then in the end my tenacity paid off!' Over the years he's collected a staggering list of more than twenty awards – two Sonys, four BAFTAs, three British comedy awards, three from the Royal Television Society, and so on. David quips, 'I'm thinking of building an extra room for them.'

In October 1991, filming began in Miami, Florida, on the second of a £2 million two-part 'Miami Twice' story called 'Oh to be in England'. Before he had left his post as Head of Comedy, Gareth Gwenlan had talked to Jonathan Powell, who had taken over as Controller of BBC1, about taking the programme to America for an extra-special Christmas episode. 'The show could do no wrong by that time and he agreed we could do it,' says Gareth.

The idea was that in the first episode, 'The American Dream', which also saw Damien's christening, Del would use Rodney's pension refund – or 'Maxwell money' as he topically called it – to buy two tickets to Florida so that he could hide from someone he'd stitched up over a wine deal with some dodgy Romanian Riesling.

The final moments of the first episode saw the brothers flying out of Gatwick Airport and featured a guest appearance by Virgin boss Richard Branson. 'Richard is a nice man but he can't act to save his life,' Gareth laughs. 'For the first ten minutes of filming he couldn't keep a straight face and then he had to take it seriously because he was holding up his own plane which was waiting to go to Los Angeles. In order to get him to say his line convincingly we had to shoot it quite a few times.'

In the story, Del and Rodney run into trouble when Del is spotted by a Mafia gang who realise he's a doppelgänger for the beleaguered head of the family, Don Occhetti. This meant that David Jason had to film twice as many scenes as normal for the dual role. The actual filming in Miami for 'Oh to be in England' was no fun for the cast or the crew. 'Foreign filming is always problematic because it costs a lot of money and I believe you are running a risk editorially when you take a series out of its normal environment,' says Gareth Gwenlan. 'I'm not sure it totally paid off. Although it's a very good two-parter, it's not Only Fools and Horses.'

Gareth had flown to Miami knowing that filming the show would be no

Above: The two faces of David Jason in 'Miami Twice'. Top, as Del Boy and above, as Don Occhetti, the local Mafia boss. Opposite: The Don in his impressive Florida mansion. The scenes were actually shot in a private suite at Miami's Biltmore Hotel which was regularly used by gangster Al Capone.

picnic but he hadn't expected it to be quite the nightmare that it turned into. Before filming had begun, he and Tony Dow had visited Miami and talked in detail about the project with the Florida Film Board who assured them that they would have no problems with the unions and that they could bring over their heads of departments and then hire local technicians with no difficulties.

'We had to have a crew that was made up of 60 per cent local workers, which was fine because we didn't want to have to take loads of people over from the UK,' says Gareth. 'So we ended up taking the heads of make-up, costume and design and the cameraman and sound recordist. Everyone else we employed there.'

However, problems arose when they needed to hire vehicles for props and costumes and for make-up and changing rooms. Having been assured by the Film Board that they could just hire vans that had owner-drivers who would drive them around, Gareth and his team soon found that they had crossed the all-powerful Teamsters [drivers] Union.

'We started shooting, then on the third day I got a call from production manager Sue Longstaff saying that we had problems with the Teamsters. This guy had just come down and said that they were going to start picketing our set. I was literally summoned to go down and see the head of the Teamsters Union in Miami and, I swear to God, had it not been so serious, I would have thought I was in a bad American B movie.

'I was shown into this very sombre, dark, wood-panelled office with heavy leather furniture, where I found this great fat, balding guy sitting at his desk. He had a real James Cagney-at-his-worst accent and he said, "So what are yous doing in my town?" I explained how much money we were spending in the city and that we were employing some sixty local technicians and he said, "Yeah, but you ain't employing any of my members." I said that we weren't

THE SECRET GULF WAR SPECIAL

During the 1991 Gulf War a special 15-minute episode of *Only Fools and Horses* was shot at RAF Strike Command at High Wycombe in Buckinghamshire. A special Trotter van was decked out in brown and yellow desert camouflage, complete with a machine gun mounted on the roof, with Peckham scrawled out and Kuwait written in. 'I wrote the script,' says John Sullivan, 'Gareth Gwenlan came down and directed it, and the van was sent out to the boys in the Gulf with the message: "Don't worry – the secret weapon is coming. The Iraqis will start running when they see this!"'

The episode starred David, Nicholas and Buster, and everyone gave up their time for free for the one-day shoot. 'It was great fun and after we finished filming they laid on a buffet for us,' recalls John. There was no time to edit the material and it was immediately dispatched to the Gulf to entertain British forces. 'It went out just as we filmed it mistakes and all,' adds John.

The film was done like a home movie, straight to camera, with David Jason saying, 'This is Derek Trotter, reporting from a secret location somewhere in southern England.' Explaining that the specially adapted Trotter van is a secret weapon, Del says. 'This is the Concorde of three wheelers. It's just that you don't know how to drive it. See the van is like a woman… It needs caressing and a bit of gentle persuasion.'

Rodney chips in: 'You could be right. It reminds me of some of your ex-birds – it drinks too much, makes funny noises and is old enough to know better.' At the end, Del turns serious and, with cut-ins of wives and families at the base, David, as Del, says, 'We're all very proud of what you've achieved over there. Proud of your courage, your efficiency and the way you've carried it out. All we want you to do now is to get home as quick as possible. So, from all of us here, Gawd bless you all. And don't worry about the wives and girlfriends. I'll look after them. They're safe in my hands. You know it makes sense!'

because we had owner-driver vehicles and we were told that that was fine.

'He said, "Well, I'm here to tell you that it ain't fine. I want twelve of my drivers on that set tomorrow, otherwise I shut you down." I know it sounds like something out of a film but it's absolutely true. I thought, "Do I laugh or do I take this seriously?" I was worried because we'd spent or committed a lot of our budget and if everything went wrong then that would go down the drain.

'Eventually I said, "Well if you are saying we have to do this then I'll have to shut the unit down and I'll have to go back to England," and he said, "I'll drive yous to the airport." I said, "I'll talk to you again tomorrow." Then I went back to the office.'

'Gareth was ashen when he came back,' John Sullivan recalls. 'He was as grey as his hair. His cigar light had obviously gone out a long time before! He said to me, "I've never been so frightened in all my life." This guy terrified him.'

'I phoned this useless Florida Film Board and they said that I was going to have to come to a compromise,' says Gareth. 'I said, "Why? You told me I could do this, you tell him to sod off." They said they couldn't do that and then it just dawned on me how much the union system out there is still in the Dark Ages. As expected, the following day the union picketed us and completely shut production down because none of our American crew would cross the picket line.'

At 7a.m. the following morning Gareth had another meeting with the Union boss and they came to a compromise. The unit would employ three Teamster Union drivers. 'So after that these three guys would arrive in the morning, do nothing all day and then go home,' says Gareth. 'As you can imagine, I was far from happy about it but there was little else I could do.

'Everyone was under huge pressure anyway because it was costing so much to be out there that there was no way we could overrun and stay longer. We were working fourteen-hour days, six days a week, and we did not have time to enjoy ourselves. The bar at our hotel wasn't open so on Saturday nights, when we had Sundays off, we'd all chip $20 into a kitty and Robin Stubbs, our costume designer, would go off and buy bottles of gin, Scotch and vodka. Then we'd all sit round in the bar and chat and just drink to oblivion!'

The unit had no work for the Teamsters drivers so one

of them was assigned to be a chauffeur for John Sullivan, instead of him running up big taxi bills. 'He was a stocky guy, of about 5 foot 11, in his early forties, and he was a very nice, polite man,' says John. 'We got on quite well and one day I was talking to him about petrol being measured in gallons, not litres. Suddenly this mild-mannered man started effing and blinding and I was quite shaken. It was a real Jekyll and Hyde thing.

'By the time he dropped me off he was back to his old gentle self. I had my family over with me, and just before I flew home this American woman on the set asked me how I was getting to the airport. I said that this guy Charlie was going to be taking us. She asked me if I knew that Charlie had just come out of prison after sixteen years, after serving time for armed robbery, murder and something else. And this guy was going to be taking my family and me to the airport.

'When he dropped us off he was polite as hell. He came across as a really nice man and I gave him a ridiculously big tip because I thought if they had any problems on the set I might have to come back and Charlie would be waiting for me. It was like I gave him a protection money bung. I thought I ought to keep on the right side of him. He'd once asked me where I lived in England and I'd said it was a quiet little village with twelve shops and 200 horses and one policeman on a bike. He said, "It sounds like my kind of town," and it was only later I realised what he meant!'

John Challis and Sue Holderness had an easier time. 'We went out there for ten days but only did about four days' work,' John recalls. 'So we had a sort of holiday which was great because I'd never been there before.' It wasn't all fun and games, filming scenes in the Everglade swamps on airboats though, as John explains. 'We were being driven by a guy called Wayne who had a Confederate flag and a cowboy hat and fancied himself as a bit of a rebel. He was a complete lunatic and after we'd filmed our bit he sank one of the other boats by going too fast and swamping it with the wash from his boat. Fortunately there was no one on it because, if there had been, they might have been eaten by alligators which wouldn't be a very nice way to go!'

Sue Holderness nearly didn't make it back to England. She had decided to take a camcorder to film a memento of the production and on one occasion was taping Nick Lyndhurst and David Jason, who were filming a scene in the Everglades where an alligator was creeping up behind them and they'd leap up and run off.

I was so close to having my legs bitten off.

'I was filming this with my camcorder,' Sue recalls. 'And I'm hopeless with it and I lost this alligator out of my view-finder and I was trying to find it again. When I finally took the camera away from my eyes the alligator was heading straight for me. I hadn't seen it coming because I'd been looking through the camera. Luckily the trainer, who had great presence of mind and strength, grabbed hold of this alligator's tail and it stopped about 6 inches from my feet. I was so close to having my legs bitten off. It was very scary – but could have been a lot worse.'

Nick and David filmed the scene sitting on a log, with the 6-foot alligator less than 8 feet behind them. 'Some people think we shot it behind a glass screen but we didn't – we were genuinely just a few feet away from some big old jaws,' says Nick. 'We knew it was close because we could hear it breathing, but when it came to start filming it wouldn't do anything. It just sat there and then, when they needed it to react and move a bit, they got a ranger with a long stick to jab it in its private parts and of course then it snarled! But just in case it reacted too violently and went for us, precautions were taken.

'We had a guy off to my left with a rifle pointing at the alligator's head. And then in front of us, just to the side of the camera, was a ranger with a 44 magnum pointing just past us, again at its head. I said, "Quite honestly I'd rather have the 'gator than a gun 5 feet away waving at my head." I knew it wasn't pointing right at me but it wasn't far away!'

It was one of the bravest things I've ever seen…

The script also called for Del to fall into a swamp at one point, although when he wrote it John Sullivan had no idea that the scene would be shot in the real Everglades. 'We were pushed for time and David ended up filming it in alligator infested water,' John says. 'It was one of the bravest things I've ever seen because we had no idea what was underneath the surface and splashing in like he did would alert every alligator around. That took some guts.'

Back in the UK, with filming over, David Jason found out that that Christmas he would be competing against himself for ratings, with 'Miami Twice' up against his other hit *The Darling Buds of May,* on ITV. The *News of the World* reported that rival television executives were taking the unusual step of arranging that the two programmes didn't clash in the schedules. Vernon Lawrence, then entertainment chief at Yorkshire TV, makers of *The Darling Buds of May*, declared, 'It would be suicidal to screen both at the same time.'

The *Daily Express* later reported that the deal was personally brokered by David Jason. 'I was very fortunate to have been asked to do Christmas specials of two very popular shows,' he told the paper, 'so I asked if Mr ITV and Mr BBC could speak to each other. So that I, or the British public, was not put in an embarrassing position, could they make sure that the two specials were not going out against each other.'

The first part of 'Miami Twice' scooped the 1991 Christmas Eve TV top spot, and viewers switching on kettles after the show caused a massive 700-megawatt power surge on the National Grid. The critics had mixed views of the show. The *Sun*, as usual, offered solid support, with TV Editor Andy Coulson calling the two-parter 'a double delight'. He went on, '*Only Fools* would have missed the hysterical moment when Del Boy, complete with shades and Bermuda shorts, disappeared off towards Cuba on an out-of-control jet-ski.'

Garry Bushell, writing in the *Daily Star*, said the show started, 'Slower than Trigger on *Mastermind*' but went on to say that, 'Minor moans aside, the Trotters have been brightening up the festivities for a decade.' The *Independent* said, 'Instead, of exploring the potential embarrassments and excitements of Del Boy deploying his entrepreneurial skills in the Sun Belt, it lapsed into a preposterous and long-winded thriller yarn.'

Part one of the show was watched by 17.7 million viewers but part two slipped to 14.88 million. Nevertheless it was still the number one show in the Christmas Day ratings, beating the multi-million-pound film *Batman*. Unusually, though, the show was beaten to the overall Christmas ratings top spot by BBC 1's *Auntie's Bloomers*, fronted by Terry Wogan, which got 18.24 million viewers. *The Darling Buds of May*, in which David Jason starred as Pop Larkin, attracted 16.44 million viewers but was narrowly beaten to the ITV top spot by *Coronation Street*.

... And More

The New Year, however, brought bad news for *Fools* fans with *The Sun* reporting on 3 January, in a story headlined 'Game is up for Del Boy', that the show might have reached the end of the road. David Jason, the article said, was busy on other projects, and John Sullivan, then busy writing his sitcom *Sitting Pretty* and his wartime comedy drama *Over Here*, confirmed there were no plans for another series at that time and that remained the case.

Nevertheless, on 25 November filming began on a Christmas special, 'Mother Nature's Son', and even before it was finished bookies William Hill were giving odds of 13–8 on it coming first in the Christmas viewing stakes, with *Coronation Street* close behind at 9–4. Anyone who backed *Only Fools and Horses* would have been quids in when the show topped the Christmas ratings, scooping a colossal 20.13 million viewers, the highest ever at that time. The figure was more than double the 9 million which *The Darling Buds of May* attracted and more than 3 million ahead of its nearest rival, an episode of *Birds of a Feather*.

Unusually, the episode in which Del sees there's money to be made by selling mineral water was filmed not in Bristol but in Brighton, East Sussex. This was because a key part of the story involved the Trotters spending a weekend at the stunning Victorian Grand Hotel on the seafront, most famous for the 1984 bombing when the IRA tried to assassinate Prime Minister Margaret Thatcher.

The story also required the Trotters to clear up Grandad's old allotment so when Gareth Gwenlan spotted the ideal location on the Moulsecoomb Estate, Lower Bevendean, in Brighton, while filming a series of the BBC comedy *Waiting for God,* it made sense to shoot everything in the one area. Other locations were found, like the White Admiral Pub also in Lower Bevendean, which doubled as the exterior of the Nag's Head, and Swaine's Farm Shop in nearby Henfield which appeared as Rodney's friend Myles' shop. The poshest location was, of course, the Presidential

Above: The Trotters at Grandad's allotment in 'Mother Nature's Son', the episode in which Del sets up his own business flogging Peckham Spring Water.
Opposite top: A make-up artist checks that David Jason's hair is right before filming begins on location in Bristol.
Bottom: Filming the riot scene in 'Fatal Extraction'. Producer Gareth Gwenlan controlled 100 extras while on horseback playing the police chief.

Suite at the Grand Hotel and the total bill for filming there came to £2500.

Loyalty to the series has always been strong in Del's fictional stomping ground of South London, and in December 1993 a Peckham man was so sure he was on to a winner with it that he staked £2000 on that year's Christmas special 'Fatal Extraction' being the most watched Christmas Day show. Sadly, his hunch didn't pay off. His 2–1 on bet went down the drain, when the show was just marginally pipped to the number one ratings spot. It was beaten by a special Victor Meldrew story 'One Foot in the Algarve', written by David Renwick, who – like John Sullivan – had begun his comedy writing career on *The Two Ronnies*. 'One Foot' attracted 20 million viewers, to *Only Fools* 19.59 million.

Nevertheless 'Fatal Extraction' was a cracking episode which saw Del running into trouble when he asked out a blonde dental receptionist called Beverley, played by actress Mel Martin. Perhaps the most memorable scene, though, was the riot outside Nelson Mandela House, with the twist that many of the 100 people involved – both police and rioters – were wearing Del Boy's latest line in ski masks. The actors hired to play the rioters were all students from the famous Old Vic drama school in Bristol, among them Aled Jones, the ex-choirboy singer, who was studying there at the time.

The riot scene was filmed under strict controls, to make sure no one got hurt. However one extra, who played a policeman, later complained to a newspaper that the students had got carried away and had been too rough, a claim which producer Gareth Gwenlan dismisses. 'We did the first rehearsal and it was supposed to be a riot for Christ's sake, and I'd seen bigger upsets at the Women's Institute,' laughs Gareth. 'So we said to the drama students, "We don't want anyone being silly or getting hurt but we do want it to look a bit more realistic." That's what happened and no one got hurt.' And Gareth should know. After all, he was literally in

the thick of the action, as a riot policeman on horseback. Gareth, who is still a member of Equity from his days as an actor, played the cop, who temporarily broke up the riot to let Del, Raquel and Damien through, in Del's new car, a 'tasteful' Capri Ghia, by announcing over the megaphone, 'Hold it, hold it, hold it – it's Del Boy.'

'We couldn't find an actor who could ride,' he says. 'So I did it, and I was keeping a firm eye on what was going on, and they were having a bit of a go but nobody was injured at all. And we were well covered if anything had gone wrong because we had first aid there, ambulances, the police – even a helicopter! The whole thing was done very carefully. The students were bloody marvellous. They were

being real but within the bounds of being safe and no one was even bruised.'

After 'Fatal Extraction' was transmitted Gareth Gwenlan assumed that it would be the last episode of the series. David Jason was then under an eighteen-month contract with Yorkshire Television to make his hugely successful police drama *A Touch of Frost*, in which he played downbeat Detective Inspector Jack Frost. Nicholas Lyndhurst meanwhile became busy with his new series *Goodnight Sweetheart*, in which he plays TV repairman-turned-shopkeeper Gary Sparrow who finds himself able to switch between the present day and the 1940s and begins living a double life with women in both time zones.

But neither Gareth nor John Sullivan wanted the show to end without having rounded it off in a manner befitting Britain's favourite comedy series. Gareth recalls, 'Eventually I said to John, "It would be a shame if we just let it bleed away. Shouldn't we try to do just one final one?" He said he would be very happy to. We then had to find a time when both Nick and David were free and that had proved very difficult over the years as their careers had developed and they'd become increasingly busy. I spoke to Nick and he would have done it the following day. He would turn down almost anything to do it.'

In the spring of 1996 Gareth was busy working on the pilot episode of John Sullivan's new comedy drama *Roger, Roger,* based around the drivers working at Cresta Cabs minicab firm, when he learned that David Jason would have a two-month gap in his schedule in the autumn. He seized his moment and arranged for David, John Sullivan, director Tony Dow and himself to go out for dinner at upmarket restaurant The Greenhouse in London's Mayfair. Nick Lyndhurst was busy filming elsewhere and couldn't attend but Gareth already knew his view.

The four men ate, drank and talked about the show, and John Sullivan outlined a few ideas he had for rounding off the series. Several hours and a number of decent bottles of wine later, they agreed to make one last feature-length episode. 'I knew John wanted to tie it all up and he wanted the Trotters to become millionaires,' says David. 'That had always been his plan. There was talk of making a series but I couldn't because of my other commitments. Then, at the end of the dinner, John said to me, "What do you think?" And I just said, "Yeah, come on, let's go for it!"'

The following morning Gareth Gwenlan was straight on the phone to David's agent Meg Poole to confirm that he wanted to book him for two months. He discovered that she knew all about it, as David had called her even earlier to tell her what he'd agreed to do. He'd cleared his time even before mundane details like money had been discussed.

Gareth's second call was to his boss Geoffrey Perkins, the new Head of Comedy at BBC Television, just to check that they did actually want a final *Only Fools and Horses* story for Christmas '96. Of course they did, came the immediate response. John Sullivan, delighted and excited to be writing for Del and Rodney again, temporarily put aside his other projects and got down to work sketching out his storylines.

After a week he realised he was having trouble so he called Gareth Gwenlan. 'I can't do it in one episode,' he told him. 'I can see a two- or maybe even a three-parter coming on.' Gareth's immediate response was to wonder whether they could film three cracking episodes of *Only Fools and Horses* in the two months without rushing it and jeopardising the results. Not only that but he'd need to get an increase in his budget and check that his cast were happy with the extra work.

'I needn't have worried,' he says. 'Because by the time the scripts came through I'm sure they would have done six episodes had we had the time.' By July matters had been settled and it was decided to make three 50-minute episodes of the show, later extended to an hour each, to be filmed between October and early December, which would round off the series.

…*Lovely jubbly… Del's back on the telly.*

Word got out and the *Daily Mirror* announced the good news with the headline: 'Lovely jubbly…Del's back on the telly'. Details also emerged of the sacrifices both Nick Lyndhurst and David Jason had made so that the shows could be made. Nick had postponed a new series of *Goodnight Sweetheart* and David had turned down a lucrative offer from Yorkshire Television to film an extra episode of *A Touch of Frost*.

Location filming for the three episodes began in Bristol on the morning of Thursday 3 October 1996 and started with scenes showing Del and Rodney and Dr Singh outside Nelson Mandela House. Later filming would briefly move back to London for the scenes in Rodney's apocalyptic futuristic dream at the beginning of 'Heroes and Villains', which will remain among the most classic moments of the series. Del and Raquel are in their dotage, Rodney is a messenger boy, Cassandra a maid, Albert has been preserved for posterity and Damien is now the boss of the all-powerful global TIT Co, barking orders to US President Keanu Reeves and announcing that 'War is Good'. The scenes were shot at the Royal Horticultural Hall in London. Filming began at 6p.m. and went on right through the night, until 8a.m. the following morning. Damien was played by Tessa Peake-Jones' real-life partner, actor Douglas Hodge, best known for his roles in the TV series *Middlemarch* and *Capital City*.

'Tony Dow rang up and asked if Doug would like to do it and he was delighted because he's a huge fan of the programme and he thought it would be a great laugh to be in it,' says Tessa Peake-Jones. 'We didn't have any lines together, and if we had had then it would have been pretty weird. But it was a bit odd seeing him as part of the team, although he knew everyone anyway. He practised his David Jason impersonations at home the week before we filmed it, trying to be Derek Trotter, and I thought he was great, except that he has blue eyes and Damien has dark brown ones so Doug had to wear brown contact lenses.'

Filming the memorable Batman and Robin scene in 'Heroes and Villains' required David Jason and Nick Lyndhurst to make complete fools of themselves. 'You have to have a tremendous sense of fun and self-deprecation and you can't take yourself too seriously and do things like that,' grins David. 'You've got to be a bit daft in the head to do it. When I got the script I read it for a while, then I had to stop. I closed the page and laughed out loud. I had to put it down. I could see in my mind what John had written and it was priceless.'

Filming it, in the early hours of a cold November morning, was another matter. David recalls, 'Nick and I had to film it about six times because we couldn't do it for laughing. I'd be looking at him in all his gear and he'd be trying to say serious lines and I just found it very funny. He'd say, "What are you laughing at?" and I'd say, "Well you've got to see you from where I see you."'

The production team went to great lengths to make sure the press didn't get pictures of David and Nick as Batman and Robin and spoil the surprise. They kept their costumes covered up until the last minute, and when camera lenses were spotted the unit electricians dazzled them with powerful film lights. Finally one persistent photographer was encouraged to leave the area with a security guard with an impeccably trained Rottweiler.

Above: Director Tony Dow with the portrait of Lord Trotter from Rodney's futuristic dream sequence in 'Heroes and Villains'.
Below: Also from 'Heroes and Villains', Douglas Hodge as Rodney's nightmare – a war-mongering adult Damien.

Even so, one snapper did get pictures of David, Nick and Buster filming scenes from the final episode with the boys' new cars. Seeing the Rolls-Royce made some papers leap to the conclusion that the Trotters had won the lottery. Although they would have preferred nothing to have leaked, Gareth Gwenlan decided not to knock down the story, in the hope that the papers would then stop digging for the real storyline. 'We didn't feed the lottery idea to them,' he says. 'They said, "Is it this?" and we said, "Could be." We didn't deny it, nor did we agree with it, but we said it in such a way that made them feel that they were on to something. They printed it and it worked for us because after that everyone else gave up trying to find out what the plot was.'

After location filming was completed, the focus moved to London where the three episodes were to be recorded at BBC Television Centre in front of studio audiences over three nights from Thursday 14 November, with the final episode to be filmed on Friday 6 December.

One of the most poignant scenes ever in the series came in 'Modern Men', when Del engineers a lift breakdown in order to get Rodney talking about Cassandra's recent miscarriage. 'I wanted to go for the tears because I thought it would be realistic,' says Nick Lyndhurst. 'We only recorded the scene once because it worked right first time and that was the one that was used.'

There have been no fewer than five Damiens in the series. Newborn baby Patrick McManus in 'Three Men, a Woman and a Baby', Grant Stevens in 'Miami Twice', Robert Liddement in 'Mother Nature's Son' and Jamie Smith from 'Fatal Extraction' onwards. Douglas Hodge played him as an adult in 'Heroes and Villains'.

Goodbye?

'Awful' is how Nick Lyndhurst describes rehearsals for the studio recording of the final episode, 'Time On Our Hands'. 'We were at the BBC rehearsal rooms at a tower block in North Acton, which is somewhere where I grew up really, and I just couldn't imagine that this was going to be our last time there doing *Only Fools and Horses*,' says Nick.

'Rehearsals were very hard,' agrees David Jason. 'When I'd read the script at home it took me ages because, every time I tried to read it, it made me cry. I knew I couldn't do that in rehearsals and I needed to have more control, although everyone seemed to have tears in their eyes.'

The atmosphere in Studio Six was subdued, as preparations for the final recording of *Only Fools and Horses* went ahead. In the dressing rooms, emotions were already running high. Feelings of nervousness are commonplace before a performance in front of a live audience, although for the last episode it was to be filled almost exclusively by fans and friends and relatives of the cast, but this time it was different. This was to be the last episode and very much the end of an era.

A little before 6.45p.m. the studio audience began arriving and filling up the seats. At 7.15p.m. warm-up man Bobby Bragg came on and did his usual routine of being cheeky about the cast and crew and generally trying to make the audience feel at ease. That night his job was not a hard one. Everyone in the studio was delighted to be there and knew they were seeing television history in the making. He introduced the cast and a clearly moved David Jason said a few words to the audience before bounding off to prepare for his first scenes.

Cameras moved into position. The familiar theme tune rang out for the last time in a BBC studio and the lights came up on the set. The final recording was underway. A little over an hour later it was almost over. The recording had gone well. The audience had been in hysterics when Del, then Rodney fainted at Sotheby's. Then they'd almost cried with laughter as the Trotter boys screamed with excitement, as they sat in the van when the auction was over realising that they'd become multi-millionaires.

As the actors filmed the final Nag's Head scene, when all their friends and pub regulars clapped and cheered them, the props team and scene shifters cleared the flat set of everything except the carpets and Del's cocktail bar, in preparation for the last studio scene. For Nick Lyndhurst it was the final reminder that the show was at an end – and it wasn't a pleasant feeling. 'The flat was all lit up with full studio lighting, and seeing it stopped me in my tracks,' he says. 'It was really horrid. It was like seeing an old friend and thinking, "What have they done to you?" It was a shell. It didn't look like a flat any more. It looked like what it was – just a studio set. It was three walls propped up. It was very sad.

'The final scene of Del, Rodney and Albert walking off into the sunset had already been shot some weeks before in Bristol, so the scene in the flat was our last scene ever. As we did it, I was fighting so hard to try to stop the tears that my voicebox just dried up completely. My last line was: "We're not in business any more, mate" and I had trouble getting it out because I was so choked up and I ended up sounding like a woman.'

'I cried before I made my entrance,' admits Buster Merryfield. 'Then I wiped the tears away and went on. I was so moved and I really felt the lines I was saying.'

...I had to fight very hard all night to keep control.

David Jason, too, spent the whole night struggling with his emotions. 'Doing the final scene was so sad. It was the realisation that you'd actually done the last scene and said goodbye to them forever. I had to fight very hard all night to keep control,' he says. 'And when it was all over and the final credits went up I shed more than a tear or two.'

As the credits rolled, the audience thundered their applause and then did something that no one can remember happening before in a studio recording of any show. They took to their feet and gave the cast a standing ovation which lasted many minutes. 'I'd never seen it before and nor had anyone else,' says David Jason. 'It was very moving and it seemed to go on for ever. It rounded off one of the most unusual nights I've ever had and I'll never forget it.'

As the cheering died away and the studio audience trooped out, still chattering excitedly about what they'd seen, the crew began clearing the studio, ready for the following morning's edition of the kids' show *Live and Kicking*. The set was taken down and removed. The contents of the flat were boxed up and sent to the various warehouses from where they had been hired, and the costumes were taken away and hung up for the final time.

The action for the cast and crew moved upstairs to the Reception Suite on the sixth floor of Television Centre, where BBC Television boss Alan Yentob threw a party and

Del's father-in-law James (Michael Jayston) explains that he thinks the watch is valuable. After it was auctioned Del never again had to say, 'This time next year we'll be millionaires'.

thanked everyone for their efforts. Familiar faces from the show's history, like Ray Butt, Martin Shardlow and Jim Broadbent, had come up specially.

However, work wasn't yet over for John Sullivan, Gareth Gwenlan or Tony Dow. They still had to edit the show and get it ready for transmission three weeks later. 'When we were editing we knew we had something special,' Gareth recalls. 'But, then again John and I sat down on Christmas Eve to do a final sound edit. Everyone had been saying it was going to be the greatest thing ever. Ladbroke's were offering odds on it being the most-watched show at Christmas and the Beeb had gone overboard, saying, "This is the BBC's Christmas present to the nation."

'I turned to John and I said, "What happens if they don't like it?" and he said, "I've been thinking about that" and I said: "It's a possibility, isn't it?" We've all done shows in the past where you've been convinced that they are going to be OK and they've bombed. I said, "The only time that I'm going to

know is after about half an hour when it is going out tomorrow, when I'm sitting at home with friends and family."'

Half an hour into transmission the following day, Gareth picked up the phone and called John Sullivan. As he expected, he got the ansaphone, so he left a message. 'John, I'm telling you, it's OK!' he said.

It certainly was. 'Heroes and Villains' chalked up a staggering 21.3 million viewers and, amazingly, exactly the same figure was achieved by 'Modern Men'. But it was 'Time On Our Hands' that really took the biscuit, becoming the most-watched television programme in British history, bar none, with 24.3 million viewers.

It was a better send-off than anyone on the production could have dreamed of. For the next few days the programme dominated tabloid newspapers. The *Sun* kicked off, after the transmission of part one, with a front page splash headed 'Del-Namic Duo', announcing the huge ratings success. And after the last episode went out, the *Daily Mirror*,

☆ MISSING SCENE ☆

This scene comes from the final episode, 'Time On Our Hands', but was cut out at rehearsal stage because the episode was over-running. It wasn't actually filmed. It followed the post-auction scene at Boycie's showroom.

SCENE 3/21. TROTTER LOUNGE. INT STUDIO. (DAY 3). DAYLIGHT. PM.

RAQUEL, ALB AND CASSANDRA WAIT ANXIOUSLY FOR DEL AND ROD'S RETURN. ALB IS ON PHONE.

RAQ: (Checking her watch) Where the hell are they??

CASS: Perhaps they're in discussion with the directors at Sotheby's.

RAQUEL GIVES HER A WITHERING LOOK.

CASS: No, perhaps not.

RAQ: Maybe they're talking with the curator at the museum.

CASS: Maybe.

ALB: (On phone) Thanks a lot. (Replaces receiver) They're not at the Nag's Head.

CASS: I guessed Rodney wouldn't be in the Nag's Head, Albert.

RAQ: Has he stopped drinking?

CASS: No he's been barred.

WE HEAR THE FRONT DOOR CLOSE AND NOW DEL AND ROD ENTER. RAQ, CASS AND ALB LOOK AT THEM EXPEC-TANTLY – IS IT GOOD NEWS OR BAD NEWS? DEL AND ROD DON'T WANT TO JUST BLURT THE NEWS OUT AND CAUSE HEART ATTACKS AND SO WE HAVE A KIND OF MEXICAN STAND-OFF. FINALLY…

RAQ: Well?

DEL: Yeah, fine thanks.

RAQ: No! I meant, what happened?

ROD: Oh, at the auction?

CASS: Yes, at the auction! Did it sell?

ROD: Yeah, it sold, didn't it, Del?

DEL: Yes, we sold it.

ALB: I knew it. Beautiful piece of machinery… How much'd you get?

DEL: Guess.

RAQ: Oh come on, just tell us!

ROD: No, go on, guess.

ALB: Five thousand pounds?

DEL: No.

RAQUEL AND CASS'S SPIRITS VISIBLY SAG IN DISAPPOINTMENT.

ALB: Six thousand.

DEL: Close. Add a nought.

CASS: Sixty thousand pounds??

DEL: You can tell she works in a bank, can't you?

ROD: Hardly any hesitation… No, not sixty thousand. Add another nought.

ALB: But that's… what is that Cassandra?

CASS: Six hundred thousand pounds??

DEL: …No! …Will you tell 'em or shall I?

ROD: Erm… You can have the privilege, Derek.

DEL: Thank you, Rodney. You two girls hold on to your stays… Add one more nought.

RAQ, CASS AND ALBERT EXCHANGE DISBELIEVING GLANCES. CASSANDRA JUST STARES WIDE-EYED AT ROD. ROD RETURNS A GENTLE NOD. RAQUEL LOOKS AT DEL AND SHAKES HER HEAD. DEL SMILES AND NODS HIS HEAD. DEL HANDS THEM THE SOTHEBY'S PAPERWORK.

RAQ, CASS AND ALBERT READ THE PAPERWORK. THEY NOW LOOK UP AT DEL AND ROD.

DEL: (To Rod) Call intensive care.

RAQUEL STANDS

RAQ: Six million pounds???

DEL: Mmmh.

PAUSE. RAQUEL NOW BURSTS INTO TEARS, RUSHES TO COCKTAIL BAR FOR A TISSUE.

DEL: (To Rod) Told you she'd be happy.

ALB AND CASSANDRA SIT IN STUNNED SILENCE. WE NOW SEE DAMIEN STARING AT ROD. ROD REACTS. DAMIEN NOW SMILES AT ROD. ROD'S REACTION IS ONE OF 'DID DAMIEN TURN THIS THING ROUND FOR US?'

DEL: Now we've all gotta take things nice and easy – no going mad and splashing it around on anything that grabs our fan-cies. I know six million sounds a lot but it'll be very easy to blow it on silly luxuries.

RAQ: But we can go out in the week and look for a house, can't we?

DEL: Of course we can, Darling. Any day except Wednesday, that's when my Rolls-Royce is being delivered.

TYING UP LOOSE ENDS

John Sullivan's attention to detail is second to none. In the final episode Rodney finds the receipt confirming that the Harrison watch legally belongs to him and Del. Way back in the first scene of the first episode Del castigates Rodney for keeping receipts and records in case the tax man comes snooping. Of course, among the pile of receipts Rodney is leafing through is the one for the watch with the neat twist that they would have been millionaires back in 1981 if they'd known they were sitting on a priceless antique watch!

using a picture of Rodney and Del's emotional lift scene, ran the headlines 'Luvvly Blubbly' and 'Del of a Way to Go'.

By the end of January 1997 the clamour for more was deafening. Everyone on the production had had so much fun on the last three episodes that no one was prepared to keep saying that it was really over for good. Talk began of a special episode to celebrate the millennium. That remains only a possibility, not a probability, and nothing will be finalised until much closer to the time, if indeed ever.

The show's stars say they'd be willing to do one more. 'I think we could do it,' says David Jason. 'Mind you, Del and Albert will have identical zimmer frames before too long.' Nick Lyndhurst is certain John Sullivan could engineer a great script. 'If I know two characters who could lose £6 million, it's Del and Rodney. I'd love to do more.'

So, there it is. Will it ever return? Only fools would claim they knew for sure. Anything is possible with John Sullivan's writing. After all, this time next year those plonkers from Peckham might be millionaires no more!

THAT WATCH – THE TRUE STORY

Only Fools and Horses might be fiction but the story of the missing antique watch that enables the Trotters to become millionaires in the final episode is absolutely true.

The pocket-watch, the fabled H6 made by English inventor John Harrison, really is lost and anyone who found it would be in line for a Del Boy-style payout which could easily match the £6.2 million Del and Rodney got for it in the show. 'It's a real possibility that it's out there somewhere, so I'd advise people to have a root around for it,' says watch expert Jonathan Betts, of the National Maritime Museum at Greenwich.

'I don't like putting exact values on things but it would certainly be worth millions. The *Only Fools and Horses* team said to me, "If it sold for £6 million, would you be surprised?" and I said, "No, I can imagine the bidding getting very silly if two collectors at an auction really wanted it." It's totally unique. I'd be incredibly excited if it was found. I'd jump on the next plane to anywhere in the world to see it, if it turned up somewhere. Someone who found it, who, like Del Boy, could prove they owned it, would be an extremely wealthy person. It would be like winning the lottery.'

Back in the eighteenth century, sea captains found it almost impossible to plot their position out of sight of land until Pontefract-born horologist John Harrison invented the first accurate marine timekeeper to tell seafarers exactly where they were on the globe. His invention won him a £20,000 prize – a fortune in those days and equivalent to about £2 million in today's money – and he went on to make five more watches. The whereabouts of five of them are known but his last one – the lesser watch, as he called it – disappeared.

The designs for it are kept at the National Maritime Museum, but the watch itself has never been found and people have been searching for it for over 200 years. In the final episode of *Only Fools and Horses* Del's father-in-law James spots it among the junk in the Trotters' garage. It has been there for sixteen years, since Del bought it with a load of junk after a house clearance and left it there, thinking it was a Victorian egg timer. When it is sold at auction in the show it goes for £6.2 million, making Del and Rodney instant millionaires.

The *Only Fools and Horses* production team went to great lengths to make sure the story in the show was believable. They first approached the National Maritime Museum and asked them for help in identifying something that the Trotters could realistically find which would make them millionaires.

'It was all very mysterious and they kept the nature of the programme very secret at that time but their brief was to find an object that was extremely valuable but was known to exist, but which had been lost and could possibly be re-found,' explains Mr Betts, the Museum's Curator of Horology (the study of time-keeping and time-telling). 'They said it had to be worth millions rather than thousands, because it had to be something that would give Del Boy a real fortune. They were really determined to find something that actually could be found.'

They rejected one suggestion, a jewelled brooch that Nelson had worn in his hat, which would be worth millions, because it had belonged to the National Maritime Museum but had been stolen. 'So if Del Boy had found it, it would have had to be returned to us,' says Mr Betts. 'And he wouldn't have been able to keep the cash. Then they asked me if I could think of anything and it was then that I suggested the missing Harrison watch. I was very impressed by the way they used the information in the programme. They'd obviously listened carefully to what we told them.'

'Harrison dedicated his whole life to building these watches, because all the watches around at the time were hopelessly inaccurate. But he believed it would be possible to make a portable timekeeper that was accurate enough and he proved that it was. He made his first – H1 – in 1730. And for the next forty-five years he dedicated his life to improving and developing it, and his fourth one was the one that solved the problem and won the enormous prize of £20,000 and gained him worldwide fame.

'He had to make a fifth to prove it was possible to make others and to get his money, and he records that he made another smaller watch. We've got drawings of it but nobody knows quite what happened to it. We've got the first four watches here at the museum and the fifth is with the Worshipful Company of Clockmakers in London.'

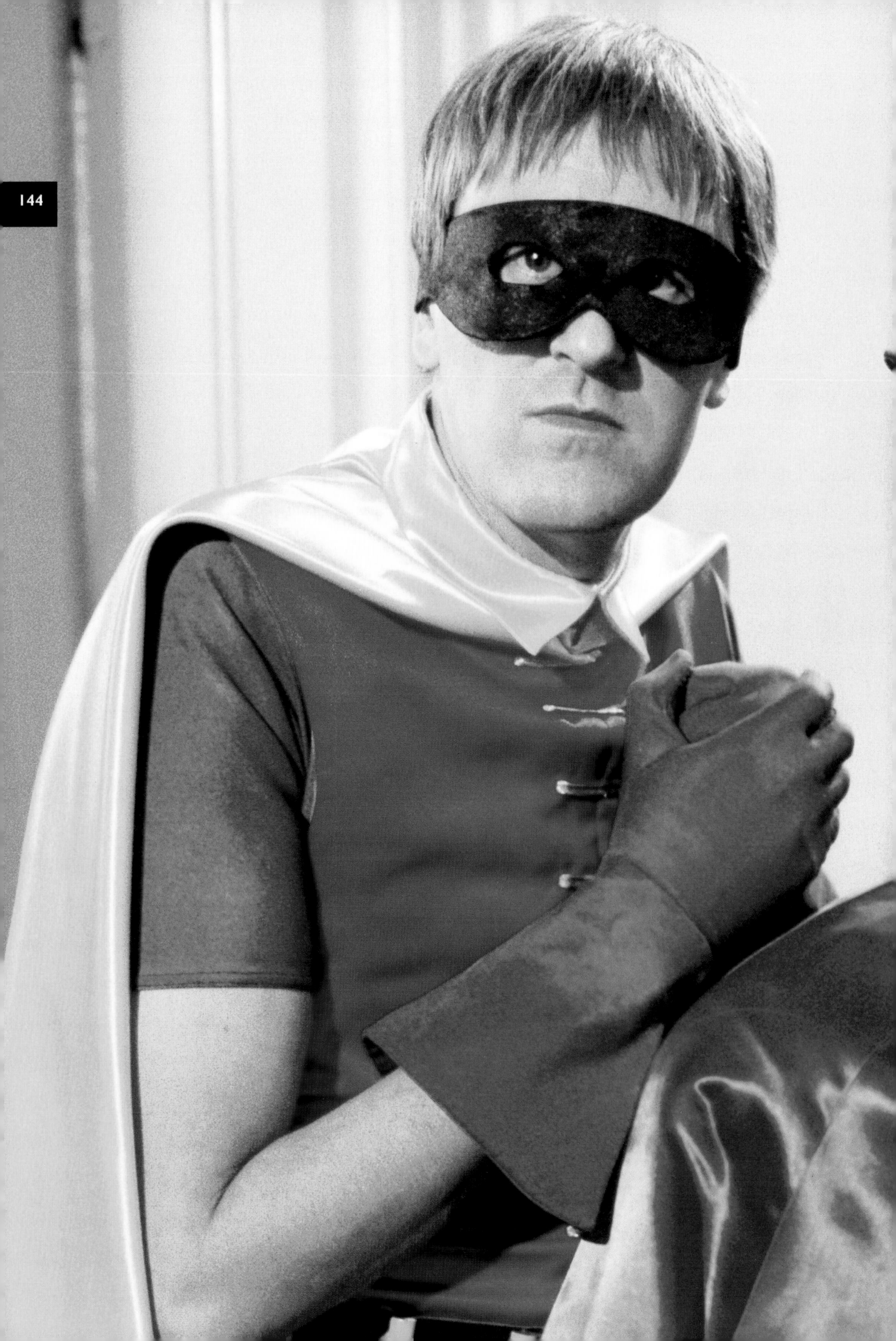

PART
4

Page 146

EPISODE
GUIDE

EPISODE GUIDE

REGULAR CAST

Del Trotter David Jason – all series
Rodney Trotter Nicholas Lyndhurst – all series
Grandad Trotter Lennard Pearce – series 1–3
Uncle Albert Buster Merryfield – series 4 onwards

KEY PRODUCTION TEAM

Producers: Ray Butt (1981–87); Gareth Gwenlan (1988–96)
Directors: Martin Shardlow (1981); Bernard Thompson ('Christmas Crackers'); Ray Butt (1982, 1983, 'Video Nasty', 'Who Wants to be a Millionaire', 'To Hull and Back', 'The Royal Flush', 'The Frog's Legacy'); Susan Belbin (1985); Mandie Fletcher (1986); Tony Dow (1988–96); Gareth Gwenlan ('Miami Twice', part one 'The American Dream').

SERIES ONE

Episode 1 **'Big Brother'**

After flogging one-legged turkeys from the back of a three-wheeled van, Del is confident he's on a winner at last with Trigger's consignment of Old English vinyl briefcases. At the same time his brother Rodney is thinking of abandoning the high-flying world of trading for a real job.

Cast *Joyce the barmaid* Peta Bernard, *Trigger* Roger Lloyd Pack
Transmitted Tuesday 8 September 1981 at 8.30p.m.
Viewing figures 9.2 million
Running time 30 minutes

Episode 2 **'Go West Young Man'**

Del enters the second-hand car market with a lethal vehicle that quite literally goes like a bomb. After a night on the town the boys are on their way home in a borrowed sports car when they run into the buyer of Del's old banger.

Cast *Boycie* John Challis, *Aussie Man* Nick Stringer, *Waiter* Barry Wilmore, *Nicky* Jo-Anne Good, *Michelle* Caroline Ellis
Transmitted Tuesday 15 September 1981 at 8.30p.m.
Viewing figures 6.1 million
Running time 30 minutes
Music 'Ain't No Stopping Us Now' performed by Enigma

Episode 3 **'Cash and Curry'**

Del is swooping in on the deal of a lifetime – which could keep them all in pilau rice forever. All he has to do is get hold of £2,000 to buy a priceless Indian relic. But he hasn't reckoned on a touch of gang warfare.

Cast *Mr Ram* Renu Setna, *Vimmal* Malik Armhed Khalil, *Indian restaurant manager* Babar Bhatti
Transmitted Tuesday 22 September 1981 at 8.30p.m.
Viewing figures 7.3 million
Running time 30 minutes
Music 'Money' performed by Pink Floyd from album *Dark Side Of The Moon*

Episode 4 **'The Second Time Around'**

When Del's old flame, and Achilles' heel, Pauline Harris returns from America the flames of passion are quickly rekindled. Pauline moves in with the Peckham trio, but Rodney and Grandad are on hand to make sure the course of true love runs anything but smooth and save Del.

The Trotter brothers as they appeared in the first series.

Cast *Trigger* Roger Lloyd Pack, *Joyce the barmaid* Peta Bernard, *Pauline* Jill Baker, *Auntie Rose* Beryl Cooke
Transmitted Tuesday 29 September 1981 at 8.30p.m.
Viewing figures 7.8 million
Running time 30 minutes

Episode 5 'A Slow Bus To Chingford'

What a great deal – a night-watchman in exchange for the use of an open-topped touring bus! So begins Trotter's Ethnic Tours of Chingford and Croydon. No one turns up, but Grandad displays the family genius for making money.

Cast *Janice* Gaynor Ward
Transmitted Tuesday 6 October 1981 at 8.30p.m.
Viewing figures 7 million
Running time 30 minutes
Music 'Layback' – Rock Spectrum

Episode 6 'The Russians Are Coming'

Another lucky deal makes Del the proud owner of three tons of lead. The information sheet reveals it is a self-assembly nuclear fallout shelter. Del is persuaded that the real value lies not only in the metal but in the protection the shelter offers – just in case World War 3 breaks out.

Cast *Eric the policeman* Derek Newark
Transmitted Tuesday 13 October 1981 at 8.30p.m.
Viewing figures 8.8 million
Running time 30 minutes

☆ CHRISTMAS SPECIAL 'Christmas Crackers'

The season of good cheer is upon the family but Del and Rodney are dreading the gastronomic experience of Christmas lunch, as cooked by Grandad. In desperation they decide to go to the Monte Carlo Club in search of a 'sacré blue chef' after Grandad goes to his old folks do.

Cast *Earl* Desmond McNamara, *Anita* Nora Connolly
Transmitted Monday 28 December 1981 at 9.55p.m.
Viewing figures 7.5 million
Running time 35 minutes
Music 'Three Times A Lady' performed by Brotherhood of Man, 'Daddy's Home' performed by Cliff Richard, 'Shakin' All Over' performed by Cliff Richard, 'Wordy Rappinghood' performed by Tom Tom Club, 'Christmas Wrapping' performed by The Waitresses, 'Bright Eyes' performed by Brotherhood of Man

SERIES TWO

Episode 1 'The Long Legs of the Law'

Rodney has the Trotter household in a panic when he announces that his hot date is a woman in uniform – a police uniform! He invites her back to the flat for a drink, then discovers to his horror that even the drink has been illegally procured.

Cast *Sid* Roy Heather, *Sandra* Kate Saunders
Transmitted Thursday 21 October 1982 at 8.30p.m.
Viewing figures 7.7 million
Running time 30 minutes

Episode 2 'Ashes to Ashes'

Trigger's grandmother has died, so the Trotter family offer their support by agreeing to sell off some of her old possessions, including a pair of precious urns. The trouble starts when they notice that the urns contain the ashes of Trig's grandfather. Del's idea of a final resting place is outrageous.

Cast *Trigger* Roger Lloyd Pack, *River policeman* John D. Collins, *Council cleansing lorry driver* Terry Duggan
Transmitted Thursday 28 October 1982 at 8.30p.m.
Viewing figures 9.8 million
Running time 30 minutes

Episode 3 'A Losing Streak'

Del can't even win a few pounds with a flip of his double-headed coin. But when Boycie challenges him, not to mention his pride, to a winner-takes-all poker match, he wages everything he owns to stay in the game. It's crook against crook in this match of the century.

Cast *Trigger* Roger Lloyd Pack, *Boycie* John Challis, *pub customer* Michael G. Jones
Transmitted Thursday 4 November 1982 at 8.30p.m.
Viewing figures 7.5 million
Running time 30 minutes

Episode 4 'No Greater Love'

Rodney has lost his heart to a not-so-young woman and with her on his arm he thinks he's man enough to stand up to her violent jailbird husband who is about to be released. But Del is ready to ship them both to the far ends of the earth.

Cast *Irene* Gaye Brown, *Julie the barmaid* Julie La Rousse, *Marcus* Steve Fletcher, *Ahmed* Raj Patel, *Leroy* David Rhule, *Tommy Mackay* David Daker, *Zoe* Lisa Price
Transmitted Thursday 11 November 1982 at 8.30p.m.
Viewing figures 8.6 million
Running time 30 minutes

The stakes are high when Del and Boycie have a game of poker that could cost them dear in 'A Losing Streak'. Pictured are David Jason, Roger Lloyd Pack, Lennard Pearce and John Challis.

Episode 5 'The Yellow Peril'

Del has done his good deeds for the day. He's arranged for Rodney to paint the kitchen of a Chinese takeaway, and then decides to do a little paint job of his own...sprucing up their mother's tombstone. But how could he know that the stolen paint was luminous?

Cast *Mr Chin the Chinese takeaway owner* Rex Wei, *Trigger* Roger Lloyd Pack
Transmitted Thursday 18 November 1982 at 8.30p.m.
Viewing figures 8.2 million
Running time 30 minutes

Episode 6 'It Never Rains...'

It's holiday time as the Trotters head for Spain but while Del and Rodney are soaking up the sun, Grandad is hiding away in the hotel room in a peculiar sort of mood. At first the boys dismiss his behaviour as a reaction to too much squid. But bit by bit, the real cause is revealed with a shocking revelation.

Cast *Alex the travel agent* Jim McManus, *French girl* Anne Bruzac, *English girl* Jillianne Foot, *Englishman* Michael Attwell, *Spanish guard* Anthony Jackson
Transmitted Thursday 25 November 1982 at 8.30p.m.
Viewing figures 9.5 million
Running time 30 minutes
Music 'In The Summertime' performed by Mungo Jerry

Episode 7 'A Touch of Glass'

Del rubs shoulders with the high and haughty only to find that they are giving him the cold one. It's only when he presents some of his recently 'acquired' porcelain do they find him useful...as a chandelier cleaner!

Cast *Lady Ridgemere* Elizabeth Benson, *Wallace the butler* Donald Bisset, *Lord Ridgemere* Geoffrey Toone
Transmitted Thursday 2 December 1982 at 8.30p.m.
Viewing figures 10.2 million
Running time 30 minutes

☆ CHRISTMAS SPECIAL
'The Funny Side of Christmas: Christmas Trees'

Del's latest line, telescopic Christmas trees, aren't selling well. So he tells Rodney to take one and deliver it to the local church. However Del's gesture isn't quite as benevolent as it first appears and Rodney is furious when he finds his brother selling them as 'The only Christmas tree used and recommended by the Church of England itself.'

Cast *Vicar* John Pennington, *Sid* Roy Heather
Transmitted Monday 27 December 1982 at 8.05p.m.
Viewing figures 7.2 million
Running time 8 minutes

☆ CHRISTMAS SPECIAL
'Diamonds Are For Heather'

There's nothing like a heart-wrenching tune played late in the evening to kindle a romance between strangers. Del catches the eye of the lovely Heather after a moving rendition of Old Shep at a Spanish Night at the Nag's Head and suddenly it's love. It looks like she might just become the future Mrs Trotter. That is, until her husband shows up!

Cast *Enrico* John Moreno, *Heather* Rosalind Lloyd, *Brian* Roger Brierley, *Waiter in the Indian restaurant* Dev Sagoo
Transmitted Thursday 30 December 1982 at 7.55p.m.
Viewing figures 9.3 million
Running time 30 minutes
Music 'Zoom' performed by Fat Larry's Band

Left: Del (David Jason) chats-up an English girl (Jillianne Foot) while on holiday in Spain in 'It Never Rains...' but she doesn't quite understand his French.
Opposite, top: David Jackson as Irish painter and decorator, Brendan, in 'Who's a Pretty Boy?'
Opposite, bottom: Rodney goes on the run in 'Wanted' – and runs as far as the top of Nelson Mandela House.

SERIES THREE

Episode 1 'Homesick'

Lugging the shopping up those twelve flights of stairs is proving too much for Grandad. The doctor recommends a new council bungalow for the Trotter dynasty. Over to Rodney, the new chairman of the Housing Committee.

Cast *Baz* Ron Pember, *Trigger* Roger Lloyd Pack, *1st old lady* Gilly Flower, *2nd old lady* Renee Roberts, *Doctor* John Bryans, *Miss Mackenzie* Sandra Payne, *Small boy* Miles Rinaldi
Transmitted Thursday 10 November 1983 at 8.30p.m.
Viewing figures 9.4 million
Running time 30 minutes

Episode 2 'Healthy Competition'

Rodney's decided to go it alone and leave Peckham's own multinational conglomerate – Trotters Independent Traders. By the end of the week he's already cornered the market in used lawn mower engines and with Mickey Pearce as his Financial Director, the sky's the limit...

Cast *Auctioneer* Glynn Sweet, *Mickey Pearce* Patrick Murray, *Harry the foreman* Rex Robinson, *Indian waiter* Dev Sagoo, *Young Towser* Mike Carnell
Transmitted Thursday 17 November 1983 at 8.30p.m.
Viewing figures 9.7 million
Music Theme from *Jaws* by John Williams

Episode 3 'Friday the 14th'

Del, Rodney and Grandad are bound for Cornwall to Boycie's weekend cottage and a spot of salmon poaching. It should be a relaxing weekend if they can forget about the mad-axe-salmon-fisherman-killer who's just escaped from the local institute, that is...

Cast *Policeman on moorland road* Ray Mort, *Gamekeeper Tom Witton* Bill Ward, *Chief of security/madman* Christopher Malcolm, *Police sergeant* Michael Stainton
Transmitted Thursday 24 November 1983 at 8.30p.m.
Viewing figures 9.7 million
Running time 30 minutes

Episode 4 'Yesterday Never Comes'

Del's into art dealing in a big way, especially when it involves a 'posh tart' like the glamorous Miranda. Has she really been wooed by his tequila sunsets or are her motives rather more mercenary...

Cast *Mrs Murphy* Lucita Lijertwood, *Miranda Davenport* Juliet Hammond, *Harry the furniture restorer* Robert Vahey, *Auctioneer* Garard Green
Transmitted Thursday 1 December 1983 at 8.30p.m.
Viewing figures 10.6 million
Running time 30 minutes

Episode 5 'May The Force Be With You'

A ripple of panic runs through the Nag's Head. Del's old school enemy, Slater, is back in town, hell bent on revenge and now brandishing a police warrant card.

Cast *Trigger* Roger Lloyd Pack, *Detective Inspector Roy Slater* Jim Broadbent, *Boycie* John Challis, *PC Hoskins* Christopher Mitchell, *Karen the barmaid* Michele Winstanley
Transmitted Thursday 8 December 1983 at 8.30p.m.
Viewing figures 10.7 million
Running time 30 minutes

Episode 6 'Wanted'

Watch out! The Peckham Pouncer's about! Alias Rodney Trotter…? Surely there must be some mistake? Try telling that to Rodders, London's most wanted criminal…

Cast *Mickey Pearce* Patrick Murray, *Blossom* Toni Palmer, *Trigger* Roger Lloyd Pack, *Boycie* John Challis, *Karen the barmaid* Michele Winstanley
Transmitted Thursday 15 December 1983 at 8.30p.m.
Viewing figures 11.2 million
Running time 30 minutes
Music 'Funky Moog' – Disco Happening

Episode 7 'Who's a Pretty Boy?'

Del decides he can make a fast buck by persuading his old friend Denzil to let him, Grandad and Rodney decorate his flat in preference to Brendan, the Irish painter. Denzil's wife is far from keen on the idea and leaves clear instructions for them to stay out of her kitchen. They don't, of course, and mistakes will always happen with the Trotters around. But what are they going to do about Corinne's canary…?

Cast *Brendan* David Jackson, *Karen the barmaid* Michele Winstanley, *Denzil* Paul Barber, *Corinne* Eva Mottley, *Louis the pet shop owner* Anthony Morton, *Mike Fisher, Nag's Head landlord* Kenneth MacDonald
Transmitted Thursday 22 December 1983 at 8.30p.m.
Viewing figures 11.9 million
Running time 30 minutes
Music 'High Fly' – Contemporary Orchestra

☆ CHRISTMAS SPECIAL 'Thicker Than Water'

It might be the season of goodwill to all men, but to Del that doesn't extend to Rodney and his long-lost father Reg when he comes back to the fold after 18 years – especially when Reg Trotter starts casting doubt on Del's parentage.

Cast *Reg Trotter* Peter Woodthorpe, *Karen the barmaid* Michele Winstanley
Transmitted Sunday 25 December 1983 at 9.35p.m.
Viewing figures 10.8 million
Running time 30 minutes
Music From the film *Sleepless Nights*

SERIES FOUR

Episode 1 'Happy Returns'

Rodney's in love with Debbie from the newsagents. Could this mean the end of his dirty magazine fetish? Trouble is, she's only 19 and 19.5 years ago Del was pretty friendly with her mum June…

Cast *June* Diane Langton, *Trigger* Roger Lloyd Pack, *Mickey Pearce* Patrick Murray, *Debby* Oona Kirsch, *Maureen* Nula Conwell, *Old lady in newsagents* Lala Lloyd, *Jason* Ben Davis
Transmitted Thursday 21 February 1985 at 8.00p.m.
Viewing figures 15.2 million
Running time 30 minutes

Episode 2 'Strained Relations'

Grandad's funeral brings relations from as far away as North London, including Uncle Albert whose intentions leave Del feeling 'like a turkey who's just caught Bernard Matthews grinning at him.'

Cast *Trigger* Roger Lloyd Pack, *Boycie* John Challis, *Mike* Kenneth MacDonald, *Vicar* John Pennington, *Cousin Jean* Maureen Sweeney, *Cousin Stan* Mike Kemp, *Old Lady* Lala Lloyd, *Maureen* Nula Conwell
Transmitted Thursday 28 February 1985 at 8.00p.m.
Viewing figures 14.9 million
Running time 30 minutes

Episode 3 'Hole in One'

Rodney's none-too-shrewd investment in suntan oil during 'the worst winter in two million years' demands emergency measures and Uncle Albert decides that it is time to display his only talent – that of falling down holes without any real injury.

Cast *Solly* Colin Jeavons, *Mike* Kenneth MacDonald, *Judge* Dennis Ramsden, *Mr Gerrard* Andrew Tourell, *Mr Fraser* James Woolley, *Maureen* Nula Conwell, *Cockney man* Michael Roberts, *Clerk* Les Rawlings
Transmitted Thursday 7 March 1985 at 8.00pm
Viewing figures 13.4 million
Running time 30 minutes

Episode 4 'It's Only Rock and Roll'

Instead of the Albert 'all, Rodney's pop group were heading for 'sod all' until Del discovers their commercial potential. As usual, it doesn't quite work out as they'd like…

Cast *Policeman* Geoffrey Leesley, *Mental*

Mickey Daniel Peacock, *Charlie* Marcus Francis, *Stew* David Thewlis, *DJ* Mike Read
Transmitted Thursday 14 March 1985 at 8.00p.m.
Viewing figures 13.6 million
Running time 30 minutes
Music 'Diane' performed by The Bachelors, 'Toot the Shoot' performed by Shakatak, 'Drivin' Hard, Boys Will Be Boys' performed by Daniel Peacock – written by John Sullivan

Episode 5 'Sleeping Dogs Lie'

Del is on to a great new money-making scheme – looking after Boycie and Marlene's new puppy Duke for a steal at £60 a week should be a doddle, a bit of the old Pedigree Chum and they should be away. Then Dukie falls victim to salmonella poisoning.

Cast *Boycie* John Challis, *Marlene* Sue Holderness, *Dog owner* Linda Barr, *Receptionist* Debbie Blyth, *Vet* John D. Collins, *Doctor* Brian Jameson
Transmitted Thursday 21 March 1985 at 8.00p.m.
Viewing figures 18.7 million
Running time 30 minutes

Episode 6 'Watching the Girls Go By'

Rodders is desperate to find a woman for a party at the Nag's Head. Nothing new? This time he's got a bet on with Mickey and Del's gonna make sure he wins…

Cast *Trigger* Roger Lloyd Pack, *Mike* Kenneth MacDonald, *Maureen* Nula Conwell, *Mickey Pearce* Patrick Murray, *Yvonne* Carolyn Allen
Transmitted Thursday 28 March 1985 at 8.00p.m.
Viewing figures 14.4 million
Running time 30 minutes

Episode 7 'As One Door Closes'

When the bottom falls out of louvre doors, times get hard for the Trotters. But nature will find a way as Del and Rodders go butterfly collecting…

Cast *Denzil* Paul Barber
Transmitted Thursday 4 April 1985 at 8.00p.m.
Viewing figures 14.2 million
Running time 30 minutes

Opposite: Del (David Jason) with old flame June (Diane Langton) in 'Happy Returns'. Below: Rodney (Nicholas Lyndhurst) thinks he's got a new girlfriend (Carolyn Allen) in 'Watching the Girls Go By'.

Episode 1 'From Prussia With Love'

When a German damsel turns up in the Nag's Head she's definitely in distress – and nine months pregnant at that. Rodney's all beer and sympathy but Del's got an idea – could this be the answer to Boycie and Marlene's dreams of a child and a golden opportunity to make a few bob along the way?

Cast *Boycie* John Challis, *Marlene* Sue Holderness, *Mike* Kenneth MacDonald, *Anna the German girl* Erika Hoffman, *Maureen* Nula Conwell, *Baby* Michael Peters
Transmitted Sunday 31 August 1986 at 8.35p.m.
Viewing figures 12.1 million
Running time 30 minutes
Music 'I Didn't Mean To Turn You On' performed by Robert Palmer, 'Lady In Red' performed by Chris de Burgh

Episode 2 'The Miracle of Peckham'

Del reckons he's discovered a miracle. The statue of the Virgin Mary at the local church has been spotted weeping. Del soon has the cream of the world's media paying to film the event – and, of course, it's nothing at all to do with a leaky church roof…

Cast *Father O'Keith* P. G. Stephens, *Biffo* John Pierce Jones, *Australian reporter* Peter Wickham, *American reporter* Carol Cleveland, *Man in the church* James Richardson
Transmitted Sunday 7 September 1986 at 8.35p.m.
Viewing figures 14.2 million
Running time 30 minutes

Episode 3 'The Longest Night'

A robber makes a raid on the local supermarket just as Del and family are out doing their weekly shopping. What's worse – Del sold him a duff watch down the market and it's that that's got them into trouble in the first place.

Cast *Tom, the security officer* John Bardon, *Mr Peterson the store manager* Max Harvey, *Lennox* Vas Blackwood, *Woman in kiosk* Jeanne Mockford, *Checkout girl* Catherine Clarke
Transmitted Sunday 14 September 1986 at 8.35p.m.
Viewing figures 16.7 million
Running time 30 minutes

☆ CHRISTMAS SPECIAL 'To Hull and Back'

Del is reluctant to get involved with Boycie and Abdul's diamond smuggling scheme until he's offered £15,000 for his trouble. He then ropes Rodney and Uncle Albert into the enterprise that will either leave them rich or in jail. They end up taking to the high seas in a dodgy old boat and sailing over to Holland with old sea dog Albert at the helm. They get back to England exhausted only to find that Del's adversary Chief Inspector Slater seems to be on to them in a big way.

Cast *Smuggler* Jane Thompson, *Mike* Kenneth MacDonald, *Vicky* Kim Clifford, *Teddy* Johnny Wade, *Ruby* Annie Leake, *Boycie* John Challis, *Abdul* Tony Anholt, *Trigger* Roger Lloyd Pack, *Denzil* Paul Barber, *Slater* Jim Broadbent, *Hoskins* Christopher Mitchell, *Sid* Roy Heather, *Colin* Mark Burdis, *PC Parker* Jeff Stevenson, *Bridge attendant* Alan Hulse, *Lil* Rachel Bell, *Boatman* Joe Belcher, *Gas rigger* David Fleeshman, *Van Kleefe* Philip Bond, *Hussein* Lorence Ferdinand
Transmitted Wednesday 25 December 1985 at 7.30p.m.
Viewing figures 16.9 million
Running time 90 minutes

Top: The Trotters in the middle of an armed raid when Lennox (Vas Blackwood) tries to hold up the supermarket in 'The Longest Night'. Above: Andy (Mark Colleano), Lisa (Gerry Cowper) and Rodney (Nicholas Lyndhurst) watch as Del disappears into the distance on a hang-glider in 'Tea for Three'.

Episode 4 **'Tea for Three'**

Look out! Del's tampered with the sunbed controls and Rodney's seeing red – literally! His face is done to a turn. He'll hardly wow Trigger's lovely niece, Lisa, with his handsome good looks now which leaves the way pretty clear for Del himself. But revenge should certainly be sweet when he volunteers Del for a spot of hang-gliding…

Cast *Trigger* Roger Lloyd Pack, *Mike* Kenneth MacDonald, *Lisa* Gerry Cowper, *Andy* Mark Colleano, *Pianist* Fred Tomlinson, *Singer* Joan Baxter, *Drummer* Derek Price, *Stuntman/Double* Ken Barker, *Stuntman* Graham Walker

Location Hang-gliding scenes filmed at Butser Hill near Petersfield, Hampshire
Transmitted Sunday 21 September 1986 at 8.35p.m.
Viewing figures 16.5 million
Running time 30 minutes
Music 'I Who Have Nothing' performed by Joan Baxter

Episode 5 **'Video Nasty'**

Rodney has gained a grant from the council to make a community film and Del soon sees its earning potential. Mickey Pearce on the other hand sees the chance to make a far more dodgy type of movie.

Cast *Trigger* Roger Lloyd Pack, *Mike* Kenneth MacDonald, *Boycie* John Challis, *Marlene* Sue Holderness, *Mickey Pearce* Patrick Murray, *Amanda* Dawn Perlman, *Vicar* Rex Robinson, *Chinese takeaway owner* Chua Kahjoo
Transmitted Sunday 28 September 1986 at 8.35p.m.
Viewing figures 17.5 million
Running time 30 minutes
Music 'West End Girls' performed by The Pet Shop Boys, 'Red Sky' performed by Status Quo, 'Avalon' performed by Brian Ferry and Roxy Music

Episode 6 **'Who Wants to be a Millionaire'**

Del's old pal Jumbo Mills is back with tales of his booming business in Australia. What's more he wants Del to go back down under with him as his partner in the enterprise. Could Del really leave Peckham for good?

Cast *Mike* Kenneth MacDonald, *Boycie* John Challis, *Jumbo Mills* Nick Stringer
Transmitted Sunday 5 October 1986 at 8.35p.m.
Viewing figures 18.8 million
Running time 30 minutes

☆ CHRISTMAS SPECIAL 1986 **'A Royal Flush'**

Del decides a visit to the opera is the perfect opportunity for Rodders to impress his new 'friend', the daughter of the Duke of Malebury. However, munching a packet of crisps through the duet and whistling along to the aria is more Peckham Astoria than Covent Garden. So when she invites him to a shooting weekend, he hardly needs Del to arrive with a borrowed sawn-off shotgun.

Cast *Man in market* Paul McDowell, *Vicky* Sarah Duncan, *Trigger* Roger Lloyd Pack, *Policeman* Andy Readman, *Sid* Roy Heather, *Dosser* Robert Vahey, *Eric* Geoffrey Wilkinson, *Ticket collector* Alan Cody, *Programme seller* Christina Michaels, *June* Diane Langton, *Man at opera* Robin Hereford, *Lady at opera* Richenda Carey, *St Johns ambulance man* Gordon Salkilld, *Mr Dow* Roger Davidson, *Henry* Jack Headley, *Charles* Peter Tuddenham, *Patterson* Arnold Peters, *Carter* Ifor Gwynne-Davies, *Mrs Miles* Kate Williams, *Lady at dinner* Daphne Goddard, *Giles* Stephen Riddle
Locations include Scenes at the Duke of Malebury's stately home were filmed at Clarendon Park, Wiltshire, however neither the house nor the grounds are open to the public
Transmitted Thursday 25 December 1986 at 7.05p.m.
Viewing figures 18.8 million
Running time 80 minutes
Music 'Ask' performed by The Smiths, 'Sometimes' performed by Erasure, 'Handel's Overture for the Royal Fireworks', extracts from Bizet's *Carmen* performed by Kent Opera

☆ CHRISTMAS SPECIAL 1987 **'The Frog's Legacy'**

At the wedding of Trigger's niece his Aunt Renee tells Del and Rodney about their mum's old friend Freddie The Frog. Rodney wants to know why this charming villain left his ill-gotten gains to the Trotters and why everyone notes his resemblance to him. Del is more interested in what happened to his hoard of gold bullion.

Cast *Boycie* John Challis, *Trigger* Roger Lloyd Pack, *Mr Jahan* Adam Hussein, *Vicar* Angus Mackay, *Auntie Renee* Joan Sims, *Mike* Kenneth MacDonald, *Marlene* Sue Holderness, *Andy* Mark Colleano, *Lisa* Gerry

Episode 1 'Yuppy Love'

'80s fever is spreading fast! Del's on the up and up into the exciting world of red braces and yuppy shirts. Armed with his filofax and briefcase he's ready to take on the City — well Peckham, anyway. Meanwhile Rodney's on the pull, with a classy new girlfriend called Cassandra. But what will she think of Nelson Mandela House?

Cast *Trigger* Roger Lloyd Pack, *Cassandra* Gwyneth Strong, *Micky Pearce* Patrick Murray, *Jevon* Steven Woodcock, *Emma* Francesca Brill, *Marsha* Laura Jackson, *Dale* Diana Katis, *Snobby girl* Hazel McBride, *Barman* William Thomas, *Girl in disco* Tracey Clarke
Transmitted Sunday 8 January 1989 at 7.15p.m.
Viewing figures 13.9 million
Running time 50 minutes
Music 'Love Goes Up And Down' performed by Errol Brown, 'Enchanted Lady' performed by The Passadenas, 'Lady In Red' performed by Chris de Burgh

Episode 2 'Danger UXD'

Just faking a signature on a delivery note means that Del can take possession of 50 dolls for absolutely nothing. The only problem is that 'Lusty Linda' and 'Erotic Estelle' are not exactly what he had in mind and would seem more appropriate to Dirty Barry's dubious trade rather than the local toyshop...

Cast *Cassandra* Gwyneth Strong, *Mike* Kenneth MacDonald, *Denzil* Paul Barber, *Barry* Walter Sparrow, *Boycie* John Challis,

Cowper, *Man in market* Duncan Faber, *Woman in market* Angela Moran
Transmitted Friday 25 December 1987 at 6.25p.m.
Viewing figures 14.5 million
Running time 60 minutes
Music 'Never Gonna Give You Up' performed by Rick Astley, 'FLM' performed by Mel and Kim, 'Faith' performed by George Michael, 'Wake Me Up Before You Go' performed by Wham, 'So Macho' and 'Toy Boy' performed by Sinitta, 'Smoke Gets In Your Eyes' performed by Brian Ferry

☆ CHRISTMAS SPECIAL 1988 'Dates'

When Del sees the sort of girl Trigger meets through a new computer dating agency he decides it's worth giving it a try and through them he meets budding actress Raquel. Rodney meanwhile is out to impress Nag's Head barmaid Nerys by acting tough. Del's romance is progressing smoothly and all is well until Albert's birthday bash is interrupted by a couple in naval uniform.

Cast *Boycie* John Challis, *Mike* Kenneth MacDonald, *Trigger* Roger Lloyd Pack, *Marlene* Sue Holderness, *Raquel* Tessa Peake-Jones, *Micky Pearce* Patrick Murray, *Jevon* Steven Woodcock, *Chris* Tony Marshall,

Above: Del Boy waits for his computer date under the clock at Waterloo Station in 'Dates'. The episode introduced Tessa Peake-Jones as Raquel.
Right: The new trendy yuppified Del Boy with Rodney in 'Yuppy Love'. Del caught 80s fever in a big way.

Nerys Andree Bernard, *Technomatch agent* Christopher Stanton, *Sonia* Jean Warren, *Charles* Nicholas Courtney, *Policeman* Paul Beringer, *Policewoman* Margaret Norris, *Sid* Roy Heather, *Naval officer* Martin Cochrane, *Mrs Sansom* Jean Challis, *Stunt arranger* Colin Skeaping, *Stunt performers* Graeme Crowther, Nick Gillard, Paul Heasman, Alan Stuart, Tip Tipping, Chris Webb, Tina Maskell
Locations include Del and Raquel met under the clock at Waterloo Station, London. The Trotter van was seen being chased by yobs and 'flying' over the bridge (with the aid of a ramp) at Talbot Road, Isleworth
Transmitted Sunday 25 December 1988 at 5.05p.m.
Viewing figures 16.6 million
Running time 80 minutes
Music 'Burning Bridges' performed by Status Quo, 'Nothing Can Come Between Us', 'Clean Heart' and 'Haunt Me' performed by Sade, 'Smokey Blues' performed by Aswad, 'Sad Song' performed by the Christians

Trigger Roger Lloyd Pack, *Waiter* Paul Cooper, *Adrian* Michael Shallard, *Chinese takeaway owner* Takashi Kawahara, *TV presenter* David Warwick, *Clayton* Tommy Buson
Transmitted Sunday 15 January 1989 at 7.15p.m.
Viewing figures 16.1 million
Running time 50 minutes
Music 'Come Out To Play' performed by UB40, 'Stop' performed by Erasure, 'Tribute (Right on)' performed by The Pasadenas, 'Fisherman's Blues' performed by The Waterboys, 'Is You Is Or Is You Isn't My Baby' and 'Jack You're Dead' performed by Joe Jackson

Episode 3 **'Chain Gang'**

Faced with the opportunity of buying 250 18-carat gold chains from a retired jeweller, Arnie, Del just can't resist. Hastily, a multi-million-dollar business consortium is formed – well, Mike from the Nag's Head, Trig, Boycie, Uncle Albert and a reluctant Rodney, anyway. Everything is fine until Arnie is taken ill just as the deal is about to be sealed and Del is left feeling that all that glitters...

Cast *Cassandra* Gwyneth Strong, *Mike* Kenneth MacDonald, *Denzil* Paul Barber, *Arnie* Philip McGough, *Boycie* John Challis, *Trigger* Roger Lloyd Pack, *Otto* Mick Oliver, *Grayson* Peter Rutherford, *Mario* Frank Coda, *Woman in crowd* Marie Lorraine, *Steven* Sam Howard, *Gary* Steve Fortune
Locations include Tandoori Nights Indian restaurant in Kings Road, Hammersmith played itself in the scene where jewellery dealer Arnie fakes a heart attack
Transmitted Sunday 22 January 1989 at 7.15p.m.
Viewing figures 16.3 million
Running time 50 minutes
Music 'My One Temptation' performed by Mica Paris, 'Sweet Little Mystery' performed by Wet Wet Wet

Episode 4 **'The Unlucky Winner is...'**

Rodney has won a holiday for three in the Mediterranean courtesy of Del and Megaflakes drawing competition. The only snag is he's got to pretend he's fourteen years old all week. Should be a doddle – all he's got to do is keep his head down. Then the skateboarding and breakdancing competitions begin.

Cast *Cassandra* Gwyneth Strong, *Mike* Kenneth MacDonald, *Mr Perkins* Michael Fenton Stevens, *Carmen* Gina Bellman, *Trudy* Lusha Kellgren
Transmitted Sunday 29 January 1989 at 7.15p.m.
Viewing figures 17 million
Running time 50 minutes

Music 'That Ole Devil Called Love' performed by Alison Moyet, 'Why Does Love Got To Be So Sad' performed by Buckwheat Zydeco, 'Strange Kind Of love' performed by Love and Money, 'Love Train' performed by Holly Johnson, 'Lucy' performed by Habit, 'Hold Me In Your Arms' performed by Rick Astley, 'Birdie Song' performed by The Tweets, 'Y Viva Espagna' performed by Sylvia

Episode 5 **'Sickness and Wealth'**

While excruciating stomach cramps and a constant diet of health salts might drive some people to visit a doctor, but not Del. Oh no, he knows he's only suffering from that scourge of all serious yuppies, PMA – Positive Mental Attitude! In the end he pays the doctor a visit and the news is not good...

Cast *Cassandra* Gwyneth Strong, *Boycie* John Challis, *Mike* Kenneth MacDonald, *Trigger* Roger Lloyd Pack, *Marlene* Sue Holderness, *Mickey* Patrick Murray, *Jevon* Steven Woodcock, *Nerys* Andree Bernard, *Elsie Partridge* Constance Chapman, *Dr Shaheed* Josephine Welcome, *Dr Meadows* Ewan Stuart, *Nurse* Ann Bryson
Transmitted Sunday 5 February 1989 at 7.15p.m.
Viewing figures 18.2 million
Running time 50 minutes
Music 'Where Is Your Love?' performed by Gail Ann Dorsey, 'I Don't Want A Lover' performed by Texas, 'Fine Time' performed by Yazz, 'Big Area' performed by Then Jericho, 'It's Only Love' performed by Simply Red

Episode 6 **'Little Problems'**

With his diploma in computer science, new job in Cassandra's father's firm and impending marriage, Rodney's certainly on the up. Del's even promised to take care of his share of the flat deposit. Only problem is, Del's gone and got himself in a bit of bother over some hooky mobile phones with the less than understanding Driscoll brothers and unless he comes up with £2000 sharpish, they're going to take care of him...

Cast *Cassandra* Gwyneth Strong, *Boycie* John Challis, *Trigger* Roger Lloyd Pack, *Mike* Kenneth MacDonald, *Marlene* Sue Holderness, *Mickey* Patrick Murray, *Jevon* Steven Woodcock, *Danny Driscoll* Roy Marsden, *Tony Driscoll* Christopher Ryan, *Alan Parry* Denis Lill, *Pamela Parry* Wanda Ventham, *Comedian* Jeff Stevenson himself, *Registrar* Derek Benfield
Transmitted Sunday 12 February 1989 at 7.15p.m.
Viewing figures 18.9 million
Running time 50 minutes
Music 'Only Want To Be With You' per-

formed by Sam Fox, 'Tender Hands' performed by Chris de Burgh, 'Love Follows' performed by Steven Dante, 'Tracie' performed by Level 42, 'Looking For Linda' performed by Hue and Cry, 'Bring Me Some Water' performed by Melissa Etheridge, 'Buffalo Stance' performed by Neneh Cherry, 'Something's Got Hold Of My Heart' performed by Marc Almond and Gene Pitney, 'Where Is The Love' performed by Mica Paris and Will Downing, 'Holding Back The Years' performed by Simply Red

☆ CHRISTMAS SPECIAL 1989 **'The Jolly Boys' Outing'**

Del has organised the annual Jolly Boys' Outing to Margate. A fun day out is marred when their coach blows up. The lads can't get a train home because there's a strike on and most of the guest houses in Margate are chocker. The gang split up and the Trotters end up at the spooky Villa Bella and Rodney and Albert have to share a bed. Del and his brother decide to head into town where Del meets an old flame.

Cast *Cassandra* Gwyneth Strong, *Boycie* John Challis, *Mike* Kenneth MacDonald, *Trigger* Roger Lloyd Pack, *Denzil* Paul Barber, *Marlene* Sue Holderness, *Raquel* Tessa Peake-Jones, *Mickey* Patrick Murray, *Jevon* Stephen Woodcock, *Sid* Roy Heather, *Alan* Denis Lill, *Pamela* Wanda Ventham, *Stephen*

Daniel Hill, *Joanne* Gail Harrison, *Trainee* Jake Wood, *Harry* Roy Evans, *Mrs Baker* Katharine Page, *Helen* Dawn Funnell, *Mrs Creswell* Rosalind Knight, *Inga* Bridget Erin Bates, *Ramondo* Robin Driscoll, *Policeman* Del Baker, *Singer* Lee Gibson, *Drummer* Alf Bigden, *Bass player* Dave Richmond, *Organist* Ronnie Price, *Eddie* Steve Alder

Locations include The forecourt of Margate Station played itself as did Benbom Brothers Theme Park in Margate. The pub where the boys stop for a pint was The Roman Galley, Thanet Way, Canterbury. The market scenes were filmed at Ramsgate Greyhound Stadium
Transmitted Monday 25 December 1989 at 4.05p.m.
Viewing figures 20.1 million
Running time 85 minutes
Music 'Night Nurse' performed by Gregory Isaacs, 'Now That We've Found Love' performed by Third World, 'Over You' performed by Roxy Music, 'Everybody Wants To Rule The World' performed by Tears for Fears, 'Help' performed by Bananarama, '2.4.6.8. Motorway' performed by Tom Robinson Band, 'This Changing Light' performed by Deacon Blue, 'Turn It Up' performed by Simply Red, 'Everybody's Talkin'' performed by Harry Nilsson, 'Move On Out' performed by Simply Red, 'Just The Way You Are' performed by Lee Gibson, 'I May Be Wrong' and 'Sunshine of My Life'' performed by Alf Bigden, Ronnie Price and Dave Richmond

Above: *Rodney becomes a fully fledged member of the 'Groovy Gang' and goes skateboarding in 'The Unlucky Winner is…'*
Left: *Del, Rodney and Albert find that there is no room at the inn in Margate – except, that is, at the spooky-looking Villa Bella, whilst Jevon (Steven Woodcock), Mickey (Patrick Murray) and Denzil (Paul Barber) have better luck in 'The Jolly Boys' Outing'.*

☆ CHRISTMAS SPECIAL 1990
'Rodney Come Home'

Rodney has gone up in the world and has landed a job at Cassandra's Dad's printing firm. Albert has taken over Rodney's old job as Del's look-out and is helping Del sell some dodgy talking dolls. Rodney and Cassandra aren't getting on well and Del decides to help heal the rift but only succeeds in making it worse. Things are looking good for Del though as Raquel has moved into the flat.

Cast Cassandra Gwyneth Strong, *Raquel* Tessa Peake-Jones, *Mickey* Patrick Murray,

Alan Denis Lill, *Michelle* Paula Anna Bland, *Frank* Philip Blaine, *Chris* Tony Marshall, *Woman in club* Jean Harrington, *Neighbour* Linda James, *TV announcer* Patrick Lunt
Locations include The nightclub was the Parkside Nightclub, Bath Road, Bristol. Scenes at Alan Parry's printing firm were filmed at Gemini Graphics and Print Ltd, York Street, Bristol. The shopping precinct where Del tries to sell his dodgy dolls was the Broadwalk Shopping Centre in Knowle
Transmitted Tuesday 25 December 1990 at 5.10p.m.
Viewing figures 18 million
Running time 75 minutes
Music 'Reckless Man, Born To Be King' performed by Magnum, 'Let Me Be' performed by Feargal Sharkey, 'True' performed by Spandau Ballet, 'Fascinating Rhythm' performed by Bassomatic, 'Don't Be A Fool' performed by Loose Ends, 'This Is The Right Time' performed by Lisa Stanfield, 'Rebel Yell' performed by Billy Idol, 'Did I Happen To Mention' and 'Your Lovely Face' performed by Julia Fordham, 'Somebody Who Loves You' performed by Joan Armatrading

SERIES SEVEN

Episode 1 'The Sky's the Limit'

Boycie's new satellite dish has been stolen and he asks Del to try to buy it back from whoever has nicked it. It doesn't take Del long to find it and he thinks he's in line for a few quid from Boycie. What he doesn't realise is that the satellite dish on his balcony isn't Boycie's one at all and that it is the main cause of the chaos at Heathrow Airport which has resulted in Cassandra's flight being diverted and Rodney's romantic plans ruined.

Cast *Raquel* Tessa Peake-Jones, *Alan* Denis Lill, *Boycie* John Challis, *Mike* Kenneth MacDonald, *Trigger* Roger Lloyd Pack, *Marlene* Sue Holderness, *Bronco* Ron Aldridge, *Henry* Gordon Warnecke, *Stewardess* Lucy Hancock, *Newsreader* Richard Whitmore, *Baby Tyler* Elliot Russell
Locations include Airport scenes were filmed at Stansted Airport
Transmitted Sunday 30 December 1990 at 7.15p.m.
Viewing figures 15 million
Running time 50 minutes
Music 'Float On' performed by The Floaters, 'Opposites Attract' and 'Straight Up' performed by Paula Abdul, 'Reckless Man' performed by Magnum

Del's latest bargain, a satellite dish, isn't such a good deal after all. It's actually come from the main runway at Heathrow Airport and planes are homing in on Nelson Mandela House in 'The Sky's the Limit'.

Episode 2 'The Chance of a Lunchtime'

Del dreams of shifting a thousand 'National Anthem' musical doorbells. Raquel's audition sets her dreaming of stardom. While she gets the chance to join the world of cravats and codpieces, Rodders loses his job in true plonker style. But Raquel might have to wait that bit longer for fame – just when Del was thinking that the best thing in life is a door bell that plays 'Long Live Swaziland' his greatest dream comes true.

Cast *Raquel* Tessa Peake-Jones, *Cassandra* Gwyneth Strong, *Alan* Denis Lill, *Boycie* John Challis, *Mike* Kenneth MacDonald, *Trigger* Roger Lloyd Pack, *Marlene* Sue Holderness, *Man in the pub* Ian Barritt, *Trudy* Helen Blizard, *Jules* Paul Opacic, *Adrian* Ian Redford, *Baby Tyler* Elliot Russell
Locations include The restaurant used for Raquel's meeting with a theatre producer was actually Henry Africa's Hothouse, Whiteladies Road, Bristol. The floating restaurant where Rodney and Cassandra went for dinner was called Shoots and was moored at Cannons Road and is now located at Hotwell Road, Bristol
Transmitted Sunday 6 January 1991 at 7.15p.m.
Viewing figures 16.6 million
Running time 50 minutes
Music 'All Around The World' performed by Lisa Stansfield, 'Promised Land' performed by Style Council, 'Do The Strand' performed by Roxy Music, 'Love And Affection' performed by Joan Armatrading, 'Old Friends' performed by Guitar Moods, 'Where Are You Baby' performed by Betty Boo, 'Eyes Without A Face' performed by Billy Idol, 'Masquerade' performed by Swing Out Sister

Episode 3 'Stage Fright'

With Raquel pregnant, Del's plan to achieve millionaire status must move up a gear. So the chance to supply the cabaret at the Starlight Rooms for an old 'friend' Eric to the tune of 600 quid is too good to miss. With Raquel dusting off her vocal cords in the kitchen and Trig's mate Tony the singer dustman, waiting in the wings, everything's sorted. Until Del discovers who really owns the club and the extent of Tony's vocal range.

Cast *Raquel* Tessa Peake-Jones, *Boycie* John Challis, *Mike* Kenneth MacDonald, *Trigger* Roger Lloyd Pack, *First woman* Lyn Langridge, *Eric* Trevor Byfield, *Eugene* Roger Blake, *Tony Angelino* Philip Pope
Locations include Scenes at The Down on the Riverside Club were filmed at a club called The Studio which was demolished in 1988. Raquel's audition took place at The Courage Social Club at Willway Road, Bedminster, Bristol
Transmitted Sunday 13 January 1991 at 7.15p.m.

Philip Pope in 'Stage Fright'.
Opposite: Boycie (John Challis) and Marlene (Sue Holderness) take to the water on an airboat in the Florida Everglades in 'Miami Twice – Oh to be in England'.

Viewing figures 16.6 million
Running time 50 minutes
Music 'Peace Through The World' performed by Maxi Priest, 'Love Is The Drug' performed by Roxy Music, 'Kick It In' performed by Simple Minds, 'Looking Out For Linda' performed by Hue and Cry, and, of course, 'Delilah' and 'I'll Never Fall In Love Again' sung by Philip Pope as Tony Angelino, 'Do You Know The Way To San Jose' sung by Tessa Peake-Jones as Raquel and their duet 'Crying'

Episode 4 'The Class of '62'

A Dockside Secondary Modern class of '62 reunion in the Nag's Head signals Roy Slater's return to Civvy Street after years in the 'Nick'. But why has this crooked ex copper decided to come back to Peckham when he is universally loathed? Just as Trig, Del, Boycie and Denzil begin to believe that he really has changed for the better, Del discovers the real reason for his return…

Cast *Raquel* Tessa Peake-Jones, *Boycie* John Challis, *Trigger* Roger Lloyd Pack, *Mike* Kenneth MacDonald, *Denzil* Paul Barber, *Roy Slater* Jim Broadbent
Transmitted Sunday 20 January 1991 at 7.15p.m.
Viewing figures 16.2 million
Running time 50 minutes
Music 'Never Enough' performed by The Cure, 'People' performed by Soul II Soul, 'Mighty Quinn' performed by Manfred Mann, 'All Around The World' performed by Lisa Stansfield, 'Valentine's Day' performed by Betty Boo

Episode 5 'He Ain't Heavy, He's My Uncle'

Albert is pumping iron and looking like a born-again Teddy Boy, while Rodders' drinking bouts leave him looking like one of the living dead. Del attempts to pamper the pregnant Raquel by buying a bargain banger from Boycie and takes on the unemployable Rodney as Director of Commercial Development. As Rodney gets to his first project – washing the car – Albert gets mugged on his way home from the over-60s club.

Cast *Raquel* Tessa Peake-Jones, *Boycie* John Challis, *Trigger* Roger Lloyd Pack, *Marlene* Sue Holderness, *Mike* Kenneth MacDonald, *Dora* Joan Geary, *Knock Knock* Howard Goorney, *Mechanic* Herb Johnson, *Ollie* Tony London
Locations include The scenes of Del and Rodney looking for Albert were shot at Tower Bridge, HMS *Belfast*, Portobello Green, Acklam Road East, Malton Road and Portobello Road Market, London
Transmitted Sunday 27 January 1991 at 7.15p.m.
Viewing figures 17.2 million
Running time 50 minutes
Music 'Uncle Albert' performed by Paul and Linda McCartney

Episode 6 'Three Men, a Woman and a Baby'

Del's about to become a father but even that can't cheer Rodney the vegetarian up. The polar cap is melting, the rain forest is dying, the sea is being poisoned, and he hasn't had a 'bit for months'. Not even one of Del's new ponytail wigs could enhance his image in Cassandra's eyes…

Cast *Raquel* Tessa Peake-Jones, *Cassandra* Gwyneth Strong, *Trigger* Roger Lloyd Pack, *Mike* Kenneth MacDonald, *Midwife* Ken Drury, *Sister* Constance Lamb
Locations include The hospital was the West Middlesex Hospital, Hillingdon
Transmitted Sunday 3 February 1991 at 7.15p.m.

Viewing figures 18.9 million
Running time 50 minutes
Music 'Movies' performed by Hothouse Flowers, 'You Don't Have To Say You Love Me' performed by Dusty Springfield, 'Street Life' performed by Roxy Music, 'Nothing Compares To You' performed by Sinead O'Connor, 'Concerto in D Major' by Vivaldi on *Classical Music Volume 1*

☆ CHRISTMAS SPECIAL 1991 'Miami Twice'
Part one: 'The American Dream'

It's time for Damien's christening and the chance for his godparents Rodney and Cassandra to get together. Their marriage is still having problems and they are only seeing each other at weekends when Rodney gets an unexpected windfall. Del kindly uses the money to book two non-refundable tickets to Miami for Rodney and Cassandra. The trouble is she can't go. Step forward a volunteer to take her place – Del Boy.

Cast *Raquel* Tessa Peake-Jones, *Cassandra* Gwyneth Strong, *Alan* Denis Lill, *Pam* Wanda Ventham, *Mickey* Patrick Murray, *Vicar* Treva Etienne, *Trigger* Roger Lloyd Pack, *Boycie* John Challis, *Marlene* Sue Holderness, *Mike* Kenneth MacDonald, *Denzil* Paul Barber, *Sid* Roy Heather, *Baby Tyler* Danny Rix, *Baby Damien* Grant Stevens, *Richard Branson* himself
Locations include The interior of the church was St John's Church, Ladbroke Grove and the exterior was St John's Church, Kentish Town
Transmitted Tuesday 24 December 1991 at 7.30 p.m.
Viewing figures 17.7 million
Running time 50 minutes
Music 'Every Heartbeat' performed by Amy Grant, 'Hot Summer Salsa' performed by Jive Bunny and the Mastermixers, 'Englishman In New York' performed by Sting, 'White Wedding' performed by Billy Idol, 'Cold, Cold Heart' performed by Midge Ure, 'Let There Be Love' performed by Simple Minds

'Miami Twice'
Part two: 'Oh to be in England'

Over in Florida, Del can't quite get his head around the idea that they drive on the other side of the road and nearly kills Rodney and himself in the dilapidated camper van they've hired. They then run into trouble when the local Mafia see Del and realise he's a dead-ringer for their boss, Don Occhetti, who is in big trouble with the law. They see the answer to all their prayers in Del but the trouble is he'll have to be shot in order to help them.

Cast *Raquel* Tessa Peake-Jones, *Cassandra* Gwyneth Strong, *Boycie* John Challis, *Marlene* Sue Holderness, *Trigger* Roger Lloyd Pack, *Mike* Kenneth MacDonald, *Alan* Denis Lill, *Mickey Pearce* Patrick Murray, *Denzil* Paul Barber, *Sid* Roy Heather, *Baby Damien* Grant Stevens, *Vicar* Treva Etienne, *Barry Gibb* himself
Transmitted Wednesday 25 December 1991 at 3.10p.m.
Viewing figures 14.9 million
Running time 95 minutes
Music 'Rockin' All Over The World' performed by Status Quo, 'Summer In The City' performed by The Gutter Brothers, 'Baby Baby' performed by Amy Grant, 'Hyperreal' performed by The Shamen, 'Killer' performed by Seal, 'Rush Rush' performed by Paula Abdul, 'Saltwater' performed by Julian Lennon, 'Born Free' performed by Vic Reeves

☆ CHRISTMAS SPECIAL 1992 'Mother Nature's Son'

When Del finds out just how much bottles of mineral water sell for he decides to 'discover' his own spring on Grandad's old allotment. It's not long before business is booming in Peckham Spring Water and the Trotters have money rolling in. But how long will it be before anyone realises that it's only really tap water? Not long when there's a chemical leak in the local reservoir.

Cast *Raquel* Tessa Peake-Jones, *Cassandra* Gwyneth Strong, *Denzil* Paul Barber, *Boycie* John Challis, *Myles* Robert Glenister, *Marlene* Sue Holderness, *Mike* Kenneth MacDonald, *Trigger* Roger Lloyd Pack, *Alan Parry* Denis Lill, *Chris* Tony Marshall, *Mickey Pearce* Patrick Murray, *Pam Parry* Wanda Ventham, *Damien* Robert Liddement, *Newscaster* Richard Whitmore, *Diver* Luke Brannigan, *Stunt arranger/performer* Michael Potter
Locations include The exterior of the Nag's Head was the White Admiral Pub, Lower Bevendean, Brighton. Allotment scenes were filmed off Natal Road, Lower Bevendean
Transmitted Friday 25 December 1992 at 6.55p.m.
Viewing figures 20.1 million
Running time 65 minutes
Music 'Merry Christmas Everybody' per-

formed by Slade, 'Crocodile Rock' performed by Elton John, 'Who's Gonna Ride Your Wild Horses' performed by U2, 'Could It Be Magic' performed by Take That, 'Santa Claus Is Coming To Town' performed by Bjorn Again, 'Money' performed by The Beatles

☆ CHRISTMAS SPECIAL 1993
'Fatal Extraction'

Del has gone back to his old ways of drinking, gambling and staying out late. Raquel leaves him taking Damien with her and on the rebound Del fixes up a date with Beverley, his dentist's receptionist. He soon realises his mistake and stands her up at the last minute. When he's back with Raquel, he becomes convinced that Beverley is following him...

Cast *Raquel* Tessa Peake-Jones, *Cassandra* Gwyneth Strong, *Boycie* John Challis, *Trigger* Roger Lloyd Pack, *Mike* Kenneth MacDonald, *Denzil* Paul Barber, *Sid* Roy Heather, *Mickey* Patrick Murray, *Damien* Jamie Smith, *Beverley* Mel Martin, *The Dentist* Andrew Charleson, *Lady on the bus* Kitty Scopes, *Arthur* Derek Martin, *Mick* Nick Maloney, *Vi* Lyn Langridge, *Policeman* Linford Brown, *Texo* Bryan Brittain, *Casino waitress* Lorraine Parsloe
Transmitted Saturday 25 December 1993 at 6.05p.m.
Viewing figures 19.6 million
Running time 85 minutes
Music 'Hands Up' performed by Right Said Fred, 'Step Into Christmas' performed by Elton John, 'Hope In A Hopeless World' performed by Paul Young, 'One Voice' performed by Barry Manilow, 'Whisper A Prayer' performed by Mica Paris, 'It's Alright' performed by East 17, 'Twist and Shout' performed by Chaka Demus and Pliers, 'Babe' performed by Take That, 'Stay (Faraway, So Close)' performed by U2, 'Mars, the Bringer of War' by Gustav Holst

☆ CHRISTMAS TRILOGY 1996
1 'Heroes and Villains'

Del's home improvement grant is rejected and Rodney is on a sex programme that would leave Roger Rabbit knackered in attempts for Cassandra to conceive. But there's always the fancy dress party to cheer them up and while dressed as the caped crusaders the pair inadvertently become street vigilantes and find that for once being on the right side of the law has positive advantages.

Cast *Raquel* Tessa Peake-Jones, *Cassandra* Gwyneth Strong, *Boycie* John Challis, *Trigger* Roger Lloyd Pack, *Mike* Kenneth MacDonald, *Marlene* Sue Holderness, *Denzil* Paul Barber, *Sid* Roy Heather, *Councillor Murray* Angela Bruce, *Old Damien* Douglas Hodge, *Damien* Jamie Smith, *Kenny* Steve

An unusual picture of Tessa Peake-Jones as a much older Raquel in 'Heroes and Villains'.

Weston, *Gary* Scott Marshall, *Scott* Dan Clark, *Kevin* Fuman Dar, *Dawn* Sheree Murphy, *Old lady* Bay White, *Mayor* Robin Meredith, *Photographer* Richard Hicks, *Market lads* Lee Barritt and Leonard Kirby
Transmitted Wednesday 25 December 1996 at 9.00p.m.
Viewing figures 21.3 million
Running time 60 minutes
Music 'Sight For Sore Eyes' performed by M People, 'I Got You Babe' performed by UB40 with Chrissie Hynde, 'Knocking On Heaven's Door' performed by The Children of Dunblane, 'Coming Home Now' performed by Boyzone, '2 Become 1' performed by The Spice Girls

2 'Modern Men'

Del's been reading the new man's guide to the 21st century but Raquel hasn't noticed any improvement. Meanwhile the Trotters'

finances hit an all-time low and Dr Singh is after Del's blood. Rodney and Cassandra face heart-ache when she loses the baby she's carrying. Rodney won't talk about how he feels and it falls to Del to get him to open up.

Cast *Raquel* Tessa Peake-Jones, *Cassandra* Gwyneth Strong, *Trigger* Roger Lloyd Pack, *Mike* Kenneth MacDonald, *Boycie* John Challis, *Marlene* Sue Holderness, *Denzil* Paul Barber, *Sid* Roy Heather, *Dr Singh* Bhasker Patel, *Damien* Jamie Smith, *Mickey Pearce* Patrick Murray, *Man in hospital* Phil Cornwell, *Sister* Beverley Hills, *Doctor* James Oliver, *Nurse* Corrine Britton, *Receptionist* Lorraine Ashley
Transmitted Friday 27 December 1996 at 8.00p.m.
Viewing figures 21.3 million
Running time 60 minutes
Music 'Roll With It' performed by Oasis, 'Light Of My Life' performed by Louise, 'Love Me For A Reason' performed by Boyzone, 'Country House' performed by Blur

3 'Time On Our Hands'

Raquel is nervous about her parents coming to dinner and Albert doesn't help matters by mixing up the coffee and the gravy granules. The following day Raquel's Dad James spots an old watch in amongst the junk in Del's garage which he thinks might be worth a few bob. He's absolutely right and the antique timepiece goes for more money than even Del has dreamed of. This time he really is a millionaire.

Cast *Raquel* Tessa Peake-Jones, *Cassandra* Gwyneth Strong, *Mike* Kenneth MacDonald, *Trigger* Roger Lloyd Pack, *Marlene* Sue Holderness, *Denzil* Paul Barber, *Mickey Pearce* Patrick Murray, *Damien* Jamie Smith, *James* Michael Jayston, *Audrey* Ann Lynn, *Auctioneer* Seymour Matthews, *Tony* Jotham Annan
Locations include Sotheby's, 34-35 New Bond Street, London
Transmitted Sunday 29 December 1996 at 8.00p.m.
Viewing figures 24.3 million
Running time 60 minutes
Music 'Take Me In To Your Heart Again' performed by Vince Hill, 'Together' performed by Boyzone, 'Under The Moon Of Love' and 'I Wonder Why' performed by Showaddywaddy, 'Our House' performed by Crosby, Stills, Nash and Young

'Comic Relief Special'

Del and Rodney are at the flat and talk directly to viewers about why they should support Comic Relief.

Transmitted Friday 14 March 1997 at 7.40p.m.
Viewing figures 10.6 million

PICTURE CREDITS

BBC Books would like to thank the following for providing photographs and for permission to reproduce copyright material. While every effort has been made to trace and acknowledge all copyright holders, we would like to apologise should there have been any errors or omissions.

All photographs © BBC except the following:
    Page 7 Neil Davenport; page 11 The Sun; page 19 Capital Pictures/Phil Loftus; page 23 Capital; page 24 Scope Features; page 41 © Yorkshire Television Ltd; page 57 courtesy of Buster Merryfield; page 59 above courtesy of Buster Merryfield; page 84 and 85 left courtesy of Phoebe de Gaye; page 85 right and background Donal Woods; page 137 above and below © Bristol Evening Post.